PROJECT MANAGEMENT
training

ATD Workshop Series

PROJECT MANAGEMENT
training

WES BALAKIAN

atd
PRESS

Alexandria, Virginia

ATD Press is an internationally renowned source of insightful and practical information on talent development, workplace learning, and professional development.

ATD Press
1640 King Street, Box 1443
Alexandria, VA 22313-1443 USA

Ordering information for print edition: Books published by ATD Press can be purchased by visiting ATD's website at td.org/books or by calling 800.628.2783 or 703.683.8100.

Library of Congress Control Number: 2016959628

ISBN-10: 1-60728-096-5
ISBN-13: 978-1-60728-096-5
e-ISBN: 978-1-60728-097-2

ATD Press Editorial Staff:
Director: Kristine Luecker
Manager: Christian Green
Community of Practice Manager, Learning & Development: Amanda Smith

Trainers Publishing House (TPH) Staff:
Publisher: Cat Russo
Project, Editorial, and Production Management: Jacqueline Edlund-Braun, Editorial Director
Editor: Tora Estep
Rights Associate and Data Manager: Nancy Silva
Cover and Text Design: Ana Ilieva Foreman/Design
Composition: Kristin Goble, PerfecType, Nashville, TN, and Debra Deysher, Double D Media, Reading, PA
Cover Art: Shutterstock
Presentation Slide and Handout Art: Fotolia

Printed by Data Reproductions Corporation, Auburn Hills, MI, www.datarepro.com

The ATD Workshop Series

Whether you are a professional trainer who needs to pull together a new training program next week, or someone who does a bit of training as a part of your job, you'll find the ATD Workshop Series is a timesaver.

Topics deliver key learning on today's most pressing business needs, including training for change management, coaching, communication skills, customer service, emotional intelligence, facilitation, leadership, new employee orientation, new supervisors, presentation skills, project management, and time management. The series is designed for busy training and HR professionals, consultants, and managers who need to deliver training quickly to optimize performance now.

Each ATD Workshop book provides all the content and trainer's tools you need to create and deliver compelling training guaranteed to

- **enhance** learner engagement
- **deepen** learner understanding
- **increase** learning application.

Each book in the series offers innovative and engaging programs designed by leading experts and grounded in design and delivery best practices and theory. It is like having an expert trainer helping you with each step in the workshop process. The straightforward, practical instructions help you prepare and deliver the workshops quickly and effectively. Flexible timing options allow you to choose from half-day, one-day, and two-day workshop formats, or to create your own, using the tips and strategies presented for customizing the workshops to fit your unique business environment. Each ATD Workshop book also comes with guidance on leveraging learning technologies to maximize workshop design and delivery efficiency and access to all the training materials you will need, including activities, handouts, tools, assessments, and presentation slides.

Contents

FOREWORD BY TONY BINGHAM   xv

PREFACE   xvii

INTRODUCTION: HOW TO USE THIS BOOK   1

     Why Is Project Management Training Important?   1

     What Do I Need to Know About Training?   3

     How Much Time Will Preparation Take?   4

     What Are the Important Features of the Book?   4

     How Are the Agendas Laid Out?   6

     How Do I Use This Book?   7

     Key Points   8

     What to Do Next   8

     Additional Resources   8

SECTION I: THE WORKSHOPS   9

     1 TWO-DAY PROJECT MANAGEMENT WORKSHOP   11

     Project Management: From the Beginning   11

     A Word About Pre-Work   13

     A Word About the Slides, Notes, and Handouts   13

     Two-Day Workshop Objectives   16

     Two-Day Workshop Overview   16

         Day-One Overview   *16*

         Day-Two Overview   *18*

Two-Day Workshop Agenda: Day One   20

What to Do Between Workshop Days   47

Two-Day Workshop Agenda: Day Two   48

What to Do Next   76

References   76

2   ONE-DAY PROJECT MANAGEMENT WORKSHOP   **77**

Project Management: From the Beginning   78

A Word About Pre-Work   79

A Word About the Slides, Notes, and Handouts   79

One-Day Workshop Objectives   81

One-Day Workshop Overview   81

One-Day Workshop Agenda   83

What to Do Next   116

References   117

3   HALF-DAY PROJECT MANAGEMENT WORKSHOP   **119**

Project Management: From the Beginning   119

A Word About Pre-Work   121

A Word About the Slides, Notes, and Handouts   121

Half-Day Workshop Objectives   122

Half-Day Workshop Overview   123

Half-Day Workshop Agenda   124

What to Do Next   150

Reference   151

4   CUSTOMIZING THE PROJECT MANAGEMENT WORKSHOPS   **153**

Customizing the Content and Activities   154

Customizing the Workshop Format   154

Project Management Skills Series 155

Small Bites—Lunch-and-Learn Seminars 156

Customizing Delivery With Technology 156

The Bare Minimum 156

What to Do Next 158

SECTION II: ESSENTIALS OF EFFECTIVE PROJECT MANAGEMENT TRAINING

SECTION II: ESSENTIALS OF EFFECTIVE PROJECT MANAGEMENT TRAINING **159**

5 IDENTIFYING NEEDS FOR PROJECT MANAGEMENT TRAINING **161**

Why Needs Analysis? 162

Strategic Needs Analysis 162

Structured Interviews 164

Focus Groups 164

Surveys 164

Individual Learning Needs Analysis 165

The Bare Minimum 165

Key Points 166

What to Do Next 166

Additional Resources 167

6 UNDERSTANDING THE FOUNDATIONS OF TRAINING DESIGN **169**

Basic Adult Learning Theory 170

More Theoretical Ideas Important to Learning 171

Multiple Intelligences 171

Whole Brain Learning 172

Theory Into Practice 174

Establishing a Framework 174

Identifying Behaviors 174

Practicing 175

Providing Feedback	*175*
Making It Relevant	*175*
The Bare Minimum	175
Key Points	176
What to Do Next	176
Additional Resources	176

7 LEVERAGING TECHNOLOGY TO MAXIMIZE AND SUPPORT DESIGN AND DELIVERY — 177

Why Consider Learning Technologies?	179
Opportunities to Use Learning Technologies	179
When Designing Training	*179*
Before Training	*180*
During Training	*181*
After Training	*182*
While Building a Learning Community	*183*
The Bare Minimum	184
Key Points	184
What to Do Next	184
Additional Resources	184

8 DELIVERING YOUR PROJECT MANAGEMENT WORKSHOP: BE A GREAT FACILITATOR — 187

The Learning Environment	188
Program Preparation Checklist	191
Participant Materials	192
Handouts	*192*
Presentation Slides	*192*
Workbooks and Journals	*193*

Videos   193

Toys, Noisemakers, and Other Props   193

Facilitator Equipment and Materials   194

A Strong Start: Introduction, Icebreakers, and Openers   195

Feedback   196

Role Plays   197

Participant Presentations   198

Ball Toss   199

Journaling   199

Responding to Questions   199

Training Room and Participant Management   200

A Word About Dealing With Difficult Participants   201

An Unforgettable End   204

The Bare Minimum   205

Key Points   205

What to Do Next   205

Additional Resources   205

9 EVALUATING WORKSHOP RESULTS   **207**

Levels of Measurement   208

Level 1: Measuring Participant Reactions   208

Level 2: Measuring the Extent to Which Participants Have Learned   209

Level 3: Measuring the Results of Training Back on the Job   210

Level 4: Measuring the Organizational Impact of Training   210

Return on Investment   211

Reporting Results   211

The Bare Minimum   212

Key Points   212

What to Do Next — 212

Additional Resources — 212

SECTION III: POST-WORKSHOP LEARNING — 215

10 THE FOLLOW-UP COACH — 217

Before the Workshop Begins — 218

During the Workshop — 218

At the Close of the Workshop — 219

After the Workshop — 220

What to Do Next — 222

Additional Resources — 223

Training — 223

Project Management and Interpersonal Skills — 223

SECTION IV: WORKSHOP SUPPORTING DOCUMENTS AND ONLINE SUPPORT — 225

11 LEARNING ACTIVITIES — 227

Learning Activities Included in *Project Management Training* — 227

12 ASSESSMENTS — 241

Assessments Included in *Project Management Training* — 242

13 HANDOUTS — 247

Handouts Included in *Project Management Training* — 247

14 PROJECT MANAGER TOOLKIT — 261

Tools Included in the Project Manager Toolkit — 262

15 ONLINE SUPPORTING DOCUMENTS AND DOWNLOADS   **269**

Access to Free Supporting Materials   269

Customizable Materials   270

Working With the Files   271

PDF Documents   *271*

PowerPoint Slides   *271*

ABOUT THE AUTHOR   **273**

ABOUT ATD   **275**

Foreword

In 2002, we launched the ASTD Trainer's WorkShop Series—a collection of books authored by practitioners that focused on the design and delivery of training on popular soft-skills topics. The creation of this series was a departure for us. These workshops-in-a-book were created to help internal trainers expedite their program delivery by using appropriate and exceptionally designed content that could be adapted and repurposed.

These topics, dealing with issues ranging from customer service to leadership to manager skills, continue to be important training programs offered in companies and organizations of all sizes and across the globe. The ASTD Trainer's WorkShop Series has helped more than 60,000 trainers and occasional trainers deliver top-notch programs that meet business needs and help drive performance.

And while many things about the delivery of soft skills training have not changed in the last decade, there have been advances in technology and its use in training. So, when we began talking about how to refresh this popular series, we knew we needed to incorporate technology and new topics. We also wanted to make sure that the new series was cohesively designed and had input from author-practitioners who are, after all, the heart and soul of this series.

Inside *Project Management Training* by Wes Balakian, and each of the titles in the series, you'll find innovative content and fresh program agendas to simplify your delivery of key training topics. You'll also find consistency among titles, with each presented in a contemporary manner, designed by peers, and reflecting the preferences of training professionals who conduct workshops.

We hope that you find tremendous value in the ATD Workshop Series.

Tony Bingham
President & CEO
Association for Talent Development (ATD)
December 2016

Preface

In the competitive "need it now" business environment, organizations are looking for an edge that can help them deliver products and services faster and cheaper while maintaining high quality and brand integrity. In the past 20 years as a consultant, trainer, speaker, author, and strategic adviser to global organizations, I've determined that a prime ingredient to scalability, predictability, and consistency in any organization or industry is having a proven method or process to deliver products and services on time, within budget, and within scope—that is, project management.

When leaders make job functions easier and help employees understand how their work relates to business results and to the work of others in the organization, they increase morale, engagement, and productivity for everyone in the organization. Employees become committed to a success larger than just their specific jobs. Project management training can help organizations establish standard processes, documentation, and language throughout the organization to ensure that projects deliver results and the organization thrives.

Not all templates, methods, or processes will work for every organization, but understanding the fundamentals of project management is an important start for employees and teams. The workshops in this book are not meant to be used as test preparation. They are designed from the perspective of "healthy" project management—using just the right amount of project management to achieve the desired results. This book is chock-full of easy-to-use templates and tools that learners can put to work right away. The activities provide opportunities to practice the concepts in small and large groups reminiscent of learners' work teams.

Despite increased competitive pressure, fluctuating economies, and the chaotic pace of change, healthy project management has proven to be one constant in business success. I have designed these workshops to help project managers and their teams improve performance, which will help their organizations maintain a competitive edge. These methods and tools have worked for my clients and customers, and they will work for your employees—project managers and project team members alike.

Wes Balakian
CEO, True Solutions Inc.
Fairview, Texas
December 2016

Introduction

How to Use This Book

What's in This Chapter

- Why project management matters
- What you need to know about training project managers
- Project manager skills and competencies
- Estimates of time required
- A broad view of what the book includes

Why Is Project Management Training Important?

Nearly everything we do in our professional and personal lives is a project of some sort. Whether it is rolling out a new product or initiative, collaborating on a team, or planning a vacation, a good understanding of how to deliver a project on time, in budget, and within scope is the formula for success. In today's complex, interconnected world, organizations need predictable, repeatable, and scalable processes that can maintain the blistering pace of change—precisely what project management gives employees the tools and know-how to do.

Managing projects requires the ability to set clear objectives, report, project plan, work collaboratively, navigate uncertainty, and monitor and control project outcomes. Project managers need to be adept at motivating and influencing a diverse group of people, sometimes dispersed geographically, to accomplish a common objective or goal. (Oh, and by the way, just because your job title does not have the words *project manager* in it doesn't mean that you are not performing the role of a project manager.) Project managers must know how to communicate, coach, train, listen, and deliver results while working with people from different cultures, age groups, backgrounds, and levels of knowledge. Layered on top of these attributes, they must also be leaders who are able to balance priorities, scope, budget, schedule, people management, planning, and organizational concerns. In short, project managers need a comprehensive set of knowledge, skills, and attributes to be effective.

That is a tall order. What does it take to properly prepare others to manage the countless projects in their organizations and lives?

Many people who are cast in the role of project manager have not been formally trained nor do they have a complete understanding of what project management is. Many successful project managers came up through the ranks, learning what works over time by trial and error. That is how I came to the field of project management. In many ways, experience is the best teacher, though sometimes a harsh and unforgiving one. But learning how to do your job over time without understanding the reasons why you are successful will not produce repeatable, predictable, and scalable results. It will produce habits—which, as we know, can be either good or bad.

Moreover, project management is an expansive field, touching every type of organization and industry. No one training program can begin to cover all the details and nuances of the job. (For example, we dedicate only one learning activity to communications management, when entire books have been written on that topic.)

So, the workshop agendas in this book focus on grounding participants in foundational project management concepts and methods and giving them opportunities to practice the concepts by working in teams. The workshops are *not* exam prep courses, but they will help participants to feel more comfortable delivering a successful project on their own. They will come away with effective methods and tools to put to work back at their jobs.

Whether you choose the half-day, one-day, or two-day program, you will find the resources and tools you need to create engaging, interactive sessions that will enable your participants to deliver business results using project management best practices. Each of the agendas can be used as a stand-alone workshop, or they can be used in succession, each building on the other to explore aspects of project management. Combine all three and you have a career path program, if your organization decides to pursue project management as a core competency for talent development. The programs can provide an introduction to the field that can lead to further training and even certification through an organization such as PMI (Project Management Institute).

Is there more to learn about project management than is presented in these workshops? Absolutely. Developing project management skills is a journey. It takes time, practice, and experience. The workshops in this book offer solid training programs to give participants the knowledge and resources they will need along the way. Remember that project management is a formal method of delivering business results—and project management *training* is a key component in enabling employees to deliver those results effectively.

Everything you do to prepare for and deliver your workshop needs to model these skills. Spend time building your understanding of project management methods and practice them in your preparation, design, delivery, and follow-up of the workshop.

What Do I Need to Know About Training?

The ATD Workshop Series is designed to be adaptable for many levels of both training facilitation and topic expertise. Circle the answers in this quick assessment that most closely align with your state of expertise.

QUICK ASSESSMENT: HOW EXPERT DO I NEED TO BE?			
Question	**Authority**	**Developing Expertise**	**Novice**
What is your level of expertise as a facilitator?	• More than 5 years of experience • Consistently receive awesome evaluations • Lead highly interactive sessions with strong participant engagement	• From 1 to 5 years of experience • Catch myself talking too much • May feel drained after training • Participants sometimes sit back and listen instead of engage	• Less than 1 year of experience • No idea what to do to be successful • Eager to develop a facilitative style
How proficient are you with the topic?	• Well versed • Have taken courses • Read books/ authored articles • Created training materials • Am sought out by peers on this topic • It is my passion	• On my way • Have taken courses • Read books • Created workshop materials • Would benefit from the book's support tools	• I can spell it! • Had a course in school • Received feedback from respected colleagues indicating I have a natural inclination for this topic (but feel a bit like an imposter)

Two-fold novice: Your best bet is to stick closely to the materials as they are designed. Spend extra time with the content to learn as much as possible about it. Read the examples and sample stories, and plan examples of your own to share. Also, closely read Chapter 8 on training delivery, and consider practicing with a colleague before delivering the program. Take comfort in the tested materials you are holding and confidence in your ability to apply them!

Developing your expertise in one or both areas: Logical choices for you may include using the outline and materials, and then including material you have developed that is relevant to the topic *and* your participants' workplace needs. Or, take the core content of the materials and revise the learning techniques into interactive approaches you have used with success in the past. Play to your strengths and develop your growth areas using the resources in this volume that complement your existing skills.

Authority twice over: Feel free to adapt the agendas and materials as you see fit and use any materials that you have already developed, or simply incorporate training activities, handouts, and so forth from this volume into your own agenda. Enjoy the benefits of ready-to-use processes and support tools and have fun tailoring them to your preferences and organizational needs.

How Much Time Will Preparation Take?

Putting together and facilitating a training workshop, even when the agendas, activities, tools, and assessments are created for you, can be time consuming. For planning purposes, estimate about four days of preparation time for a two-day course.

What Are the Important Features of the Book?

Section I includes the various workshop designs (from two days to a half day) with agendas and thumbnails from presentation slides as well as a chapter on customizing the workshop for your circumstances. The chapters included are

- Chapter 1. Two-Day Workshop (15 hours program time) + Agenda + PPT (thumbnails)
- Chapter 2. One-Day Workshop (7.5 hours program time) + Agenda + PPT (thumbnails)
- Chapter 3. Half-Day Workshop (3 to 4 hours program time) + Agenda + PPT (thumbnails)
- Chapter 4. Customizing the Project Management Workshops.

The workshop chapters include advice, instructions, workshop at-a-glance tables, as well as full program agendas.

Section II is standard from book to book in the ATD Workshop Series as a way to provide a consistent foundation of training principles. This section's chapters follow the ADDIE model—the classic instructional design model named after its steps (analysis, design, development, implementation, and evaluation). The chapters are based on best practices and crafted with input from experienced training practitioners. They are meant to help you get up to speed as quickly as possible. Each chapter includes several additional recurring features to help you understand the concepts and ideas presented. The Bare Minimum gives you the bare bones of what you need to know about the topic. Key Points summarize the most important points of each chapter. What to Do Next guides you to your next action steps. And, finally, the Additional Resources section at the end of each chapter gives you options for further reading to broaden your understanding of training design and delivery. Section II chapters include

- Chapter 5. Identifying Needs for Project Management Training
- Chapter 6. Understanding the Foundations of Training Design
- Chapter 7. Leveraging Technology to Maximize and Support Design and Delivery
- Chapter 8. Delivering Your Project Management Training Workshop: Be a Great Facilitator
- Chapter 9. Evaluating Workshop Results.

Section III covers information about post-workshop learning:

- Chapter 10. The Follow-Up Coach

Section IV includes thumbnail versions of all the supporting documents for reference and guidance for accessing the documents online:

- Chapter 11. Learning Activities
- Chapter 12. Assessments
- Chapter 13. Handouts
- Chapter 14. Project Manager Toolkit
- Chapter 15. Online Supporting Documents and Downloads.

The book includes everything you need to prepare for and deliver your workshop:

- **Agendas,** the heart of the series, are laid out in three columns for ease of delivery. The first column shows the timing, the second gives the presentation slide number and image for quick reference, and the third gives instructions and facilitation notes. These are designed to be straightforward, simple agendas that you can take into the training room and use to stay on track. They include cues on the learning activities, notes about tools or handouts to include, and other important delivery tips.
- **Learning activities,** which are more detailed than the agendas, cover the objectives of the activity, the time and materials required, the steps involved, variations on the activity in some cases, and wrap-up or debriefing questions or comments.
- **Assessments, handouts, and tools** are the training materials you will provide to learners to support the training program. These can include scorecards for games, instructions, reference materials, samples, self-assessments, and so forth.

- **Presentation media** (PowerPoint slides) are deliberately designed to be simple so that you can customize them for your company and context. They are provided for your convenience. Chapter 7 discusses different forms of technology that you can incorporate into your program, including different types of presentation media.

All the program materials are available for download, customization, and duplication. See Chapter 15 for instructions on how to access the materials.

How Are the Agendas Laid Out?

The following agenda is a sample from the half-day workshop.

Half Day: (8:00 a.m. to 12:00 p.m.)

TIMING	SLIDES	ACTIVITIES/NOTES/CONSIDERATIONS
8:00 a.m. (5 min)	Slide 1 **ATD** Workshop Project Management Training Half-Day Workshop	**Welcome and Introductions** Welcome the participants as they enter the room and briefly introduce yourself. Make an effort to talk to each person, which will set the tone for the session and begin to model communication as a primary skill for successful project management. Note the usual housekeeping items such as restroom locations and breaks.
8:05 a.m. (10 min)	Slide 2 My Project Management Story 1. What is your name and current position? 2. What is your project management experience? 3. What do you hope to learn today? 4. How will you define success at the end of the workshop?	**Learning Activity 1: My Project Management Story** This icebreaker partner activity will help you get a sense of your participants' level of experience with project management and what their learning needs are. It will also help your participants get to know each other better. To help participants interact with each other, divide the group into pairs and have them interview each other using the same set of questions. Then have each pair introduce each other to the group. NOTE: To conduct this activity in the time allotted, follow the instructions in the learning activity, but skip steps 1 and 2 and start the activity at step 3.

TIMING	SLIDES	ACTIVITIES/NOTES/CONSIDERATIONS
8:15 a.m. (5 min)	Slide 3 **Workshop Objectives** • Define what a project is • Develop a working definition of project management • Learn the five project process groups: initiate, plan, execute, monitor and control, close • Gain confidence to apply project management processes to a project as a project manager or project team member	**Workshop Objectives** Introduce the topic of project management to the participants. Make the point that they use project management every day—even though they may not call it that. Just about everyone is a project manager based on the definition of a project (distinctive, transitory, defined start and finish, continuously advanced). Doctors, police officers, attorneys, veterinarians, and teachers all deliver and manage projects. Briefly present the workshop objectives at a high level. Let the participants know that although the workshop will cover a lot of information, there will be opportunities to practice the concepts they are learning with each other in small groups. Explain that the session will introduce them to basic project management terminology and processes and will help them develop several key project management skills they will need to lead a project or participate as a project team member. (Slide 1 of 2)

How Do I Use This Book?

If you've ever read a "Choose Your Own Adventure" book, you will recognize that this book follows a similar principle. Think back to the self-assessment at the beginning of this introduction:

- If you chose *authority*, you can get right to work preparing one of the workshops in Section I. Use Section II as a reference. Many of the chapters in Section II feature a sidebar or other information written by the author, who has much experience in the topic under consideration. This advice can help guide your preparation, delivery, and evaluation of training.

- If you chose *developing expertise*, read Section II in depth and skim the topic content.

- If you chose *novice at training and the topic*, then spend some serious time familiarizing yourself with both Sections I and II of this volume as well as the topic content.

Once you have a general sense of the material, assemble your workshop. Select the appropriate agenda and then modify the times and training activities as needed and desired. Assemble the materials and familiarize yourself with the topic, the activities, and the presentation media.

Key Points

- The workshops in this book are designed to be effective at all levels of trainer expertise.

- Good training requires an investment of time.

- The book contains everything you need to create a workshop, including agendas, learning activities, presentation media, assessments, handouts, and tools.

What to Do Next

- Review the agendas presented in Section I and select the best fit for your requirements, time constraints, and budget.

- Based on your level of expertise, skim or read in depth the chapters in Section II.

- Consider what kind of follow-up learning activities you will want to include with the workshop by reviewing Section III.

Additional Resources

Biech, E. (2008). *10 Steps to Successful Training*. Alexandria, VA: ASTD Press.

Biech, E., ed. (2014). *ASTD Handbook: The Definitive Reference for Training & Development*, 2nd edition. Alexandria, VA: ASTD Press.

Emerson, T., and M. Stewart. (2011). *The Learning and Development Book*. Alexandria, VA: ASTD Press.

McCain, D.V. (2015). *Facilitation Basics*, 2nd edition. Alexandria, VA: ATD Press.

Piskurich, G. (2003). *Trainer Basics*. Alexandria, VA: ASTD Press.

Stolovitch, H.D., and E.J. Keeps. (2011). *Telling Ain't Training*, 2nd edition. Alexandria, VA: ASTD Press.

SECTION I

The Workshops

Chapter 1
Two-Day Project Management Workshop

What's in This Chapter

- Project management fundamentals
- Objectives of the two-day Project Management Workshop
- Two-day workshop agenda in detail

This two-day workshop will provide a solid introduction and overview of project management methods and best practices. Because project management is a broad subject that covers many industries, a two-day workshop cannot include everything project managers need to know. The workshop is *not* an exam prep course. Rather, it presents foundational project management concepts punctuated with exercises and templates that will help participants feel comfortable returning to the workplace with the knowledge that they could successfully deliver a project on their own. The two-day agenda is designed with the assumption that participants have some knowledge of project management or will have taken the half-day or one-day workshop recently before attending the two-day workshop.

Project Management: From the Beginning

Because formal project management theory, methods, and best practice standards have been employed in every conceivable governmental, military, and commercial organization and industry, the field of project management has evolved over time. This evolution (revolution, even) continues as the profession is continually refined and gains more traction globally. Project management is a methodical approach and discipline that everyone knows about but may not realize they use.

Consider the case of doctors—they see patients, they diagnose their problems, they prescribe solutions, and then they discharge the patients with possible follow-up visits. Compare that to the definition of a project: distinctive, transitory, defined start and finish, and continuously advanced. Doctors see a unique problem (patient), for a temporary time with a start and finish, and throughout the process determine the problem through diagnoses. They complete projects: They are project managers!

Project management is in the business of delivering results. Its strategies and methodologies work as well for disaster relief, fighting fires, and emergency response as they do for business goals in for-profit and nonprofit organizations. It is a proven method that will consistently deliver the results the project defines.

The workshops in this book have been designed from the perspective of healthy project management, which simply means that you do not have to use every process, procedure, template, trick, tip, and technique on every project to achieve your desired results. But you should know what tools are available before you decide which tools you don't need. Using just the right amount of project management is one of the keys to success.

The two-day workshop will cover everything needed to manage a successful small- to medium-sized project and then focus in more detail on the most crucial aspects of project management. The workshop materials provide templates for the participants to use during the workshop activities and as tools back on the job. You are welcome to use these templates or create your own that are more specific to the needs of your organization and participants. Keep in mind, however, that project management is not about filling in templates; it is also not about using project software to deliver a project. Such tools can help save time and make project management easier, but only one element can deliver a project on time, within scope, and within budget—*the project manager*. You will want to stress this point with your participants to empower their project management success.

As you prepare to deliver the workshop, think about times you have used project management to facilitate a training session, create a product, deliver a service, convene a meeting, or even plan a party. That's right—you, too, are a project manager. Add your personal experiences and successes to this workshop to make it your own. (And don't forget that people learn as much from your failures as they do from your successes.) Be willing to share whatever will make the concepts real and doable. Project managers must own their projects, and as the facilitator, you should own your role in this workshop as well. The more of "you" that you put into the sessions, the more your participants will get out of them.

Managing projects requires the ability to set clear objectives, report, project plan, work collaboratively, navigate uncertainty, and monitor and control project outcomes. Everything you do to prepare for and deliver this workshop needs to model these skills. Spend time building your understanding of project management methods and practice them in your preparation, design, delivery, and follow-up of this workshop.

A Word About Pre-Work

The two-day workshop includes a pre-work assignment to help your participants think about project management in their own specific context. When you send a welcome or confirmation message to participants, ask them to think about a project they were involved in this past year. Ask your participants to answer these questions about the project:

- What role did you play?
- What was unique about the project?
- Did it come in on time, within budget, and within scope?
- Did your project follow any specific process?

This is a great way to begin the relationship with your participants. At the start of the workshop you will debrief their pre-work by encouraging them to share one or two of their answers to the questions with the group. Not everyone has to share; you can ask everyone to keep the questions in mind as they experience the workshop.

A Word About the Slides, Notes, and Handouts

The slides for this workshop contain key learning concepts about project management. Additional and supporting information will be found in the notes column of the agenda. Because it is impossible to include every piece of information in the slide, prepare to discuss points from your own experience to help answer participants' questions. Project management is a complex topic, so I encourage you to research and learn more about the concepts covered in the workshop. See Figure 1-1 for resources that will help you sharpen your project management skills and build your project management acumen. The blogs and online resources will bolster the information presented in the workshop with cutting-edge expertise in project management topics. Also, if you are unsure about any topic in the agenda, send me an email with your questions at wes.balakian@truesolutions.com and I will be glad to help you.

Figure 1-1. Resources to Build Your Project Management Acumen

RESOURCE	NOTES
ONLINE: WEBSITES, BLOGS, AND MORE	
Business Analyst Times www.batimes.com	Business Analyst Times is a companion website to Project Times. You may not wear the business analyst hat on your project right now but who knows when you will need to don that hat in the future?
How to Manage a Camel www.arraspeople.co.uk/camel-blog/	Published by the British recruiting firm Arras People, this website covers building your internal network, project sponsorship, and other helpful topics.
ProjectsAtWork www.projectsatwork.com	Similar to Project Times, this website offers a wide range of project management articles and other resources.
Project Management Institute (PMI) www.pmi.org	The PMI website provides one of the most important project management resources online, with access to guides, whitepapers, and other resources to aid you in your career development. It also includes a directory of e-learning programs on change management, essentials of project management, organizational change, and much more.
Project Management Tips www.pmtips.net	The Project Management Tips website provides information on knowledge management, collaboration, and related project resources.
Project Times www.projecttimes.com	Project Times is a curated website that publishes helpful articles on issues such as project brainstorming, communication, leadership, requirements, management, and stakeholder management.
BOOKS	
Getting Things Done: The Art of Stress-Free Productivity, by David Allen (New York: Penguin, revised edition, 2015)	*Getting Things Done* (called GTD by enthusiasts) remains the single best book on personal productivity. At first, the GTD system may feel challenging because it requires that you change some of your habits to implement it, but I encourage you to persevere. The clarity of mind you can obtain with GTD is well worth the effort.
Making Things Happen: Mastering Project Management, by Scott Berkun (Sebastopol, CA: O'Reilly, 2008)	In this modern classic on the discipline of project management, Berkun draws heavily on his experience leading technology projects at Microsoft. If you work on software or technology projects with any regularity, you owe it to yourself to read this book.
Project Management for Trainers, 2nd edition, by Lou Russell (Alexandria, VA: ATD Press, 2015)	Russell gives expert project management advice, written especially for trainers and the unique project management challenges they encounter.

RESOURCE	NOTES
Results Without Authority: Controlling a Project When the Team Doesn't Report to You, 2nd edition, by Tom Kendrick (New York: AMACOM, 2012)	Kendrick gives helpful guidance about how to motivate people when you lack formal authority over them—a challenge most project managers face every day.
The Economist Guide to Project Management: Getting It Right and Achieving Lasting Benefits, 2nd edition, by Paul Roberts (Hoboken, NJ: Wiley, 2013)	Now in its second edition, this book covers the fundamentals of project management.
PODCASTS	
Project Management for the Masses www.pmforthemasses.com	Hosted by Cesar Abeid, this podcast includes a variety of guest contributors who discuss a wide range of project management topics.
The People and Projects Podcast www.peopleandprojectspodcast.com	Hosted by Andy Kaufman, this site offers podcasts and a helpful guide to recommended books on project management. Past episodes have explored project failure, feedback, negotiating skills, and numerous other pertinent topics.
The Project Management Podcast www.project-management-podcast.com	Hosted by Cornelius Fichtner, the site offers podcasts, with a special focus on interviews with experts in the field.

The handouts provided in this volume are another source of information for you as the facilitator and for your participants. In some cases, the handouts provide templates to be used in the learning activities. In other cases, they include "must-know" concepts that summarize the key learning in the modules or provide tips, examples, flowcharts, and so on. And still other handouts provide useful information you won't have time to present within the scope of this workshop but that will help participants once they are back in their workplaces. Encourage participants to review these valuable resources to increase their project management knowledge and skills.

Also included in this volume is a Project Manager Toolkit (Chapter 14) that includes all the templates from the two-day agenda plus additional templates, all created by True Solutions Inc. (TSI). You can distribute a print copy of the Project Manager Toolkit to your participants at the close of the workshop or send it to them digitally a week or two after the workshop is completed as follow-up support for their learning. (In addition, TSI publishes a set of more than 100 templates on a wide range of project management processes and tasks to help project managers.)

The agenda notes are not highly scripted. They are crafted in a natural voice that you can make your own when you deliver the content. Avoid just reading the slides—or your participants will immediately see that you are not comfortable with the subject and begin a contest to uncover what you don't know.

As an instructor, author, consultant, and experienced corporate executive, I can talk for days about project management, but when I get in front of people what they see is my passion. Show them yours. If you are confident with project management principles and content, you will find navigating the agenda very easy. If you are more of a novice to the field, rely on the agendas to help guide you through the material but plan to spend some time broadening your knowledge base with the resources noted in Figure 1-1.

Two-Day Workshop Objectives

After completing the two-day workshop, participants will be able to

- Define what a project is
- Develop a working definition of project management
- Explore the project process groups: initiate, plan, execute, control, and close
- Practice using tools and techniques within the project process groups
- Identify the knowledge and skills required to be effective project managers
- Create a detailed action plan for developing project management skills and knowledge.

Two-Day Workshop Overview

Day-One Overview

TOPICS	TIMING
Welcome and Introductions	10 minutes
Learning Activity 1: My Project Management Story	30 minutes
Workshop Objectives	10 minutes
What Is Project Management?	
What Is a Project?	5 minutes
Continuous Advancement	5 minutes
What Is Project Management?	5 minutes
The Project Management Process	
Project Management Process Groups	5 minutes
Project Phases	5 minutes
Initiate Project Module	
Initiate: Objectives	5 minutes
Initiate: Key Tasks	5 minutes
Initiate: Project Charter	5 minutes
Learning Activity 2: Create a Project Charter	15 minutes

TOPICS	TIMING
BREAK	**15 minutes**
Initiate: Identify Stakeholders	5 minutes
Learning Activity 3: Create a Stakeholder Register	15 minutes
Initiate: Module Wrap-Up	10 minutes
Plan Project Module	
Plan: Objectives	5 minutes
Plan: Processes	5 minutes
Plan: Create Stakeholder Management Plan	5 minutes
Plan: Collect Requirements	10 minutes
Plan: Define Scope	5 minutes
Learning Activity 4: Create a Scope Statement	15 minutes
Plan: Product Scope vs. Project Scope	5 minutes
Plan: Scope Management Plan	5 minutes
LUNCH	**60 minutes**
Learning Activity 5: Communication Interference	20 minutes
Plan: Communications Management Plan	5 minutes
Plan: Work Breakdown Structure	5 minutes
Plan: Sample Work Breakdown Structures	5 minutes
Plan: WBS Key Definitions	5 minutes
Learning Activity 6: Create a Simple WBS	20 minutes
Plan: Develop Schedule	5 minutes
Learning Activity 7: Create a Schedule Management Plan	20 minutes
BREAK	**15 minutes**
Plan: Define Activities	5 minutes
Plan: Sequence Activities	10 minutes
Plan: Precedence Relationships	10 minutes
Plan: Estimate Activity Durations	5 minutes
Plan: Human Resource Planning	5 minutes
Learning Activity 8: Create a Human Resource Plan	20 minutes
Plan: Cost Management	5 minutes
Plan: Estimate Costs	5 minutes
Plan: Procurement Management	10 minutes
Learning Activity 9: Create a Contract Award	15 minutes
Plan: Quality Management	5 minutes
Plan: Grade vs. Quality	5 minutes
Plan: Impact of Poor Quality	5 minutes
Day-One Debrief	10 minutes
TOTAL	**480 minutes**

Day-Two Overview

TOPICS	TIMING
Welcome and Reconnect	5 minutes
Day-One Review	5 minutes
Plan Project Module (continued)	
Plan: What Is Project Risk?	5 minutes
Plan: Risk Management Planning	5 minutes
Plan: Project Risk Management Integrated With Other Project Areas	10 minutes
Plan: Risk Management	5 minutes
Plan: Identify Risks	5 minutes
Plan: Cause-and-Effect Diagram Example	10 minutes
Learning Activity 10: Process Flowcharting Exercise	10 minutes
Learning Activity 11: Risk Categorization Exercise	15 minutes
Plan: Qualitative Risk Analysis	10 minutes
Plan: Risk Responses	5 minutes
Plan: Create Multiple Strategies	10 minutes
Plan: Project Management Plan	5 minutes
Plan: Module Wrap-Up	10 minutes
BREAK	**15 minutes**
Execute Project Module	
Execute: Objectives	5 minutes
Execute: Purpose	5 minutes
Execute: Processes	5 minutes
Execute: Manage Communications	5 minutes
Learning Activity 12: Matrix Game: Communication 101	20 minutes
Execute: Quality Assurance	5 minutes
Execute: Direct and Manage Project Work	5 minutes
Execute: Module Wrap-Up	10 minutes
Monitor and Control Project Module	
Monitor and Control: Objectives	5 minutes
Monitor and Control: Purpose	5 minutes
Monitor and Control: Control Scope	5 minutes
Monitor and Control: Control Schedule	5 minutes
Monitor and Control: Control Costs	5 minutes
LUNCH	**60 minutes**
Monitor and Control: Four Key Data Points for Controlling Project Costs	10 minutes
Monitor and Control: Control Communications	5 minutes
Monitor and Control: Control Risks	5 minutes

TOPICS	TIMING
Monitor and Control: Control Quality	5 minutes
Learning Activity 13: Create a Quality Management Plan	15 minutes
Monitor and Control: Run Chart Example	5 minutes
Monitor and Control: Control Procurements	5 minutes
Monitor and Control: Control Stakeholder Engagement	5 minutes
Monitor and Control: Perform Integrated Change Control	5 minutes
Monitor and Control: Monitor and Control Project Work	5 minutes
Monitor and Control: Module Wrap-Up	10 minutes
BREAK	**15 minutes**
Close Project Module	
Close: Objectives	5 minutes
Close: Purpose	5 minutes
Close: Close Procurements	5 minutes
Close: Close Contract and Close Project Interactions	5 minutes
Close: Close Project or Phase	5 minutes
Close: Module Wrap-Up	5 minutes
Project Management Knowledge Requirements	
Project Management Knowledge Requirements	5 minutes
Project Management Knowledge	5 minutes
General Management Knowledge	10 minutes
Ability to Perform and Interpersonal Skills	5 minutes
Learning Activity 14: Project Management Interpersonal Skills Quick Assessment	15 minutes
Workshop Wrap-Up	
Learning Activity 15: Action Planning	30 minutes
Project Manager Toolkit (Chapter 14)	5 minutes
What Do Great Project Managers Do?	10 minutes
TOTAL	**480 minutes (8 hours)**

Two-Day Workshop Agenda: Day One

Day One: (8:00 a.m. to 4:00 p.m.)

TIMING	SLIDES	ACTIVITIES/NOTES/CONSIDERATIONS
8:00 a.m. (10 min)	Slide 1 **ATD** Workshop Project Management Training Two-Day Workshop Day One	**Welcome and Introductions** Welcome the participants as they enter the room and briefly introduce yourself. Make an effort to talk to each person, which will set the tone for the session and begin to model communication as a primary skill for successful project management. Note the usual housekeeping items such as restroom locations and breaks.
8:10 a.m. (30 min)	Slide 2 My Project Management Story 1. What is your name and current position? 2. What is your project management experience? 3. What do you hope to learn today? 4. How will you define success at the end of the workshop?	**Learning Activity 1: My Project Management Story** This icebreaker partner activity will help you get a sense of your participants' level of experience with project management and what their learning needs are. It will also help your participants get to know each other better. Ask participants to answer the questions on the slide on their own and then to write their answer to question 4 on a sticky note. Have them place their notes on a flipchart at the front of the room. Briefly review their answers with the group. Let students know that you will be referring to their notes throughout the workshop. Make an effort to connect participants with the topics they consider important to their learning success. To help participants interact with each other, divide the group into pairs and have them interview each other using the same set of questions. Then have pairs introduce each other to the group. Follow the instructions in the learning activity to facilitate this activity.

TIMING	SLIDES	ACTIVITIES/NOTES/CONSIDERATIONS
8:40 a.m. (10 min)	**Slide 3** Workshop Objectives • Define what a project is • Develop working definition of project management • Learn the project process groups: initiate, plan, execute, control, and close • Practice using tools and techniques within the project process groups • Identify the knowledge and skills required to be effective project manager • Create a detailed action plan for developing project management skills and knowledge	**Workshop Objectives** Introduce the topic of project management to the participants. Make the point that they use project management every day—even though they may not call it that. Just about everyone is a project manager based on the definition of a project (distinctive, transitory, defined start and finish, continuously advanced). Doctors, police officers, attorneys, veterinarians, and teachers all deliver and manage projects. Briefly present the workshop objectives at a high level. Point out where they overlap with the participants' responses in Learning Activity 1. Let the participants know that the workshop will need to cover a lot of information, although there will be opportunities to practice the concepts they are learning with each other in small groups. Explain that the session is not intended to prepare them to take a certification exam, but it will enable them to lead a project, participate as a project team member, and understand the terminology, theory, and application of project management. (Slide 1 of 2)
	Slide 4 Pre-Work Assignment Think of a project that you have been involved with recently: •What role did you play? •What was unique about the project? •Did it come in on time, budget, and within scope? •Did your project follow any specific process?	Wrap up your overview of the objectives by asking, by a show of hands, how many of the participants have had some experience with project management before, perhaps having attended other workshops, read books about it, or worked as team members on projects. Take a moment to review the pre-work assignment you gave the participants to identify a project they were involved in this year. Ask for a few volunteers to briefly share their project examples with the group. Ask them: • What role did you play? • What was unique about the project? • Did it come in on time, within budget, and within scope? • Did your project follow any specific process? (Slide 2 of 2)

TIMING	SLIDES	ACTIVITIES/NOTES/CONSIDERATIONS
8:50 a.m. (5 min)	Slide 5 What is a Project? Project Program Company	**Learning Content/Lecture and Discussion** **What Is a Project?** To understand what project management is, you have to start even further back and ask what a project is. Ask participants: What is the difference between a project and a program? Use the slide to explain that a program is an ongoing set of activities, such as a car company that produces a fleet of vehicles. A project, however, has four specific characteristics: • Distinctive • Transitory • Defined start and finish • Continuously advanced. A project, using the example on the slide, would be the development of a single model of car in a single model year. Briefly discuss the first three characteristics (distinctive, transitory, and defined start/finish), which are mostly self-explanatory. Then introduce the fourth characteristic: *continuous advancement*. Emphasize that it is a key element in defining a project. Open the discussion by asking participants what they think the term means. Once they have shared their ideas with the group, use the next slide to help explain it further.

TIMING	SLIDES	ACTIVITIES/NOTES/CONSIDERATIONS
8:55 a.m. (5 min)	Slide 6 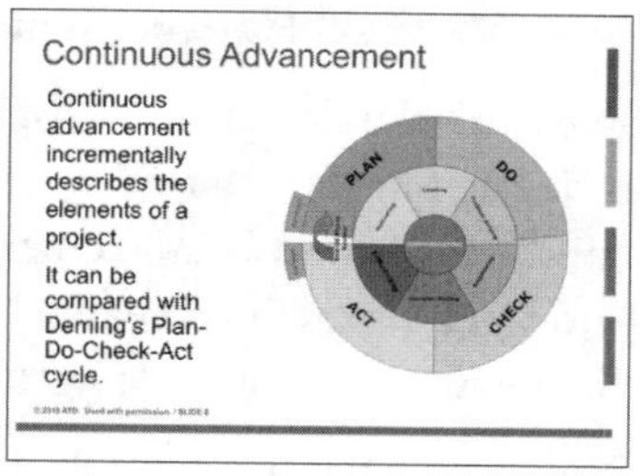 Continuous Advancement Continuous advancement incrementally describes the elements of a project. It can be compared with Deming's Plan-Do-Check-Act cycle.	**Learning Content/Discussion** **Continuous Advancement** Continuous advancement works in a manner similar to the Plan-Do-Check-Act cycle made popular by W.E. Deming. We *plan*, we *do*, we *check*, and we *act* the plan. As we progress through the chart, we get increasingly more detailed as we gather information. Walk the participants step by step through the Plan-Do-Check-Act cycle shown on the slide: • **Plan:** planning the project • **Do:** executing the project work • **Check:** the monitoring portion of the M&C (monitoring and control) process, checking to determine status • **Act:** the controlling portion of the M&C process, taking corrective or preventive action. The entire model is built on a wheel, with communicating—the most critical interpersonal skill for a project manager—as the hub. Other interpersonal skills make up the various spokes of the wheel. Discuss the interpersonal skills listed in the diagram and point out that any interpersonal skill could be part of this wheel diagram. Explain that at the end of the cycle, there is a review, and the process starts over—representing the end-of-phase review.

TIMING	SLIDES	ACTIVITIES/NOTES/CONSIDERATIONS
9:00 a.m. (5 min)	Slide 7 	**Learning Content/Discussion** **What Is Project Management?** Share the classic definition of *project management* as defined in the *PMBOK® Guide*. PMBOK stands for Project Management Body of Knowledge, which is created by the Project Management Institute (PMI). Discuss this definition with the participants by asking them to share other definitions they may have of project management. Ideally, this will spark some lively discussion that will reveal their views and thoughts about project management. It has been suggested, for example, that project management is the art and science of getting things done. What do they think about that definition compared to the *PMBOK® Guide* definition?
9:05 a.m. (5 min)	Slide 8 	**Learning Content/Discussion** **Project Management Process Groups** • **Handout 1: Project Management Process Groups** • **Handout 2: My Project Management Action Plan** Use this slide and Handout 1 to transition from definitions to learning about the process of managing projects. Explain that PMI and a few other large organizations have developed global standards for project management and the process of project management. The model in the slide shows PMI's five project management process groups, which will be the focus of the next five learning modules. They include initiate, plan, execute, monitor and control, and close. Each process group contains multiple activities and processes. Planning, the most important process group, comprises the majority of the content in the workshop.

TIMING	SLIDES	ACTIVITIES/NOTES/CONSIDERATIONS
	Slide 8, *continued*	Introduce Handout 2, which presents an action plan that participants will refer to throughout the training and use to keep track of ideas for implementation back on the job. Let them know that they will also be expected to share some ideas from their action plans during the final wrap-up of the workshop.
9:10 a.m. (5 min)	Slide 9 Project Phases	**Learning Content/Discussion** **Project Phases** A *project phase* is a collection of activities that creates one or more *deliverables* and ends with a *review* (*PMBOK® Guide*). A project might have any number of phases in it. Reviews are often termed *stage gates, phase exits,* or *kill points.* Phases are generally named for the type of work being performed and can be sequential or overlapping. Ask participants to think of a good kill point on a three-month project (for example, end of month, end of major deliverable, or anything that makes sense to the project team or stakeholder).
9:15 a.m. (5 min)	Slide 10 Initiate: Objectives • Understand how to initiate a typical project • Identify processes used to initiate a typical project • Identify and practice the tools and documentation required to initiate a typical project	**Learning Content/Lecture** **Initiate: Objectives** Introduce the first module, which includes the activities and processes in the first project management process group: initiate. In this module, you will help participants learn how to initiate a project, what purpose initiation serves, and why initiation is important to a project's success. A defining characteristic of the initiate project step is that it is *high level.* When a project is started, the sponsor, project manager, and stakeholders take a high-level view of the project—a vision of what is about to happen—because at this early stage, not enough is known yet to be able to define the complete, detailed project. Briefly review the slide, which gives the learning objectives of the module.

TIMING	SLIDES	ACTIVITIES/NOTES/CONSIDERATIONS
9:20 a.m. (5 min)	Slide 11 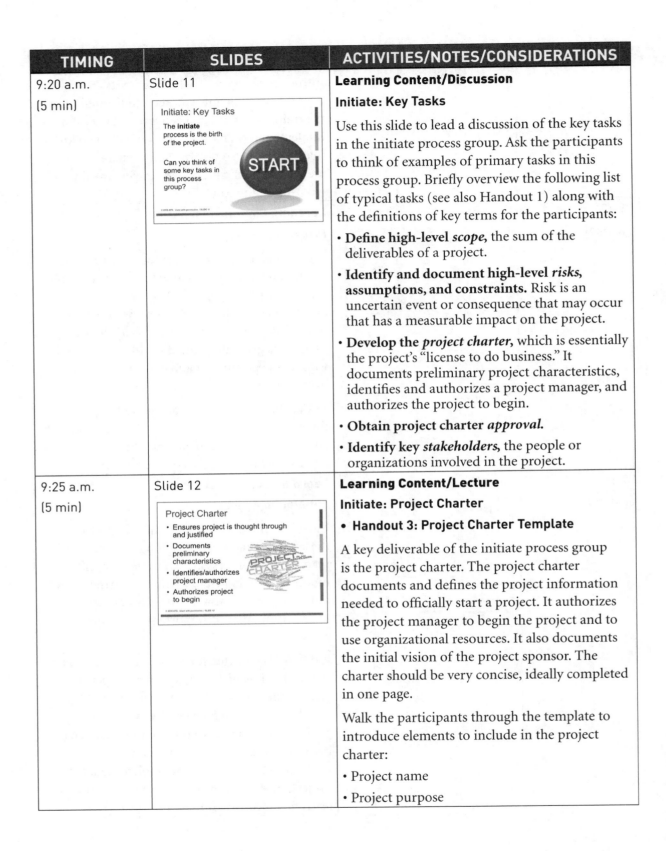	**Learning Content/Discussion** **Initiate: Key Tasks** Use this slide to lead a discussion of the key tasks in the initiate process group. Ask the participants to think of examples of primary tasks in this process group. Briefly overview the following list of typical tasks (see also Handout 1) along with the definitions of key terms for the participants: • **Define high-level *scope,*** the sum of the deliverables of a project. • **Identify and document high-level *risks,* assumptions, and constraints.** Risk is an uncertain event or consequence that may occur that has a measurable impact on the project. • **Develop the *project charter,*** which is essentially the project's "license to do business." It documents preliminary project characteristics, identifies and authorizes a project manager, and authorizes the project to begin. • **Obtain project charter *approval.*** • **Identify key *stakeholders,*** the people or organizations involved in the project.
9:25 a.m. (5 min)	Slide 12	**Learning Content/Lecture** **Initiate: Project Charter** • **Handout 3: Project Charter Template** A key deliverable of the initiate process group is the project charter. The project charter documents and defines the project information needed to officially start a project. It authorizes the project manager to begin the project and to use organizational resources. It also documents the initial vision of the project sponsor. The charter should be very concise, ideally completed in one page. Walk the participants through the template to introduce elements to include in the project charter: • Project name • Project purpose

TIMING	SLIDES	ACTIVITIES/NOTES/CONSIDERATIONS
	Slide 12, *continued*	• Business case and justification for chartering the project
		• Planned project objectives
		• High-level description of the project overall
		• High-level description of the product or service to be created by the project
		• A list of potential project risks identified at a very high level
		• Planned schedule
		• Initial budget amount
		• Results of a feasibility study or project selection analysis
		• Description of how the project links to the organization's work portfolio
		• Assignment of a project manager
		• Project manager roles, responsibilities, and authority level
		• Name and title of person(s) authorizing the project
9:30 a.m. (15 min)	Slide 13 Create a Project Charter • Select a project: – Make a cake – Build a house – Plan a vacation • Work through template with your group • Hint: Don't get bogged down in details	**Learning Activity 2: Create a Project Charter** • **Handout 3: Project Charter Template** This small group activity gives participants practice creating a project charter. Working through the template together will help them identify and document a project's purpose, objectives, descriptions, budget, schedule, and more. Use this slide and the instructions in the learning activity to complete the activity.
9:45 a.m. (15 min)	Slide 14 15-Minute Break	**BREAK**

TIMING	SLIDES	ACTIVITIES/NOTES/CONSIDERATIONS
10:00 a.m. (5 min)	Slide 15 Identify Stakeholders	**Learning Content/Lecture** **Initiate: Identify Stakeholders** • **Handout 4: Potential Stakeholders** Briefly explain that stakeholders are the people and organizations participating in the project or those who are directly or indirectly affected by the project. Stakeholders can be internal or external to the organization and can include the general public in some projects. The handout lists many potential stakeholders on projects. Ask participants to think about who else could be considered a stakeholder. Some examples of stakeholders not listed in the handout are clients, human resources, chief executive officers, chief technology officers, chief financial officers, procurement, social media team, and others.
10:05 a.m. (15 min)	Slide 16 Create a Stakeholder Register • Using your sample project, identify at least 3 stakeholders • Work through the template with your group • Hint: Don't get bogged down in details	**Learning Activity 3: Create a Stakeholder Register** • **Handout 5: Stakeholder Register Template** This small group activity introduces the stakeholder register, a key deliverable of the process of identifying stakeholders. It gives participants practice using a template to create their own stakeholder register. The relevant information project managers must document for all identified stakeholders includes the stakeholders' interests, involvement, expectations, importance, influence, and impact on the project's execution, as well as any specific communication requirements. It is important to note that they must identify all stakeholders, even if they don't actually require any communications. Follow the instructions in the learning activity.

TIMING	SLIDES	ACTIVITIES/NOTES/CONSIDERATIONS
10:20 a.m. (10 min)	Slide 17 Initiate: Module Wrap-Up	**Learning Content/Lecture** **Initiate: Module Wrap-Up** Use this slide to review the major processes included in the initiate process group (refer to Handout 1): • Define the high-level scope of a project • Identify and document high-level risks, assumptions, and constraints • Develop a project charter • Obtain project charter approval • Identify key stakeholders. Give the participants 5 minutes to make notes in their action plans (Handout 2). Ask them what actions they would like to take in the initiate process group. Encourage them to create SMART (specific, measurable, achievable, relevant, and timely) goals that they can work toward when they return to their teams and organizations.
10:30 a.m. (5 min)	Slide 18 Plan: Objectives •Identify processes to plan a typical project •Explore tools and documentation for a typical project •Plan a typical project	**Learning Content/Lecture** **Plan: Objectives** Use this slide and handout as an introduction to the planning process group. Emphasize that planning is the longest and most time-consuming process in project management. The more time is spent here, however, the less time and money will have to be spent on rework later. The objectives of this module are to identify processes needed to plan a typical project, explore tools and documentation for a project, and, finally, plan a project.

TIMING	SLIDES	ACTIVITIES/NOTES/CONSIDERATIONS
10:35 a.m. (5 min)	Slide 19 **Plan: Processes** The planning process group includes those processes performed to define and mature the project scope, develop the project plan, and identify and schedule the project activities that occur in the project.	**Learning Content/Lecture** **Plan: Processes** Briefly overview the key processes in the plan process group, referring participants to the list in Handout 1. It includes those processes performed to define and mature the project scope, develop the project plan, and identify and schedule the project activities. Explain that you will be exploring several of these processes in greater depth in this module. A key outcome of the plan process group is the *project management plan.* You will spend more time on that later in the workshop, but for now explain that it is the formal, approved document that defines the activities of the project.
10:40 a.m. (5 min)	Slide 20 Create Stakeholder Management Plan	**Learning Content/Lecture** **Plan: Create a Stakeholder Management Plan** • **Handout 6: Stakeholder Needs and Expectations Questionnaire** The process of creating a stakeholder management plan identifies how the project will manage stakeholders. It helps project managers develop ways to effectively engage stakeholders and manage their expectations so that they can achieve their project objectives. As the project progresses, the project manager may need to update this plan as circumstances change. A key component of stakeholder management is identifying stakeholder needs and expectations. Handout 6 provides a questionnaire that they can distribute to stakeholders to help them identify their needs and expectations. Walk through the handout with the participants and explain that it will help them collect valuable stakeholder input needed to create their stakeholder management plan.

TIMING	SLIDES	ACTIVITIES/NOTES/CONSIDERATIONS
10:45 a.m. (10 min)	Slide 21 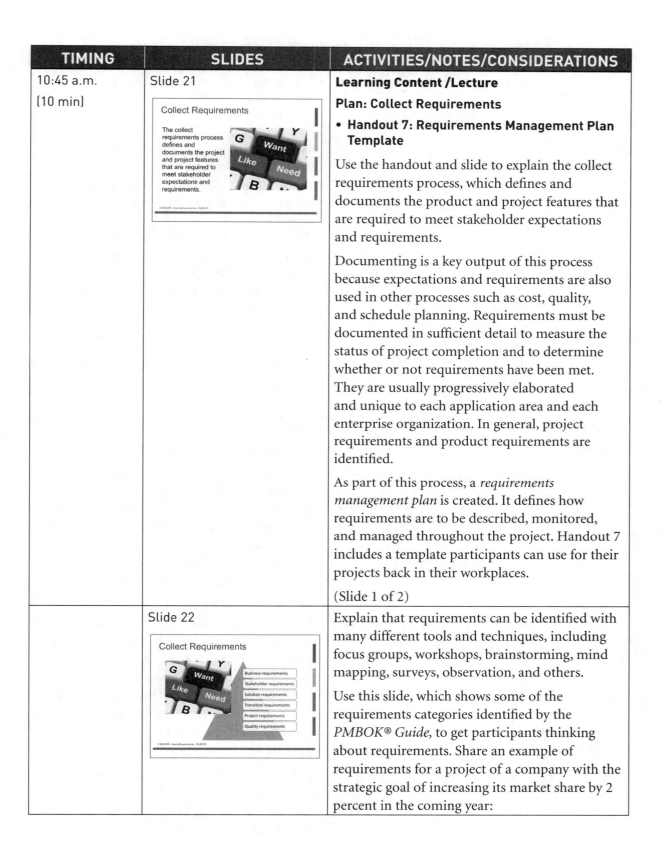 **Collect Requirements** The collect requirements process defines and documents the project and project features that are required to meet stakeholder expectations and requirements.	**Learning Content /Lecture** **Plan: Collect Requirements** • **Handout 7: Requirements Management Plan Template** Use the handout and slide to explain the collect requirements process, which defines and documents the product and project features that are required to meet stakeholder expectations and requirements. Documenting is a key output of this process because expectations and requirements are also used in other processes such as cost, quality, and schedule planning. Requirements must be documented in sufficient detail to measure the status of project completion and to determine whether or not requirements have been met. They are usually progressively elaborated and unique to each application area and each enterprise organization. In general, project requirements and product requirements are identified. As part of this process, a *requirements management plan* is created. It defines how requirements are to be described, monitored, and managed throughout the project. Handout 7 includes a template participants can use for their projects back in their workplaces. (Slide 1 of 2)
	Slide 22 **Collect Requirements** Business requirements Stakeholder requirements Solution requirements Transition requirements Project requirements Quality requirements	Explain that requirements can be identified with many different tools and techniques, including focus groups, workshops, brainstorming, mind mapping, surveys, observation, and others. Use this slide, which shows some of the requirements categories identified by the *PMBOK® Guide,* to get participants thinking about requirements. Share an example of requirements for a project of a company with the strategic goal of increasing its market share by 2 percent in the coming year:

TIMING	SLIDES	ACTIVITIES/NOTES/CONSIDERATIONS
	Slide 22, *continued*	• **Specific business objectives tied to project deliverables:** Increase sales to drive more profit by implementing a sales tracking software tool. • **Functional requirements:** The business must have sales tracking data from point of sale through inventory ordering. • **Technical specifications to achieve the functional requirements**: Manage tracking by implementing a radio frequency identification (RFID) system to scan all products. • **Quality requirements and specifications:** No more than 10 defects per 1,000 is acceptable. • **Other nonfunctional requirements:** What is needed in service levels, performance, security, or supportability? Ask participants to come up with other examples from their own projects and organizations for each type of requirement. (Slide 2 of 2)
10:55 a.m. (5 min)	Slide 23 Define Scope • Defines what *is* and *is not* included in the project • Provides project team and stakeholders with same understanding of what products will be produced and what processes will be used in producing them	**Learning Content/ Lecture** **Plan: Define Scope** Explain that scope equals work. The scope statement describes the work on the project and provides a common understanding of the project for the project stakeholders. The scope statement is progressively elaborated from initial information defined during project charter development and from requirements defined during the collect requirements process. The scope statement is a narrative document. In a typical project that is 6 months long and has a budget of $500,000, you might expect to find a 30- to 50-page scope statement document. In addition to the scope statement, there may also be separate specific technical specification documents and functional requirement documents. The scope statement is required to complete detailed project planning. The work breakdown structure, activity list, and project schedule derive from key information documented in this process.

TIMING	SLIDES	ACTIVITIES/NOTES/CONSIDERATIONS
11:00 a.m. (15 min)	Slide 24 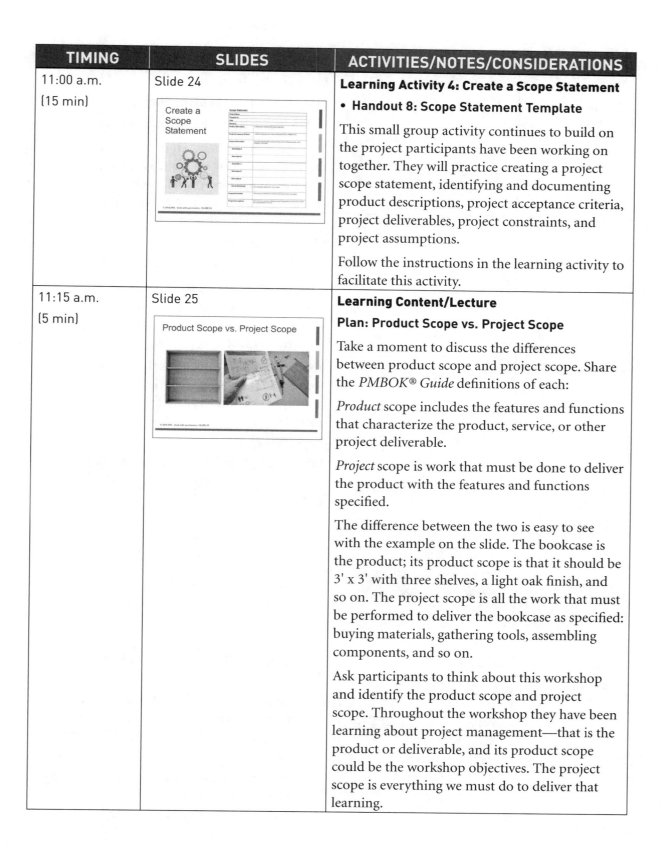	**Learning Activity 4: Create a Scope Statement** • **Handout 8: Scope Statement Template** This small group activity continues to build on the project participants have been working on together. They will practice creating a project scope statement, identifying and documenting product descriptions, project acceptance criteria, project deliverables, project constraints, and project assumptions. Follow the instructions in the learning activity to facilitate this activity.
11:15 a.m. (5 min)	Slide 25	**Learning Content/Lecture** **Plan: Product Scope vs. Project Scope** Take a moment to discuss the differences between product scope and project scope. Share the *PMBOK® Guide* definitions of each: *Product* scope includes the features and functions that characterize the product, service, or other project deliverable. *Project* scope is work that must be done to deliver the product with the features and functions specified. The difference between the two is easy to see with the example on the slide. The bookcase is the product; its product scope is that it should be 3' x 3' with three shelves, a light oak finish, and so on. The project scope is all the work that must be performed to deliver the bookcase as specified: buying materials, gathering tools, assembling components, and so on. Ask participants to think about this workshop and identify the product scope and project scope. Throughout the workshop they have been learning about project management—that is the product or deliverable, and its product scope could be the workshop objectives. The project scope is everything we must do to deliver that learning.

TIMING	SLIDES	ACTIVITIES/NOTES/CONSIDERATIONS
11:20 a.m. (5 min)	Slide 26 Scope Management Plan A scope management plan documents how the project scope will be defined, validated, and controlled.	**Learning Content/Lecture** **Plan: Scope Management Plan** • **Handout 9: Scope Management Plan Template** Use this slide and handout to briefly overview the scope management plan, which documents how the project scope will be defined, validated, and controlled. The scope management plan, at a minimum, will document • Project name • Approach to project scope changes • Who can request a scope change • Who can approve a scope change • Process description of how to request, consider, and implement a scope change. You will not have time to work through the scope management plan during the workshop, but the handout provides a template that participants can use for their projects back in their workplaces. Prior to breaking for lunch, have participants take a few moments to write in their action plans.
11:25 a.m. (60 min)	Slide 27 60-Minute Lunch	**LUNCH**
12:25 p.m. (20 min)	Slide 28 Communication Interference	**Learning Activity 5: Communication Interference** Use this activity to underline that effective communication in project management is a critical success factor. The activity is facilitated in two parts. In Part 1, lead participants in a simple listening exercise to demonstrate the importance of clear communication and good listening skills.

TIMING	SLIDES	ACTIVITIES/NOTES/CONSIDERATIONS
	Slide 28, *continued*	In Part 2, help participants explore the idea of communication "blockers"—things that can get in the way of effective communication. Lead a group brainstorm to identify factors that interfere with communication.
		Record their ideas and insights on a flipchart and post in the room as a reminder of the critical role of communication in the success of a project. Supplement their list with these communication blockers, which can be either attitudinal/behavioral or external factors:
		• **Attitudinal/behavioral:** accusing, judging, insulting, diagnosing, sarcasm, globalizing ("all" or "never")
		• **External:** language differences between sender and receiver, cultural differences, physical distance, physical background noise
		Follow the instructions in the learning activity to complete this activity.
12:45 p.m. (5 min)	Slide 29 Communications Management Plan	**Learning Content/Lecture** **Plan: Communications Management Plan** • **Handout 10: Communications Management Plan Template** Share that when troubled projects are evaluated, poor communication is typically at the heart of the conflict and negative outcomes. A common rule of thumb is that good project managers spend up to 90 percent of their time communicating. Communication provides vital connections between people, concepts, and information throughout the project environment. Good communication management ensures that important information is generated, gathered, disseminated, and warehoused in an appropriate and effective manner. It can facilitate success in projects, whereas the lack of it almost always contributes to project confusion, deficiencies, and failure.

TIMING	SLIDES	ACTIVITIES/NOTES/CONSIDERATIONS
	Slide 29, *continued*	The communications management plan helps the project manager determine the communication needs of project stakeholders, including • What information is needed • When it is needed • How it will be delivered. Briefly review the communication management plan template in Handout 10. Highlight the different kinds of information they will want to include in their plans. Point out that when putting together a communications management plan, they can save time by reusing information and materials from previous projects, but they must consider the specific needs of their current project because each project will have needs that are unique to it.
12:50 p.m. (5 min)	Slide 30 How to Eat an Elephant	**Learning Content/Lecture** **Plan: Work Breakdown Structure** Use this slide to introduce the work breakdown structure (WBS) process. Introduce the topic with this old joke: Q: How do you eat an elephant? A: One bite at a time. How does this relate to the next topic? It is much the same with projects, especially complex projects. Explain that experienced project managers understand that it is simply not possible to visualize and manage an entire project without some sort of effective tool and process. Instead of trying to manage the whole project at once, project managers break it down into bite-sized pieces, which can then be managed more easily. This process is typically the first process applied after the project scope statement has been developed.

TIMING	SLIDES	ACTIVITIES/NOTES/CONSIDERATIONS
12:55 p.m. (5 min)	Slide 31	**Learning Content/Lecture** **Plan: Sample Work Breakdown Structure** • **Handout 11: Work Breakdown Structures** Explain that the primary deliverable from the work breakdown structure process is the work breakdown structure (WBS) itself—which may well be the most important tool for management of any project. When properly developed, the WBS illustrates all of the work elements that define the project and serves as the basis for most planning activities from this point forward in the project. The WBS is a hierarchical, graphical representation of the work, which forms the scope baseline for the project. It is derived from the scope statement and the associated deliverables. Use this slide to demonstrate a simple WBS. This and more samples are included in Handout 11. The WBS breaks the project down into manageable pieces known as *work packages*, showing project work (scope) only—not time. Each descending level represents an increasingly detailed definition of project work: • Level 0 = name of project (top level on graphic) • Level 1 = typically the phase (second level on graphic) • Level 2 and beyond = work packages (rows of boxes under deliverables) Emphasize the point that work not in the WBS is work *outside* the scope of the project.

TIMING	SLIDES	ACTIVITIES/NOTES/CONSIDERATIONS
1:00 p.m. (5 min)	Slide 32 Key WBS Definitions • Work Products • Deliverables • Milestones • Scope Baseline Components	**Learning Content/Lecture** **Plan: Key WBS Definitions** • **Handout 12: WBS Dictionary** Use the slide and handout to show key WBS components and a sample WBS dictionary. A WBS dictionary is a document that describes each component in the work breakdown structure. For each WBS component, the WBS dictionary includes a brief definition of work products, deliverables, milestones, and scope baseline components, and so on. Briefly review these elements with the participants: • **Work Products:** Anything tangible produced by the project, including deliverables • **Deliverables:** Specific, defined, and tangible outputs from the project that the customer cares about • **Milestones:** Collections of major work (products or deliverables), typically used to measure project progress • **Scope Baseline Components:** Project scope statement.
1:05 p.m. (20 min)	Slide 33 Create a Simple WBS • Select a presenter and a timekeeper for your group. • Use chart paper to create and then present your WBS to the entire group.	**Learning Activity 6: Create a Simple WBS** This interactive team activity will help participants practice creating a WBS for a simple project by decomposing a project into more manageable pieces and identifying the WBS levels. Ask participants to turn to the scope statement (Handout 8) that they created in the earlier exercise (bake a cake, build a house, plan a vacation). They will use the information they documented there to help them create their WBS. Follow the instructions in the learning activity to complete this activity.

TIMING	SLIDES	ACTIVITIES/NOTES/CONSIDERATIONS
1:25 p.m. (5 min)	Slide 34 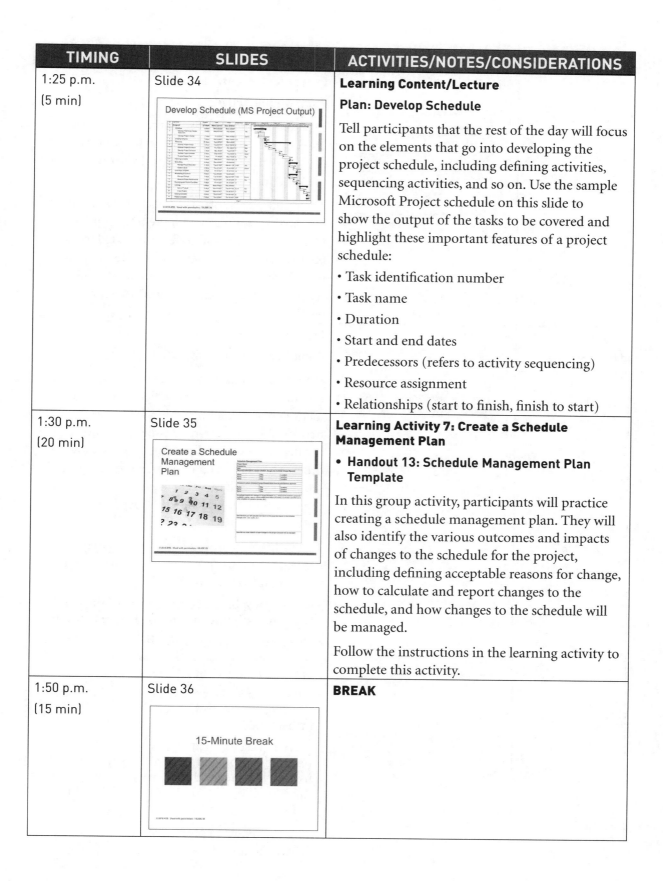	**Learning Content/Lecture** **Plan: Develop Schedule** Tell participants that the rest of the day will focus on the elements that go into developing the project schedule, including defining activities, sequencing activities, and so on. Use the sample Microsoft Project schedule on this slide to show the output of the tasks to be covered and highlight these important features of a project schedule: • Task identification number • Task name • Duration • Start and end dates • Predecessors (refers to activity sequencing) • Resource assignment • Relationships (start to finish, finish to start)
1:30 p.m. (20 min)	Slide 35	**Learning Activity 7: Create a Schedule Management Plan** • **Handout 13: Schedule Management Plan Template** In this group activity, participants will practice creating a schedule management plan. They will also identify the various outcomes and impacts of changes to the schedule for the project, including defining acceptable reasons for change, how to calculate and report changes to the schedule, and how changes to the schedule will be managed. Follow the instructions in the learning activity to complete this activity.
1:50 p.m. (15 min)	Slide 36	**BREAK**

TIMING	SLIDES	ACTIVITIES/NOTES/CONSIDERATIONS
2:05 p.m. (5 min)	Slide 37 Define Activities • Creates the detailed list of project activities/tasks by breaking down the WBS into activities • Defines the activities that will satisfy all the project work (scope)	**Learning Content/Lecture** **Plan: Define Activities** Explain that the purpose of the define activities process is to create a detailed activity list for the project, which is accomplished by breaking down the WBS into activities. The resulting activity list is part of the schedule that is often confused with the project plan. Microsoft Project and other automated tools can be used to create the activity list and eventually the schedule. Inputs to this step include the schedule management plan and the scope baseline.
2:10 p.m. (10 min)	Slide 38 Sequence Activities Define Activities → Sequence Activities → Develop Schedule	**Learning Content/Lecture** **Plan: Sequence Activities** Explain that once the activity list is created, the relationships between the activities must be identified and documented in some form of network logic diagram. This involves chronicling the dependencies and putting them in a logical order. The logic diagram in this slide shows the sequence of activities that are linked together in the logical order in which they need to be carried out. The *PMBOK® Guide* defines four types of dependencies that can exist between activities. Discuss and give examples of each: • **Mandatory:** based on the nature of the work (example: a frame on a house before the roof) • **Discretionary:** established by the project team (example: an organization's preference to do one task before another) • **External**: based on the relationship between project and nonproject activities (example: city inspections) • **Internal:** established by the organization (examples: Apple proprietary software must be used in iPhone products; every Amazon order must be shipped from an Amazon distribution center). Ask participants to give some examples of each of these kinds of dependencies.

TIMING	SLIDES	ACTIVITIES/NOTES/CONSIDERATIONS
2:20 p.m. (10 min)	Slide 39 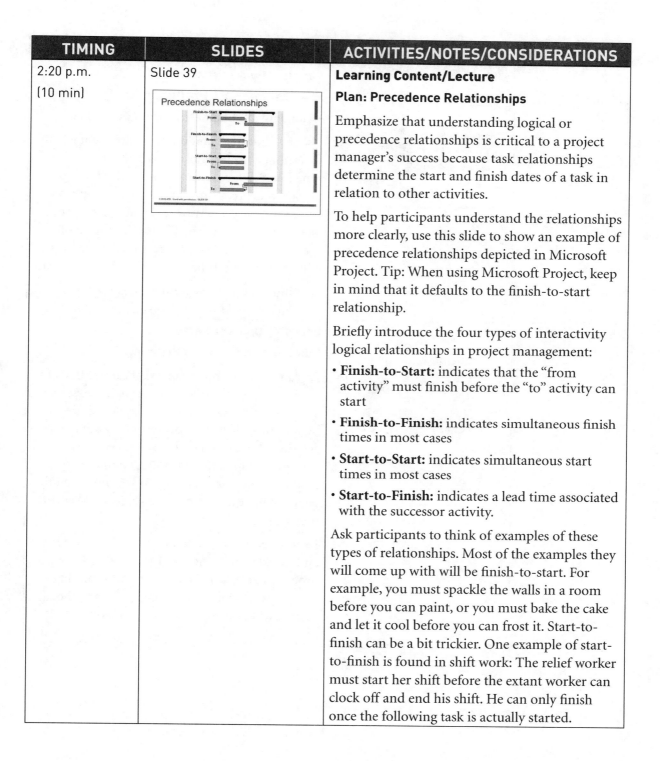	**Learning Content/Lecture** **Plan: Precedence Relationships** Emphasize that understanding logical or precedence relationships is critical to a project manager's success because task relationships determine the start and finish dates of a task in relation to other activities. To help participants understand the relationships more clearly, use this slide to show an example of precedence relationships depicted in Microsoft Project. Tip: When using Microsoft Project, keep in mind that it defaults to the finish-to-start relationship. Briefly introduce the four types of interactivity logical relationships in project management: • **Finish-to-Start:** indicates that the "from activity" must finish before the "to" activity can start • **Finish-to-Finish:** indicates simultaneous finish times in most cases • **Start-to-Start:** indicates simultaneous start times in most cases • **Start-to-Finish:** indicates a lead time associated with the successor activity. Ask participants to think of examples of these types of relationships. Most of the examples they will come up with will be finish-to-start. For example, you must spackle the walls in a room before you can paint, or you must bake the cake and let it cool before you can frost it. Start-to-finish can be a bit trickier. One example of start-to-finish is found in shift work: The relief worker must start her shift before the extant worker can clock off and end his shift. He can only finish once the following task is actually started.

TIMING	SLIDES	ACTIVITIES/NOTES/CONSIDERATIONS
2:30 p.m. (5 min)	Slide 40 Estimate Activity Durations This process estimates time durations for each defined activity resource, which will serve as an essential input for the process of developing the schedule.	**Learning Content/Lecture** **Plan: Estimate Activity Durations** • **Handout 14: Estimate Activity Durations** Use this slide and handout to explain that when we estimate activity durations, we estimate time for each defined activity to help develop the schedule. In more complex projects, it is common to use sophisticated mathematics to determine probabilistic distributions for each activity, resulting in a time range estimate instead of a single time estimate. Handout 14 gives an overview of some typical techniques used for estimating activity duration.
2:35 p.m. (5 min)	Slide 41 Human Resource Planning	**Learning Content/Lecture** **Plan: Human Resource Planning** Explain that the most important output from the human resource planning is *the human resource plan*, which defines roles and responsibilities, organizational charts, how resources will be acquired, time when each resource will be needed, any specialized training requirements, and staffing plans. Staffing plans define when the people will be assigned to the project and when they will be released. Remind participants that they must take external and market conditions into account in this process. The external conditions surrounding their organizations and the conditions of the market will influence resource availability and cost.

TIMING	SLIDES	ACTIVITIES/NOTES/CONSIDERATIONS
2:40 p.m. (20 min)	Slide 42 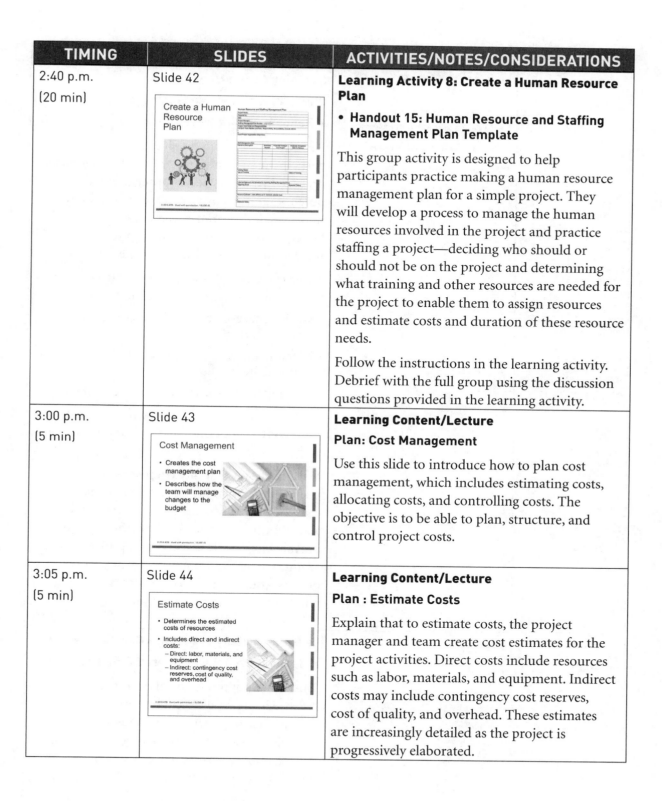	**Learning Activity 8: Create a Human Resource Plan** • **Handout 15: Human Resource and Staffing Management Plan Template** This group activity is designed to help participants practice making a human resource management plan for a simple project. They will develop a process to manage the human resources involved in the project and practice staffing a project—deciding who should or should not be on the project and determining what training and other resources are needed for the project to enable them to assign resources and estimate costs and duration of these resource needs. Follow the instructions in the learning activity. Debrief with the full group using the discussion questions provided in the learning activity.
3:00 p.m. (5 min)	Slide 43	**Learning Content/Lecture** **Plan: Cost Management** Use this slide to introduce how to plan cost management, which includes estimating costs, allocating costs, and controlling costs. The objective is to be able to plan, structure, and control project costs.
3:05 p.m. (5 min)	Slide 44	**Learning Content/Lecture** **Plan : Estimate Costs** Explain that to estimate costs, the project manager and team create cost estimates for the project activities. Direct costs include resources such as labor, materials, and equipment. Indirect costs may include contingency cost reserves, cost of quality, and overhead. These estimates are increasingly detailed as the project is progressively elaborated.

TIMING	SLIDES	ACTIVITIES/NOTES/CONSIDERATIONS

3:10 p.m.
 	
(10 min)
	Slide 45
	
	Procurement Management
	• Documents purchasing and acquisition decisions
	• Identifies potential sellers for required resources
	• Includes three primary activities:
	  – Make-or-buy decision making
	  – Selecting the type of contract
	  – Creating the Procurement Management Plan
		Learning Content/Lecture
		Plan: Procurement Management
		• **Handout 16: Contract Options**
		
		Review the points on the slide with the participants. The *plan procurement management* process documents decisions regarding the purchase and acquisition of required project resources. It determines whether resources will be acquired from outside the organization, and if so, identifies potential sellers of the resources.
		
		Three primary activities are completed during the plan procurement management process:
		
		• Making make-or-buy decisions (which can often be difficult)
		
		• Selecting the type of contract(s) to be negotiated with suppliers
		
		• Creating the procurement management plan.
		
		Briefly overview Handout 16, which presents some contract options and the best time to use them.
		
		Make the point that the required resources include more than just physical materials or components; they can also include services and labor from outside the immediate project organization. Some construction projects, for example, may require special permits. This process would be used to specify who will purchase those permits and how they will be obtained.

3:20 p.m. (15 min)	Slide 46 Create a Contract Award	**Learning Activity 9: Create a Contract Award** • **Handout 17: Contract Award Template** This small group activity gives participants practice in creating a contract award, which describes how a specific contract will be administered and defines the needs for procuring outside resources, selecting those resources, and ensuring they perform as expected on the project. Follow the instructions in the learning activity. Debrief with the full group using the discussion questions provided in the learning activity.

TIMING	SLIDES	ACTIVITIES/NOTES/CONSIDERATIONS
3:35 p.m. (5 min)	Slide 47 Quality Management • Quality must be "planned-in"—not "inspected in" • Quality means delivering precisely what is promised	**Learning Content/Discussion** **Plan: Quality Management** Review the essentials of quality management with the participants. When a project team delivers on time, within budget, satisfying all scope requirements, then quality has been achieved. To make sure that this happens, the project manager and team must define what quality means to the project and document it in the *project quality management plan,* which identifies roles and responsibilities; specific subject matter expertise; and the who, when, and where of quality management. It identifies how the project will be measured and what outcomes will constitute acceptable quality. It also identifies how the products of the project will be measured and what specific outcomes, functions, or specifications will qualify as acceptable quality. In addition, the organization may have specific quality processes and procedures that have to be applied to the project and product quality plans.
3:40 p.m. (5 min)	Slide 48 Quality vs. Grade	**Learning Content/Discussion** **Plan: Quality vs. Grade** Explain that there is a big difference between the terms *quality* and *grade. Quality,* according to the International Standards Organization, is "the degree to which a product or service fulfills its requirements" (ISO 9000). *Grade,* in contrast, is the product or service's categorization based on its characteristics or features. A product can be high grade or low grade, and as long as it fulfills its requirements, there is no problem. Low quality, however, is a problem. Share this example with the participants. Ask them to imagine buying a cheap, basic model car (*low grade*). It doesn't have any fancy features, but it works, exactly as promised, every time. It may be a *low-grade* product, but because it works well it is also *high quality.*

TIMING	SLIDES	ACTIVITIES/NOTES/CONSIDERATIONS
	Slide 48, *continued*	Now ask them to imagine buying a high-end, luxury model car (*high grade*). It has all the advanced features—navigation system, heated seats, voice activation, and so on. But how would they feel if the navigation system always got them lost or the voice activation responded as if they were speaking another language? How satisfied would they be with their *high-grade, low-quality* purchase?
		Rolex and Timex watches are another example. Both tell time and both look about the same, except one is high grade and the other is low grade. Both may be high quality, or neither may be, depending on whether they have quality built into them.
		People never buy a low-grade product and expect it to perform like a high-grade one. However, to be satisfied, they do expect high quality regardless of grade. The quality management plan will help a project team determine, in advance, acceptable levels of quality and how it will be measured.
3:45 p.m. (5 min)	Slide 49 Impact of Poor Quality ✓Increased Costs ✓Low Morale ✓Lower Customer Satisfaction ✓Increased Risk Costs of Fixing Errors Time or Phase of Project	**Learning Content/Discussion** **Plan: Impact of Poor Quality** Good quality clearly has benefits associated with it, but what about the effects of poor quality? Briefly present this graph showing poor quality and its impact over time on a project. Ask your participants to share examples from their experiences of the negative impact of poor quality on projects. Be ready to share some of your own experiences as well. Here are some ideas to get you started: • **Rework during project:** Doing the same work a second time! • **Rework when products are delivered:** Failure to meet customer requirements and expectations. • **Rework after delivery:** Product recalls, warranty work, remedy after the fact; decreased reputation and credibility.

TIMING	SLIDES	ACTIVITIES/NOTES/CONSIDERATIONS
3:50 p.m. (10 min) Ends at 4:00 p.m.	Slide 50 Day-One Debrief • Reflect on what you learned today • Share what you found most valuable Key Learning Points	**Day-One Debrief** Close Day One of the workshop by asking participants to reflect on what they learned today. Have them write some next steps in their action plans (Handout 2) and encourage them to share the one idea that they found most valuable. Close with an interactive activity. Choose your favorite or conduct a search on the Internet, which will bring up lots of ideas such as the ball toss (toss a ball around a circle, and as each person catches the ball he or she shares one thing they learned today). Another effective closing activity is called the gallery walk. If you have flipchart pages from the workshop posted on the walls (so that there is a lot of good information on the walls), have participants walk around the room and read the flipcharts, as if in an art gallery, by way of review. Encourage them to use their smartphones to take photos of the chart pages with ideas that they want to remember. Answer any questions about the first day's topics and share reminders about Day Two of the workshop.

What to Do Between Workshop Days

- Make notes about follow-up you need to do before the second day.
- Capture facilitator lessons learned from the first day of the workshop and adjust materials or your facilitation plan for the second day, if necessary.
- Address equipment, room setup, catering, or other learning environment issues that you haven't been able to address during the workshop.
- Debrief with your co-facilitator, if appropriate.
- Gather the materials required for Day Two's activities.

Two-Day Workshop Agenda: Day Two

Day Two: (8:00 a.m. to 4:00 p.m.)

TIMING	SLIDES	ACTIVITIES/NOTES/CONSIDERATIONS
8:00 a.m. (5 min)	Slide 51 **ATD** Workshop Project Management Training Two-Day Workshop Day Two	**Welcome and Reconnect** Arrive early to set up the room and make sure that everything is working properly. Adjust room configuration as needed. Welcome participants and tell them that in today's session they are going to continue learning about the project management process, picking back up with the planning process group, then exploring executing, monitoring and controlling, and finally closing the project.
8:05 a.m. (5 min)	Slide 52 Day-One Review • What did we learn on day one? • What is still unclear? **???**	**Day-One Review** Take a few moments to review what you covered in the first day of the workshop. Tell participants to look through their notes and then ask them a few of the following questions to get them warmed up: • What is the definition of a project? • What is the primary purpose of a project charter? • What is a stakeholder? • How much time should a project manager spend communicating? • Why should we collect requirements? • What does WBS stand for? • What is it used for? • What are precedence relationships? • What is the difference between quality and grade? Give participants an opportunity to ask questions about the content. Is there anything that is still unclear?

TIMING	SLIDES	ACTIVITIES/NOTES/CONSIDERATIONS
8:10 a.m. (5 min)	Slide 53 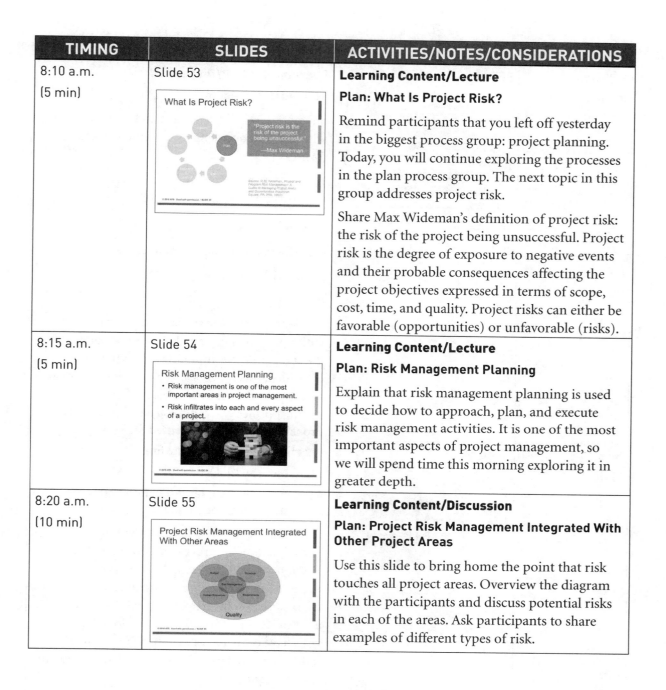	**Learning Content/Lecture** **Plan: What Is Project Risk?** Remind participants that you left off yesterday in the biggest process group: project planning. Today, you will continue exploring the processes in the plan process group. The next topic in this group addresses project risk. Share Max Wideman's definition of project risk: the risk of the project being unsuccessful. Project risk is the degree of exposure to negative events and their probable consequences affecting the project objectives expressed in terms of scope, cost, time, and quality. Project risks can either be favorable (opportunities) or unfavorable (risks).
8:15 a.m. (5 min)	Slide 54	**Learning Content/Lecture** **Plan: Risk Management Planning** Explain that risk management planning is used to decide how to approach, plan, and execute risk management activities. It is one of the most important aspects of project management, so we will spend time this morning exploring it in greater depth.
8:20 a.m. (10 min)	Slide 55	**Learning Content/Discussion** **Plan: Project Risk Management Integrated With Other Project Areas** Use this slide to bring home the point that risk touches all project areas. Overview the diagram with the participants and discuss potential risks in each of the areas. Ask participants to share examples of different types of risk.

TIMING	SLIDES	ACTIVITIES/NOTES/CONSIDERATIONS
8:30 a.m. (5 min)	Slide 56 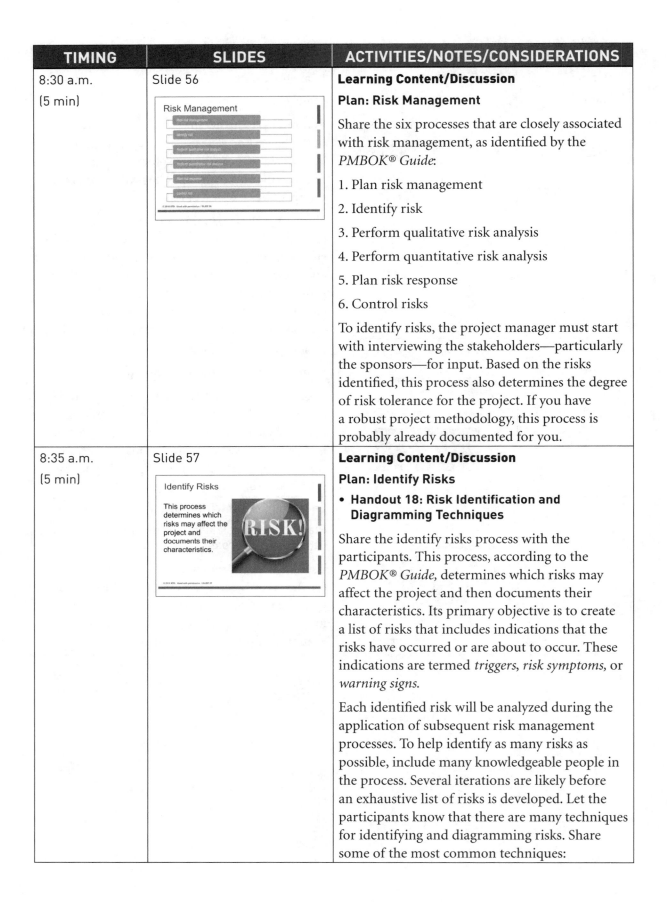	**Learning Content/Discussion** **Plan: Risk Management** Share the six processes that are closely associated with risk management, as identified by the *PMBOK® Guide*: 1. Plan risk management 2. Identify risk 3. Perform qualitative risk analysis 4. Perform quantitative risk analysis 5. Plan risk response 6. Control risks To identify risks, the project manager must start with interviewing the stakeholders—particularly the sponsors—for input. Based on the risks identified, this process also determines the degree of risk tolerance for the project. If you have a robust project methodology, this process is probably already documented for you.
8:35 a.m. (5 min)	Slide 57	**Learning Content/Discussion** **Plan: Identify Risks** • **Handout 18: Risk Identification and Diagramming Techniques** Share the identify risks process with the participants. This process, according to the *PMBOK® Guide*, determines which risks may affect the project and then documents their characteristics. Its primary objective is to create a list of risks that includes indications that the risks have occurred or are about to occur. These indications are termed *triggers*, *risk symptoms*, or *warning signs*. Each identified risk will be analyzed during the application of subsequent risk management processes. To help identify as many risks as possible, include many knowledgeable people in the process. Several iterations are likely before an exhaustive list of risks is developed. Let the participants know that there are many techniques for identifying and diagramming risks. Share some of the most common techniques:

TIMING	SLIDES	ACTIVITIES/NOTES/CONSIDERATIONS
	Slide 57, *continued*	• Brainstorming • Delphi estimation • Nominal group • Process flowcharting • Checklist analysis • Assumptions analysis • Qualitative risk analysis • Documentation review. Handout 18 gives more information about these techniques as well as examples. Remind participants that although most risk identification is done during planning, identifying risks should be encouraged frequently throughout the project life cycle. In many projects, new risks can surface daily.
8:40 a.m. (10 min)	Slide 58 Cause-and-Effect Diagram Example	**Learning Content/Discussion** **Plan: Cause-and-Effect Diagram Example** There are multiple diagramming techniques that can be used for root-cause analysis. Here are some of the most common: • Fishbone diagrams • System process flowcharts • Influence diagrams. Walk through this sample cause-and-effect diagram (also called a fishbone or Ishikawa diagram) with the participants. A fishbone diagram identifies possible causes for a problem. It immediately sorts ideas into useful categories and can be used to structure a brainstorming session. This example shows the possible causes of shipping the wrong merchandise. **Variation:** If you have time, you can share the process of creating a fishbone diagram or create a simple diagram together as a group on a flipchart.

TIMING	SLIDES	ACTIVITIES/NOTES/CONSIDERATIONS
	Slide 58, *continued*	To create a fishbone diagram, the group agrees on the problem, which goes in a box at the center right of the paper with a long horizontal line running to it. The group brainstorms the *categories* of causes of the problem, which are drawn as angled branches off the horizontal line (thus earning its name *fishbone*). Then the group brainstorms possible causes of the problem, and each idea is written as a branch off the category it fits in (it could be written in more than one place if it relates to more than one category). The group can continue to ask "Why does this happen?" and write sub-causes branching off the causes until the group runs out of ideas.
8:50 a.m. (10 min)	Slide 59 Process Flowcharting Exercise • A flowchart is a graphical representation of a process. • It identifies potential risk areas. • It is used in process improvement.	**Learning Activity 10: Process Flowcharting Exercise** Explain that a flowchart is a graphical representation of a process. It can identify potential areas of risk and can be used in process improvement. This activity will give participants practice using the process flowcharting technique to create a graphical representation of a simple process and to identify potential risks in the process. Follow the instructions in the learning activity to conduct this activity.
9:00 a.m. (15 min)	Slide 60 Risk Categorization Exercise	**Learning Activity 11: Risk Categorization Exercise** • **Handout 19: Project Risk Categorization Worksheet** In this small group exercise, participants practice using a template to identify and categorize risks for a project. Risk categorization is an important tool in analyzing and prioritizing risks. It builds on the risk information generated in the risk identification process. Risks can be categorized into several major categories: • Technical, quality, and performance risks • Project management risks

TIMING	SLIDES	ACTIVITIES/NOTES/CONSIDERATIONS
	Slide 60, *continued*	• Organizational risks • Internal risks • External risks. We prioritize risk so that we can focus efforts on those risks that most affect our project success. Follow the instructions in the learning activity to complete this activity. No debrief is needed for the activity. Transition directly into the next slide.
9:15 a.m. (10 min)	Slide 61 	**Learning Content/Discussion** **Plan: Qualitative Risk Analysis** Explain that risk analysis builds on the risk information gathered during the identification step, converting it into information that can be used in decision making. Analysis helps determine the risk's *probability* (the likelihood the risk's consequences will occur), *impact* (an estimate of the severity of adverse effects, magnitude of loss, and opportunity cost), and *exposure* (probability $\times$ impact). A probability and impact (P–I) matrix offers a way to determine whether a risk is considered low, moderate, or high by combining the two dimensions of a risk: its probability of occurrence and its impact on objectives if it occurs. Use the P–I matrix on this slide to work through a few examples of risks with the participants. Together decide where the risks would rate on the P–I matrix.

TIMING	SLIDES	ACTIVITIES/NOTES/CONSIDERATIONS
9:25 a.m. (5 min)	Slide 62 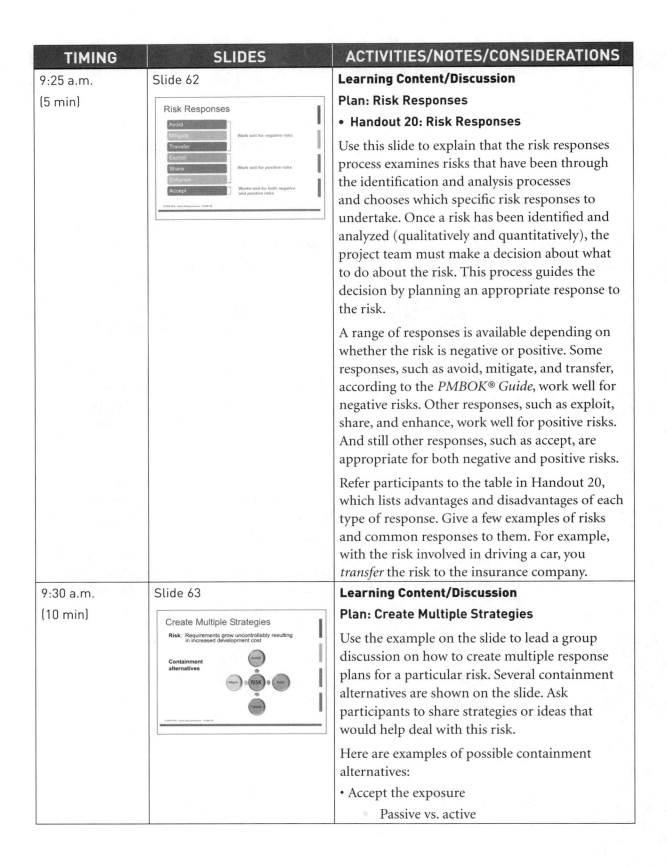	**Learning Content/Discussion** **Plan: Risk Responses** • **Handout 20: Risk Responses** Use this slide to explain that the risk responses process examines risks that have been through the identification and analysis processes and chooses which specific risk responses to undertake. Once a risk has been identified and analyzed (qualitatively and quantitatively), the project team must make a decision about what to do about the risk. This process guides the decision by planning an appropriate response to the risk. A range of responses is available depending on whether the risk is negative or positive. Some responses, such as avoid, mitigate, and transfer, according to the *PMBOK® Guide*, work well for negative risks. Other responses, such as exploit, share, and enhance, work well for positive risks. And still other responses, such as accept, are appropriate for both negative and positive risks. Refer participants to the table in Handout 20, which lists advantages and disadvantages of each type of response. Give a few examples of risks and common responses to them. For example, with the risk involved in driving a car, you *transfer* the risk to the insurance company.
9:30 a.m. (10 min)	Slide 63	**Learning Content/Discussion** **Plan: Create Multiple Strategies** Use the example on the slide to lead a group discussion on how to create multiple response plans for a particular risk. Several containment alternatives are shown on the slide. Ask participants to share strategies or ideas that would help deal with this risk. Here are examples of possible containment alternatives: • Accept the exposure ◦ Passive vs. active

TIMING	SLIDES	ACTIVITIES/NOTES/CONSIDERATIONS

	Slide 63, *continued*	• Avoid
		   ◦ Invoke contract termination
		   ◦ Restrict to well-defined parts
		• Transfer
		   ◦ Specify requirements as responsibility of the customers
		• Mitigate
		   ◦ Use phased approach
		   ◦ Use change management procedure in contract
		• Risk reserve
		   ◦ Set aside a reserve (*cost, time*)

9:40 a.m. (5 min)	Slide 64 Project Management Plan • Integrates all subsidiary plans and outputs from other planning processes into a single, interconnected document • Represents the final step in project planning	**Learning Content/Lecture** **Plan: Project Management Plan** You have spent a good deal of the workshop working through the processes in the project planning phase with your participants. Creating the project management plan is the final process in the group. Use this slide to discuss the project management plan and bring a close to the plan project phase. The project management plan integrates all the subsidiary plans and outputs from other planning processes into a single, interconnected document. It is the why, what, how, who, how much, and when of the project. Completion of this plan marks the end of the planning stage and allows the project manager and team to proceed to the execute phase of the project. The project manager and project team must meet with all of the stakeholders during a project kickoff meeting to overcome any objections and obtain final approval for the project management plan before the executing processes begin. The kickoff meeting is the last planning meeting before executing. Note that organizations may differ in the way they define the project management plan or when they hold the final approval meeting.

TIMING	SLIDES	ACTIVITIES/NOTES/CONSIDERATIONS
9:45 a.m. (10 min)	Slide 65 Plan: Module Wrap-Up	**Learning Content/Lecture** **Plan: Module Wrap-Up** Use this slide to wrap up the second and largest process group module: plan. Review the major processes in the plan project process group (Handout 1): • Create stakeholder management plan • Collect requirements • Create communications management plan • Create scope management plan • Define scope • Create work breakdown structure (WBS) • Create schedule management plan • Develop schedule • Create cost management plan • Estimate costs • Determine budget • Create risk management plan • Create quality management plan • Record details for scope, schedule, and costs • Define how to manage and control all aspects of the project • Identify key roles needed on the project • Identify, analyze, and document risks, assumptions, and constraints • Document strategies and decisions • Obtain formal approval of the project management plan Give participants 5 minutes to make some notes in their action plans (Handout 2). Ask them what actions they would like to take in the planning process group. Encourage them to create SMART goals that they can work toward when they return to their teams and organizations.

TIMING	SLIDES	ACTIVITIES/NOTES/CONSIDERATIONS
9:55 a.m. (15 min)	Slide 66 15-Minute Break	**BREAK**
10:10 a.m. (5 min)	Slide 67 Execute: Objectives • Learn to manage work on the project • Identify the purpose of developing and managing the project team • Identify tools used to execute the project management plan	**Learning Content/Lecture** **Execute: Objectives** Use this slide to introduce the next module and its objectives. The third major process group in project management is executing the project. A key word that might characterize the executing process is *deliverables*. The most important output of the entire process group is the deliverables created for the project. In addition to deliverables, there are records of the deliverables that are distributed as information to project stakeholders.

10:15 a.m.
(5 min)
	Slide 68
	
	Execute: Purpose
	• One major outcome of executing the project is deliverables.
	• The project manager will manage the project work by
	  – Encouraging the project team to work together
	  – Managing communications with stakeholders
	  – Managing issues that may arise.
		Learning Content/Lecture
		Execute: Purpose
		
		Explain that the purpose of the execute phase is to produce the project deliverables as defined by the project requirements. The various executing processes work very closely with each other. In addition, they also work closely with the processes in the monitoring and controlling process group. Executing processes focus on producing deliverables, whereas the monitoring and controlling processes concentrate on confirming that the planned deliverables are created and that they meet the planned specifications and requirements.

TIMING	SLIDES	ACTIVITIES/NOTES/CONSIDERATIONS
10:20 a.m. (5 min)	Slide 69 **Execute: Processes** • Acquire, develop, and manage project team • Manage stakeholder engagement • Conduct procurements • Perform quality assurance • Manage communications • Direct and manage work	**Learning Content/Lecture** **Execute: Processes** Use this slide and Handout 1 to overview the many tasks and processes associated with the executing project process as defined in the *PMBOK® Guide*. Remind the participants that even though they have transitioned into the executing phase, planning does not stop if a need arises. Some of the processes are PMBOK based; others are practical. The processes of acquiring, developing, and managing the project team are self-explanatory and can be interpreted literally. The next two—manage stakeholder engagement and conduct procurements—are also easily understood and performed with a general understanding of business without extensive prior knowledge. In fact, the procurement function is often handled by the procurement or purchasing department in many organizations. Explain that for this workshop, then, you will concentrate on the remaining three processes in the execute group—communications, quality assurance, and managing project work.
10:25 a.m. (5 min)	Slide 70 **Manage Communications** • Makes project information available to project stakeholders, as documented in the communications management plan • Creates, collects, distributes, stores, and retrieves project information • Requires orderly record keeping, distribution methods, information retrieval systems, and solid communications skills.	**Learning Content/Lecture** **Execute: Manage Communications** Managing communications requires orderly record keeping, distribution methods, information retrieval systems, excellent communication skills. Both the project manager and the stakeholders must possess solid communication skills. Following the communications plan (created in the project planning phase) is a key consideration for sharing information among project team members and stakeholders during the executing process. For example, if the communications plan calls for a Friday status report, the project manager must fulfill that requirement.

TIMING	SLIDES	ACTIVITIES/NOTES/CONSIDERATIONS
10:30 a.m. (20 min)	Slide 71 Matrix Game: Communication 101	**Learning Activity 12: Matrix Game:** **Communication 101** It bears repeating that effective communication is the single most important success factor in projects. It encompasses a broad set of skills that all project managers must develop. This interactive game will give participants practice tailoring their communication styles to suit their purpose and audience. Follow the instructions in the learning activity to conduct this game.
10:50 a.m. (5 min)	Slide 72 Quality Assurance • Application of quality activities intended to ensure the project will employ all processes necessary to satisfy documented requirements • Project quality management is the responsibility of the project manager	**Learning Content/Lecture** **Execute: Quality Assurance** Use this slide to explain that the quality assurance process focuses on the quality metrics associated with the project. Quality assurance measures the project in terms of scope, schedule, and cost performance. Quality *assurance* is more *project* oriented, whereas quality *control* is more *product* oriented. In quality assurance, qualified experts measure project performance against the project plan; in quality control, auditors or other subject matter experts measure quality against the product. Often project managers who are not associated with the project are used to audit the project.
10:55 a.m. (5 min)	Slide 73 Direct and Manage Project Work • Coordinating and directing all project resources to carry out the project management plan • Typically, most project costs are expended during project execution	**Learning Content/Lecture** **Execute: Direct and Manage Project Work** The direct and manage project work process has one major goal: creating the deliverables defined in the project management plan. To successfully execute the project management plan, the project manager must manage the work performed; track scope, schedule, and budget baselines; and determine performance results. The project manager and team must continually monitor and measure performance against baselines so that timely corrective action can be taken when needed. They must also periodically update final cost and schedule forecasts.

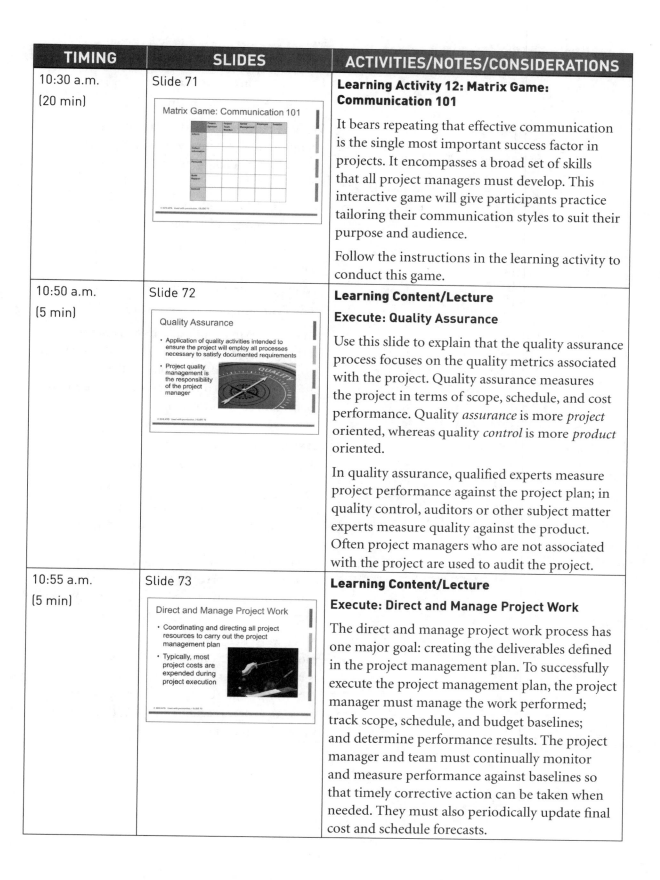

TIMING	SLIDES	ACTIVITIES/NOTES/CONSIDERATIONS
11:00 a.m. (10 min)	Slide 74 Execute: Module Wrap-Up	**Learning Content/Lecture** **Execute: Module Wrap-Up** We have reached the end of our third process group module: execute. Review the major processes included in the execute group (Handout 1): • Acquire, develop, and manage project team • Manage stakeholder engagement • Conduct procurements • Perform quality assurance • Manage communications • Direct and manage project work. Give participants 5 minutes to make some notes in their action plans (Handout 2). Ask them what actions they would like to take in the execute process group. Encourage them to create SMART goals that they can work on when they return to their teams and organizations.
11:10 a.m. (5 min)	Slide 75 Monitor and Control: Objectives	**Learning Content/Lecture** **Monitor and Control: Objectives** Use this slide to introduce the next module and its objectives. The fourth major phase in project management is controlling and monitoring the project. This module will explain how to monitor and control the project work, what purpose these processes serve, and why monitoring and controlling the project is important to a project's success. A key word that might characterize the monitoring and controlling process group is *check*. The most important element of monitoring and controlling is *checking* the project's progress against the plan to ensure that the project is on track.

TIMING	SLIDES	ACTIVITIES/NOTES/CONSIDERATIONS
11:15 a.m. (5 min)	Slide 76 **Monitor and Control: Purpose** • Ensures the work being performed is the planned work or is changed to meet the requirements of the project in a controlled manner. • The project manager monitors and controls the project by – Controlling changes – Monitoring progress	**Learning Content/Lecture** **Monitor and Control: Purpose** Explain that this process group focuses on controlling change on the project and measuring project performance. Its key deliverable is a controlled approach to managing change. The project manager will continue to manage the work on the project. Refer participants to Handout 1, which summarizes the monitoring and controlling processes as defined in the *PMBOK® Guide*. The processes have a high degree of interaction with each other and work closely with the processes in the executing process group. As noted in the previous module, executing processes focus on producing deliverables, whereas the monitoring and controlling processes concentrate on confirming that the right deliverables are created and that they meet the planned specifications and requirements. When a change occurs on the project, the project manager will return to the planning processes to update affected project documents to ensure that the entire project is continually properly documented.
11:20 a.m. (5 min)	Slide 77 **Control Scope** • This process effectively manages changes in project scope and then integrates them across the entire project. • Scope changes are identified by using the variance analysis tool. • The project manager is responsible for discouraging unnecessary scope changes.	**Learning Content/Discussion** **Monitor and Control: Control Scope** Although it may seem obvious, ask participants why it is important to control the scope of a project and then let them share their ideas. Remind them that changes in scope, if not managed well, can lead to schedule delays, cost overruns, and scope creep (uncontrolled changes or growth of a project or product's scope).

TIMING	SLIDES	ACTIVITIES/NOTES/CONSIDERATIONS
	Slide 77, *continued*	Change is a pervasive and unavoidable feature of our world, and in this environment, the project manager is responsible for minimizing unnecessary changes to the project using the control scope process, which manages necessary changes to the project work baseline. The process works closely with the other change control processes. If a change is approved, the project scope statement must be updated.
11:25 a.m. (5 min)	Slide 78 Control Schedule • Monitors the status of the project to update project progress • Manages changes to the schedule baseline	**Learning Content/Lecture** **Monitor and Control: Control Schedule** The control schedule process focuses on controlling changes to the schedule. Use the slide to share the *PMBOK® Guide* two-part definition of this process. As with scope control, the project manager is responsible for minimizing unnecessary changes to the project—in this case, the schedule. If a schedule change is approved, then project schedule must be updated. Some organizations use a change control board (CCB) to evaluate and approve change requests.
11:30 a.m. (5 min)	Slide 79 Control Costs • Effectively manages changes to the project budget • Uses the earned value technique to measure project cost performance.	**Learning Content/Lecture** **Monitor and Control: Control Costs** Briefly review the control costs process, which manages necessary changes to the project cost baseline (budget) and measures project performance using earned value. The earned value technique helps measure cost performance against the plan (earned value versus planned value). We will look more closely at the planned and earned values after lunch. The control costs process works closely with the other change control processes. The project manager is responsible for minimizing unnecessary changes to the project. If a cost change is approved, the project budget must be updated.

TIMING	SLIDES	ACTIVITIES/NOTES/CONSIDERATIONS
11:35 a.m. (60 min)	Slide 80 60-Minute Lunch	**LUNCH**
12:35 p.m. (10 min)	Slide 81 Four Key Data Points for Controlling Project Costs Planned Value / Earned Value / Actual Cost / Budget at Completion	**Learning Content/Lecture** **Monitor and Control: Four Key Data Points for Controlling Project Costs** • **Handout 21: Four Key Data Points for Controlling Project Costs** Use this slide and Handout 21 to introduce the four key data points used in controlling costs: planned value, earned value, actual cost, and budget at completion. **Planned value (PV)** is what we intend to do (*scheduled work*) and what we intend to spend to do it (*cost*). There is a dual element involved in planned value: scheduled work content and cost content. This is annotated as PV or BCWS (budget cost of work scheduled). Share this simple example of planned value: I intend to work 4 hours to install a new bedroom door. The PV of the work is $400. **Earned value (EV)** is the value of what we accomplished. EV is also annotated as BCWP (budgeted cost of work performed). It represents the value of the work in dollars (derived from original PV data). Share this example based on the bedroom door project: I worked 4 hours to install the new bedroom door (PV=$400); I only got 50 percent done so the earned value is $200.

TIMING	SLIDES	ACTIVITIES/NOTES/CONSIDERATIONS
	Slide 81, *continued*	**Actual cost (AC)** is the amount spent to achieve the earned value. AC is also annotated as ACWP (actual cost of work performed). AC represents the value of the work performed in dollars (derived from original PV data and the EV).
		Continuing with our door project, I worked 4 hours to install the new bedroom door (PV=$400); I only got 50 percent done (EV=$200). Because I worked the entire 4-hour period, I expended $400 worth of effort and so my AC is $400.
		And this provides an example of a cost overrun on a project. The opposite is also possible: If I had a PV of $400, but it only took me 2 hours to complete the work, the EV is $400 and the AC would be $200.
		Budget at completion, or BAC, represents the expected value of the work when completed.
		So, with our door project still in mind, I worked 4 hours to install the new bedroom door (PV=$400); I only got 50 percent done, so the BAC is $200.
12:45 p.m. (5 min)	Slide 82 Control Communications • Monitors and controls communications throughout the project life cycle. • The level and detail of reporting should be appropriate to the intended audience.	**Learning Content/Lecture** **Monitor and Control: Control Communications** Explain that the process of controlling communications focuses on reporting actual project performance. The project manager tracks performance using cost control and schedule control processes and then reports using data from these processes. The process uses forecasts associated with project performance reports. Many organizations choose to simplify the performance report into a "dashboard" configuration that shows a "red, yellow, or green" status based on predetermined parameters.

TIMING	SLIDES	ACTIVITIES/NOTES/CONSIDERATIONS
12:50 p.m. (5 min)	Slide 83 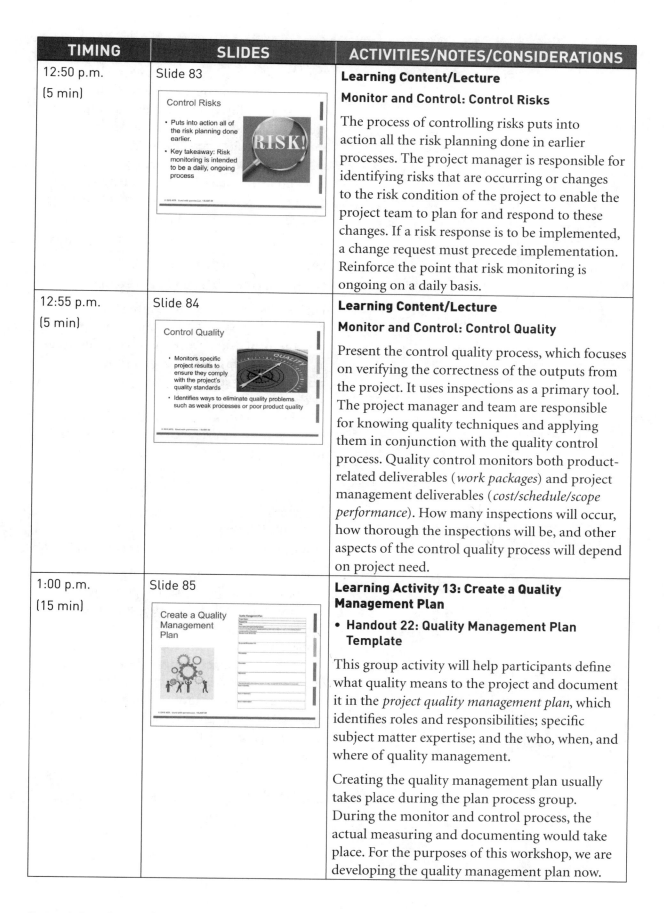	**Learning Content/Lecture** **Monitor and Control: Control Risks** The process of controlling risks puts into action all the risk planning done in earlier processes. The project manager is responsible for identifying risks that are occurring or changes to the risk condition of the project to enable the project team to plan for and respond to these changes. If a risk response is to be implemented, a change request must precede implementation. Reinforce the point that risk monitoring is ongoing on a daily basis.
12:55 p.m. (5 min)	Slide 84	**Learning Content/Lecture** **Monitor and Control: Control Quality** Present the control quality process, which focuses on verifying the correctness of the outputs from the project. It uses inspections as a primary tool. The project manager and team are responsible for knowing quality techniques and applying them in conjunction with the quality control process. Quality control monitors both product-related deliverables (*work packages*) and project management deliverables (*cost/schedule/scope performance*). How many inspections will occur, how thorough the inspections will be, and other aspects of the control quality process will depend on project need.
1:00 p.m. (15 min)	Slide 85	**Learning Activity 13: Create a Quality Management Plan** • **Handout 22: Quality Management Plan Template** This group activity will help participants define what quality means to the project and document it in the *project quality management plan*, which identifies roles and responsibilities; specific subject matter expertise; and the who, when, and where of quality management. Creating the quality management plan usually takes place during the plan process group. During the monitor and control process, the actual measuring and documenting would take place. For the purposes of this workshop, we are developing the quality management plan now.

TIMING	SLIDES	ACTIVITIES/NOTES/CONSIDERATIONS
	Slide 85, *continued*	The plan identifies how the project will be measured and what outcomes will constitute acceptable quality. It also identifies how the products of the project will be measured and what specific outcomes, functions, or specifications will qualify as acceptable quality. In addition, the organization may have specific quality processes and procedures that have to be applied to the project and product quality plans. Follow the instructions in the learning activity.
1:15 p.m. (5 min)	Slide 86 Run Chart Example	**Learning Content/Lecture** **Monitor and Control: Run Chart Example** Explain that a run chart is simply a line graph plotted over time. Collecting and charting data over time can help uncover trends or patterns in a process. Use this slide to demonstrate a sample run chart of pizza delivery times over several weeks. The chart provides a visual representation of the process, making it easy to see the peaks and valleys, so we can uncover possible issues to address. If the goal was to deliver a pizza in 20 minutes on average, the graph reveals where deliveries are over and under that time and on which days that occurs.
1:20 p.m. (5 min)	Slide 87 Control Procurements Monitors the relationships created by a project's procurement needs, contract performance, and procurement changes	**Learning Content/Lecture** **Monitor and Control: Control Procurements** The control procurements process focuses on managing the sellers' work and performance and integrating seller resources into the overall project management process. The project manager is responsible for minimizing unnecessary changes to the project. However, necessary contract changes that will improve the outcome or performance should be proactively considered and applied to the project. If a work change is approved, then the project scope statement and the sellers' contract(s) will need to be updated, which implies a return to planning and executing processes.

TIMING	SLIDES	ACTIVITIES/NOTES/CONSIDERATIONS
1:25 p.m. (5 min)	Slide 88 Control Stakeholder Engagement	**Learning Content/Lecture** **Monitor and Control: Control Stakeholder Engagement** The *PMBOK® Guide* defines this process as monitoring stakeholder relationships and adjusting strategies to engage those individuals or groups. As the project progresses and its environment changes, adjustments may need to be made to maintain or increase efficiency and effectiveness with key stakeholders. Stakeholder engagement is highest in the beginning of the project and wanes as the project progresses. The role of the project manager is to monitor that engagement and ensure it does not cause project slowdowns or stops.
1:30 p.m. (5 min)	Slide 89 Perform Integrated Change Control Effectively manages changes and integrates them appropriately across the entire project	**Learning Content/Lecture** **Monitor and Control: Perform Integrated Change Control** This process focuses on managing necessary changes to the project baseline, scope, schedule, cost, and product deliverables. It deals with the deliverables planned for the project and works closely with the other change control processes. The project manager is responsible for minimizing unnecessary changes to the project. One element of the change control process is managing product specification. Similar to how the change control process manages changes to the work to be performed, it also manages changes to the product specification to minimize unnecessary product specification changes.

TIMING	SLIDES	ACTIVITIES/NOTES/CONSIDERATIONS
1:35 p.m. (5 min)	Slide 90 Monitor and Control Project Work • Monitors all other processes through initiation, planning, executing, and closing • Takes corrective or preventive actions • Project manager is responsible for continuously monitoring project work	**Learning Content/Lecture** **Monitor and Control: Monitor and Control Project Work** This process is focused on measuring work performance against the plan—the "check" portion of the project. The project manager is responsible for continuously monitoring project work. If project managers detect some aspect of the project heading off course, they will make controlling adjustments as necessary to bring the project back in alignment to ultimately achieve the project's defined objectives.
1:40 p.m. (10 min)	Slide 91 Monitor and Control: Module Wrap-Up	**Learning Content/Lecture** **Monitor and Control: Module Wrap-Up** Wrap up the discussion of the fourth process group module: monitor and control. Review the key processes involved in the monitor and control process group (Handout 1): • Control scope • Control schedule • Control costs • Control communications • Control risks • Control quality • Validate scope • Control procurements • Control stakeholder engagement • Perform integrated change control • Monitor and control project work. Ask participants if they have any questions about the processes in this group. Give them 5 minutes to make notes in their action plans (Handout 2). Ask them to note what actions they would like to take in the monitor and control process group. Encourage them to create SMART goals that they can work on when they return to their teams and organizations.

TIMING	SLIDES	ACTIVITIES/NOTES/CONSIDERATIONS
1:50 p.m. (15 min)	Slide 92 15-Minute Break	**BREAK**
2:05 p.m. (5 min)	Slide 93 Close Project: Objectives • Define processes associated with closing a project • Understand the purpose of obtaining stakeholder approval of final deliverables	**Learning Content/Lecture** **Close: Objectives** Use this slide to introduce the final process group and its objectives: closing the project. This module will explain how to close out a project, including defining the processes associated with closing a project and understanding the purpose of obtaining stakeholder approval of final deliverables. A key word that might characterize the closing process group is *signoff*.
2:10 p.m. (5 min)	Slide 94 Close: Purpose • Carefully manages closing the project or phase • Releases contracted and internal resources • Conducts an end-of-phase review to determine whether or not the project should continue	**Learning Content/Lecture** **Close: Purpose** Use this slide and Handout 1 to overview the close project process group, which manages closing the project, releases contracted and internal resources, and conducts an end-of-phase review to determine whether or not the project should continue. The key deliverable from this process is project closure. Two processes are associated with the close project process: closing procurements and closing the project or phase. Each will be discussed in this module.

TIMING	SLIDES	ACTIVITIES/NOTES/CONSIDERATIONS
2:15 p.m. (5 min)	**Slide 95** Close Procurements Formally validates that all requirements for each project procurement activity has been met and found acceptable for both seller and buyer good business purchase departments Organization purchasing contracts	**Learning Content/Lecture** **Close: Close Procurements** Explain that the close procurements process works so closely with the close project or phase process that the two processes could be one. Here, project managers track performance, work results, quality results, and overall project status with the seller. They provide formal acceptance to the vendors when they have satisfied the terms and conditions of the project. When vendors have been provided with final acceptance in writing, their portion of the project is complete and they are formally released from the project.
2:20 p.m. (5 min)	**Slide 96** Close Contract and Close Project Interactions 	Formal Acceptance for:	Contract Closure	Close Project
Work		
Product	Given to Vendor	Received from Sponsor
Project		
Resource Release		
Documentation	Received from Vendor	Provided to Sponsor and Organization		**Learning Content/Lecture** **Close: Close Contract and Close Project Interactions** When closing the project, close contracts and close project are highly related. Review this slide with the participants to show the interrelated nature of these closing processes.
2:25 p.m. (5 min)	**Slide 97** Close Project or Phase • Documents project results to formalize the acceptance of the product of the project or project phase • Collects project records, analyzes project performance, analyzes lessons learned, and archives all project information for future review and use	**Learning Content/Lecture** **Close: Close Project or Phase** In this process, the project manager tracks performance, work results, quality results, and overall project status before requesting formal acceptance from the sponsor. When the sponsor provides formal acceptance, the project is complete and the resources are formally released from the project. Project records are archived to be used as historical information for future projects.

TIMING	SLIDES	ACTIVITIES/NOTES/CONSIDERATIONS
2:30 p.m. (5 min)	Slide 98 Close: Module Wrap-Up	**Learning Content/Lecture** **Close: Module Wrap-Up** Wrap up the discussion of the fifth and last process group module: close. At the end of this process group, project managers will have • Closed procurements • Closed the project or phase. Give participants 5 minutes to make notes in their action plans (Handout 2). Ask them to note what actions they would like to take in the close project process group. Encourage them to create SMART goals they can work on when they return to their teams and organizations.
2:35 p.m. (5 min)	Slide 99 Project Management Knowledge Requirements The project manager must possess a wide range of knowledge and skills to be successful, including • Project management and general management • Ability to perform • Interpersonal skills	**Learning Content/Lecture** **Project Management Knowledge Requirements** Use this slide to switch gears from project management processes to focus on the fundamental knowledge and skills needed by successful project managers. What should be clear from the exploration of the project management process groups over the last two days is that project managers must have a broad knowledge base in order to be successful. Specifically, according to the *PMBOK® Guide,* they need knowledge and skills in several key areas, including: • Project management and general management knowledge • Ability to perform • Interpersonal skills.

TIMING	SLIDES	ACTIVITIES/NOTES/CONSIDERATIONS
2:40 p.m. (5 min)	Slide 100 Project Management Knowledge • Project management in general • Project management standards (as depicted in the *PMBOK® Guide* or some other standard) • Industry- or organization-specific project management knowledge and methodologies	**Learning Content/Discussion** **Project Management Knowledge** Use this slide to explain the kinds of project management knowledge needed: • Project management, in general, such as the process groups we've discussed over these two days • Project management standards, such as those depicted in the *PMBOK® Guide* or other standards • Industry- or organization-specific project management knowledge and methodologies (for example, a software development project manager may need to have knowledge of coding, the processes of software development, testing, and so on). Ask participants to share examples of specific knowledge that would be needed for their own industry or organizations.
2:45 p.m. (10 min)	Slide 101 General Management Knowledge • Finance • Strategic planning • Organizing • Human resource administration	**Learning Content/Lecture** **General Management Knowledge** Ask participants why they think business is conducted. Let them share their answers with the group. Chances are they will come up with the standard answer to this question: to make money. (Making money, however, may not be the primary motivator in all cultures and organizations, so you may want to adapt this slide introduction accordingly.) To make money and provide value, the project manager must also know about these other facets of management: • **Finance:** how to budget, control, and account for the budget • **Strategic planning:** how to ensure that the project meets the strategic goals of the organization • **Organizing:** how to manage the specific roles and responsibilities defined for the project team

TIMING	SLIDES	ACTIVITIES/NOTES/CONSIDERATIONS
	Slide 101, *continued*	• **Human resource administration:** how to manage people and understand what is appropriate and legal when dealing with team members. This list is by no means exhaustive. Ask participants if they can think of other important management principles that are missing from this list.
2:55 p.m. (5 min)	Slide 102	**Learning Content/Lecture** **Ability to Perform and Interpersonal Skills** Many processes use expert judgment as the basis for decision making, which requires the project manager to have specialized application knowledge and knowledge of industry best practices. Interpersonal skills also play a key role in a project manager's ability to perform. Without good communications skills, for example, the project manager would not be able to perform successfully.
3:00 p.m. (15 min)	Slide 103	**Learning Activity 14: Interpersonal Skills Quick Assessment** • **Assessment 1: Project Management Interpersonal Skills Quick Assessment** Project managers must possess many key interpersonal skills to be able to perform. This self-reflection activity helps participants identify areas of strength as well as potential development opportunities. Emphasize that this is a personal reflection activity and that participants will not be asked to share their results with anyone else. To debrief the activity, ask participants to discuss why these skills (or competencies) are important to a project manager's success. Encourage them to share examples from their own experiences when they have used or needed these skills in a project.

TIMING	SLIDES	ACTIVITIES/NOTES/CONSIDERATIONS
	Slide 103, *continued*	Be sure to highlight communication as the key skill, because all other skills depend on effective communication. The project manager should be savvy in promoting the project and the value it brings to the organization to facilitate awareness, buy-in, and success.
		Cultural awareness provides another good discussion point. Many project managers work in a global organization, so simple awareness of how to meet and greet people, choose appropriate phrases or message content, observe food etiquette, and so on can be indispensable skills and knowledge for project managers.
		Political awareness is also critical to project management success. Project managers should be aware of the organization's values, culture, and politics. This can include the unspoken rules of "how things work" in an organization.
		Follow the instructions in the learning activity to conduct this activity.
3:15 p.m. (30 min)	Slide 104 Action Planning	**Learning Activity 15: Action Planning** Remind your participants that learning is a journey, not a destination. The learning and work that they have done in this workshop will help them build a solid foundation of management methods and best practices. Their group project activities have helped them define projects and processes, hone interpersonal skills needed for successful project management, and practice key components of the project process groups: initiate, plan, execute, control, and close. This activity will help pull together everything that they have learned in the workshop, create an action plan for going forward, and garner support for their learning goals. Follow the instructions in the learning activity.

PROJECT MANAGEMENT training

TIMING	SLIDES	ACTIVITIES/NOTES/CONSIDERATIONS
3:45 p.m. (5 min)	Slide 105 Project Management Toolkit	**Project Manager Toolkit** • **Project Manager Toolkit (Chapter 14)** During the workshop, the participants practiced using several tools and processes in their group activities. Remind them that the approach this workshop has taken is from the perspective of healthy project management. They don't have to use every process, tool, and technique on every project to achieve results. Using just the right amount of project management is a critical factor in success. And so is having a robust set of tools at the ready. To support participants' work back on the job, distribute the bonus Project Manager Toolkit that includes powerful templates for them to start implementing in their own projects and teams right away. **Optional:** An important aspect of training and support for learning is follow-up. In addition to the print copy you give them here, you could send the Project Manager Toolkit to the participants electronically in a week or two after the workshop is completed. (See Chapter 15 for more information on electronic formats and licensing issues.)
3:50 p.m. (10 min) Ends at 4:00 p.m.	Slide 106 What do great project managers do?	**What Do Great Project Managers Do?** • **Handout 23: 10 Things Great Project Managers Do Every Day** • **Assessment 2: Evaluation Form** Close the workshop on a positive note. Ask participants to help you learn by completing the evaluation form. As participants are completing the evaluation, ask them to think about what they will do *every day* to be great project managers. Handout 23 gives 10 simple but profound ideas for habits they can cultivate to be great project managers. Be available to field questions about the workshop topics. Share plans for follow-up coaching if applicable (see Chapter 10 for ideas to follow up the training with support and activities.) Thank the participants for their contributions and wish them well.

What to Do Next

If you have decided that the two-day workshop is the best choice for your participants, consider these next steps as you prepare for your workshop:

- Determine the schedule for workshops, reserve location, and order any catering you may wish to provide.

- Identify and invite participants.

- Review the workshop objectives, activities, and handouts to plan the content you will use.

- Prepare copies of the participant materials and any activity-related materials you may need. Refer to Chapter 15 for information about how to access and use the supplemental materials provided for this workshop.

- Gather tactile items, such as Koosh balls, crayons, magnets, or Play-Doh, to place on the tables for tactile learners. See Chapter 8 for other ideas to enhance the learning environment of your workshop.

- Confirm that you have addressed scheduling and personal concerns so that you can be fully present to facilitate the class.

References

ISO. (2005). *ISO 9000: 2005 Quality Management Systems—Fundamentals and Vocabulary.* Geneva: International Standards Organization.

Mulle, K. (2016). *Emotional Intelligence Training.* Alexandria, VA: ATD Press.

PMI. (2013). *A Guide to the Project Management Body of Knowledge: PMBOK™ Guide,* fifth ed. Newtown Square, PA: PMI.

Wideman, R.M. (1992). *Project and Program Risk Management: A Guide to Managing Project Risks and Opportunities.* Newtown Square, PA: PMI.

Chapter 2

One-Day Project Management Workshop

What's in This Chapter

- Project management fundamentals
- Exploration of interpersonal skills needed for project management
- Objectives of the one-day Project Management Workshop
- One-day workshop agenda in detail

While the two-day workshop approaches project management through a detailed project cycle, the length of the one-day workshop doesn't lend itself to such an approach. Simply providing a compressed project cycle would not be helpful for the learners. Instead, this workshop takes a different and complementary tack. In the one-day workshop, learners will learn about the background knowledge that is necessary for project management mastery and develop a group of critical interpersonal skills for project management success. Although many of these skills could (and have) required their own workshops (such as leadership, communication, and problem solving), their inclusion here hints at the scope of skills a successful project manager should have and should strive to develop. This workshop focuses on leadership skills through the lens of project management and only lightly touches on the project management processes. It is recommended that you pair this workshop with either the two-day or half-day workshop or require participants to have prior experience with project management before taking the one-day workshop.

Project Management: From the Beginning

Because formal project management theory, methods, and best practice standards have been employed in every conceivable governmental, military, and commercial organization and industry, the field of project management has evolved over time. This evolution (revolution even) continues as the profession is continually refined and gains more traction globally. Project management is a methodical approach and discipline that everyone knows about but may not realize they use.

Consider the case of doctors—they see patients, they diagnose their problems, they prescribe solutions, and then they discharge the patients, with possible follow-up visits. Compare that to the definition of a project: distinctive, transitory, defined start and finish, and continuously advanced. Doctors see a unique problem (patient), for a temporary time with a start and finish, and throughout the process determine the problem through diagnoses. They complete projects: They are project managers!

Project management is in the business of delivering results. Its strategies and methodologies work as well for disaster relief, fighting fires, and emergency response as they do for business goals in for-profit and nonprofit organizations. It is a proven method that will consistently deliver the results the project defines.

The workshops in this book have been designed from the perspective of healthy project management, which simply means that you do not have to use every process, procedure, template, trick, tip, and technique on every project to achieve your desired results. But you should know what tools are available before you decide which tools you don't need. Using just the right amount of project management is one of the keys to success.

The one-day workshop will introduce the topic of project management and give participants a good start toward building a solid foundation of project management processes and practices. The workshop materials provide templates for the participants to use during the workshop activities and as tools back on the job. You are welcome to use these templates or create your own that are more specific to the needs of your organization and participants. Keep in mind, however, that project management is not about filling in templates or using a particular project software. Such tools can help save time and make project management easier, but only one element can deliver a project on time, within scope, and within budget—*the project manager*. You will want to stress this point with your participants to empower their project management success.

As you prepare to deliver the workshop, think about times you have used project management to facilitate a training session, create a product, deliver a service, convene a meeting, or even plan a party. That's right—you, too, are a project manager. Add your personal experiences and successes to this workshop to make it your own. (And don't forget that people learn as much from your failures as they do from your successes.) Be willing to share whatever will make the concepts real and doable. Project managers must own their projects, and as the facilitator, you should own your role in this workshop. The more of "you" that you put into the sessions, the more your participants will get out of them.

Managing projects requires the ability to set clear objectives, report, project plan, work collaboratively, navigate uncertainty, and monitor and control project outcomes. Everything you do to prepare for and deliver this workshop needs to model these skills. Spend time building your understanding of project management methods and practice them in your preparation, design, delivery, and follow-up of this workshop.

A Word About Pre-Work

The one-day workshop includes a pre-work assignment to help your participants think about project management in their own specific context. When you send a welcome or confirmation message to participants, ask them to think about a project they were involved in this past year. Ask your participants to answer these questions about the project:

- What role did you play?
- What was unique about the project?
- Did it come in on time, within budget, and within scope?
- Did your project follow any specific process?

This is a great way to begin the relationship with your participants. At the start of the workshop you will debrief their pre-work by encouraging them to share one or two of their answers to the questions with the group. Not everyone has to share; you can ask everyone to keep the questions in mind as they experience the workshop.

A Word About the Slides, Notes, and Handouts

The slides for this workshop contain key learning concepts about project management. Additional and supporting information will be found in the notes column of the agenda. Because it is impossible to include every piece of information in the slide, you will need to be prepared to discuss points from your own experience to help answer participants' questions. Project management is a complex topic, so I encourage you to research and learn more about the concepts covered in the workshop. See Figure 1-1 in chapter 1 for resources that will help you sharpen your project management skills and build your project management acumen. The blogs and online resources noted in the figure will bolster the information presented in the workshop with leading-edge expertise in project management topics. Also, if you are unsure about any topic in the agenda, send me an email with your questions at wes.balakian@truesolutions.com and I will be glad to help you.

The handouts provided in this volume are another source of information for you as the facilitator and for your participants. In some cases, the handouts provide templates to be used in the learning activities. In other cases, they include "must-know" concepts that summarize the key learning in the modules, or they provide tips, examples, flowcharts, and so on. And still other handouts provide useful information you won't have time to present within the scope of this workshop but that will help participants once they are back in their workplaces. Encourage participants to review these valuable resources to increase their project management knowledge and skills.

Also included in this volume is a Project Manager Toolkit (Chapter 14) that includes all the templates from the two-day agenda plus additional templates, all created by True Solutions Inc. (TSI). You can distribute a print copy of the Project Manager Toolkit to your participants at the close of the workshop or send it to them digitally a week or two after the workshop is completed as follow-up support for their learning. (In addition, TSI publishes a set of more than 100 templates on a wide range of project management processes and tasks to help project managers.)

The agenda notes are not highly scripted. They are addressed to you, the facilitator, and crafted in a natural voice that you can make your own when you deliver the content. Avoid just reading the slides—or your participants will immediately see that you are not comfortable with the subject and begin a contest to uncover what you don't know.

As an instructor, author, consultant, and experienced corporate executive, I can talk for days about project management, but when I get in front of people they see my passion. Show them yours. If you are confident with project management principles and content, you will find navigating the agenda very easy. If you are more of a novice to the field, rely on the agendas to help guide you through the material but plan to spend some time broadening your knowledge base with the resources noted in Figure 1-1.

One-Day Workshop Objectives

Participants will be able to

- Define what a project is
- Develop a working definition of project management
- Identify knowledge requirements for project managers
- Explore the key interpersonal skills needed for effective project management: communicating, leading, motivating, problem solving, decision making, and influencing.

One-Day Workshop Overview

TOPICS	TIMING
Welcome and Introductions	10 minutes
Learning Activity 1: My Project Management Story	25 minutes
Workshop Objectives	10 minutes
What Is Project Management?	
What Is a Project?	5 minutes
Continuous Advancement	5 minutes
What Is Project Management?	5 minutes
Project Management Knowledge Requirements	
Knowledge Requirements	5 minutes
Project Management Knowledge	5 minutes
General Management Knowledge	5 minutes
General Management Knowledge: Planning	5 minutes
General Management Knowledge: Financial Management	5 minutes
General Management Knowledge: Organizational Skills	5 minutes
General Management Knowledge: People Management	5 minutes
Team Management Tips	5 minutes
Specialized Knowledge	10 minutes
BREAK	**15 minutes**
Learning Activity 14: Interpersonal Skills Quick Assessment	15 minutes
Communicating	
Communication Skills	5 minutes
Learning Activity 5: Communication Interference	10 minutes
Communication Model	5 minutes
Communication Types	5 minutes
Communication Planning	5 minutes
Identify Stakeholders	5 minutes

TOPICS	TIMING
Communications Management Plan	10 minutes
Learning Activity 16: Bumper Sticker Communication Tips	10 minutes
LUNCH	**60 minutes**
Leading	
Learning Activity 17: Leadership Skills: Manager or Leader?	10 minutes
Six Characteristics of Successful Leaders	5 minutes
Project Managers as Leaders	5 minutes
Learning Activity 18: Inspirational Leader	15 minutes
Leadership Power	5 minutes
Leadership Wrap-Up	10 minutes
Motivating	
Motivation Skills	5 minutes
Learning Activity 19: MBWA Exercise	15 minutes
Motivation Techniques	10 minutes
Positive Motivation	5 minutes
Motivation to Achieve Action	5 minutes
Learning Activity 20: Motivators and De-motivators	15 minutes
Motivation Wrap-Up	5 minutes
Problem Solving	
Problem-Solving Skills	5 minutes
What Is a Problem?	5 minutes
Learning Activity 21: Problem-Solving Exercise	20 minutes
Problem-Solving Wrap-Up	5 minutes
BREAK	**15 minutes**
Decision Making	
Decision-Making Skills	5 minutes
Decisions	5 minutes
Gather Information	5 minutes
Decision-Making Wrap-Up	5 minutes
Influencing	
Influencing Skills	5 minutes
Influencing Tactics and Responses	5 minutes
Learning Activity 22: Are You a Good Listener?	15 minutes
Workshop Wrap-Up	
Workshop Wrap-Up and Review	5 minutes
Action Planning	10 minutes
What Do Great Project Managers Do?	5 minutes
TOTAL	**480 minutes**

One-Day Workshop Agenda

One Day: (8:00 a.m. to 4:00 p.m.)

TIMING	SLIDES	ACTIVITIES/NOTES/CONSIDERATIONS
8:00 a.m. (10 min)	Slide 1 ATD Workshop Project Management Training One-Day Workshop	**Welcome and Introductions** Welcome the participants as they enter the room and briefly introduce yourself. Make an effort to talk to each person, which will set the tone for the session and begin to model communication as a primary skill for successful project management. Note the usual housekeeping items such as restroom locations and breaks.
8:10 a.m. (25 min)	Slide 2 My Project Management Story 1. What is your name and current position? 2. What is your project management experience? 3. What do you hope to learn today? 4. How will you define success at the end of the workshop?	**Learning Activity 1: My Project Management Story** This icebreaker partner activity will help you get a sense of your participants' level of experience with project management and what their learning needs are. It will also help your participants get to know each other better. Ask participants to answer the questions on the slide on their own and then to write their answers to question 4 on a sticky note. Have them place their notes on a flipchart at the front of the room. Briefly review their answers with the group. Let participants know that you will be referring to their notes throughout the workshop. Make an effort to connect participants with the topics they consider important to their learning success. To help participants interact with each other, divide the group into pairs and have them interview each other using the same set of questions. Then have pairs introduce each other to the group. Follow the instructions in the learning activity. You will need to shave 5 minutes off the timing noted in the learning activity to make it fit into the one-day workshop agenda.

TIMING	SLIDES	ACTIVITIES/NOTES/CONSIDERATIONS
8:35 a.m. (10 min)	**Slide 3** One-Day Workshop Objectives • Define what a project is • Develop a working definition of project management • Identify knowledge requirements for project managers • Explore key interpersonal skills needed for effective project management: communicating, leading, motivating, problem solving, decision making, and influencing	**Workshop Objectives** Introduce the topic of project management to the participants. Make the point that they use project management every day—even though they may not call it that. Just about everyone is a project manager based on the definition of a project (distinctive, transitory, defined start and finish, continuously advanced). Doctors, police officers, attorneys, veterinarians, and teachers all deliver and manage projects. Now review the objectives at a high level. Point out where these objectives overlap with the participants' responses in Learning Activity 1. Explain that although these objectives do not cover all aspects of project management, they do represent some of the most important skills involved in managing a successful project. Let the participants know that the workshop will cover a lot of information, but there will be interactive opportunities to practice the concepts they are learning with each other in small groups. (Slide 1 of 2)
	Slide 4 Pre-Work Assignment Think of a project that you have been involved with recently: •What role did you play? •What was unique about the project? •Did it come in on time, budget, and within scope? •Did your project follow any specific process?	Wrap up your overview of the objectives by asking, by a show of hands, how many of the participants have had some experience with project management before, perhaps having attended other workshops, read books about it, or worked as team members on projects. (As mentioned in the introduction to this chapter, this workshop is designed to work well with people who have taken either the two- or half-day workshop or have previous project management experience. It builds on that knowledge to develop specific knowledge and skills needed for effective project management.) Take a moment to review the pre-work assignment you gave the participants to identify a project they were involved in this year. Ask for a few volunteers to briefly share their project examples with the group. Ask them: • What role did you play? • What was unique about the project?

TIMING	SLIDES	ACTIVITIES/NOTES/CONSIDERATIONS
	Slide 4, *continued*	• Did it come in on time, within budget, and within scope? • Did your project follow any specific process? (Slide 2 of 2)
8:45 a.m. (5 min)	Slide 5 	**Learning Content/Lecture and Discussion** **What Is a Project?** To understand what project management is, you have to start even farther back and ask what a project is. Ask participants: What is the difference between a project and a program? Use the slide to explain that a program is an ongoing set of activities, such as a car company that produces a fleet of vehicles. A project, however, has four specific characteristics: • Distinctive • Transitory • Defined start and finish • Continuously advanced. A project, using the example on the slide, would be the development of a single model of car in a single model year. Briefly discuss the first three characteristics (distinctive, transitory, and defined start/finish), which are mostly self-explanatory. Then introduce the fourth characteristic: *continuous advancement.* Emphasize that it is a key element in defining a project. Open the discussion by asking participants what they think the term means. Once they have shared their ideas with the group, use the next slide to help explain it further.

TIMING	SLIDES	ACTIVITIES/NOTES/CONSIDERATIONS
8:50 a.m. (5 min)	Slide 6 Continuous Advancement Continuous advancement incrementally describes the elements of a project. It can be compared with Deming's Plan-Do-Check-Act cycle.	**Learning Content/Discussion** **Continuous Advancement** Continuous advancement works in a manner similar to the Plan-Do-Check-Act cycle made popular by W. Edward Deming. We *plan*, we *do*, we *check*, and we *act* the plan. As we progress through the chart, we get increasingly more detailed as we gather information. Walk the participants step by step through the Plan-Do-Check-Act cycle shown on the slide: • **Plan:** planning the project • **Do:** executing the project work • **Check:** the monitoring portion of the M&C (monitoring and control) process, checking to determine status • **Act:** the controlling portion of the M&C process, taking corrective or preventive action. The entire model is built on a wheel, with communicating—the most critical interpersonal skill for a project manager—as the hub. Other interpersonal skills make up the various spokes of the wheel. Discuss the interpersonal skills listed in the diagram and point out that any interpersonal skill could be part of this wheel diagram. Explain that at the end of the cycle, there is a review, and the process starts over—representing the end-of-phase review.

TIMING	SLIDES	ACTIVITIES/NOTES/CONSIDERATIONS
8:55 a.m. (5 min)	Slide 7 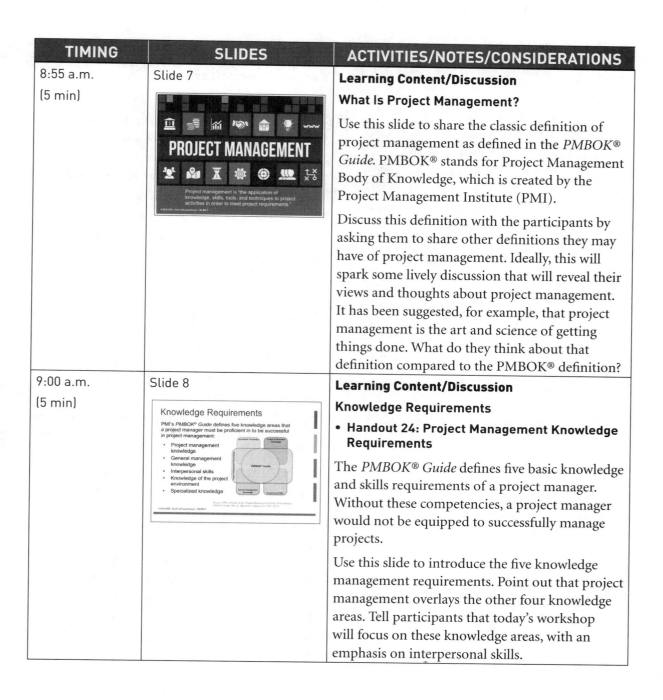	**Learning Content/Discussion** **What Is Project Management?** Use this slide to share the classic definition of project management as defined in the *PMBOK® Guide*. PMBOK® stands for Project Management Body of Knowledge, which is created by the Project Management Institute (PMI). Discuss this definition with the participants by asking them to share other definitions they may have of project management. Ideally, this will spark some lively discussion that will reveal their views and thoughts about project management. It has been suggested, for example, that project management is the art and science of getting things done. What do they think about that definition compared to the PMBOK® definition?
9:00 a.m. (5 min)	Slide 8	**Learning Content/Discussion** **Knowledge Requirements** • **Handout 24: Project Management Knowledge Requirements** The *PMBOK® Guide* defines five basic knowledge and skills requirements of a project manager. Without these competencies, a project manager would not be equipped to successfully manage projects. Use this slide to introduce the five knowledge management requirements. Point out that project management overlays the other four knowledge areas. Tell participants that today's workshop will focus on these knowledge areas, with an emphasis on interpersonal skills.

TIMING	SLIDES	ACTIVITIES/NOTES/CONSIDERATIONS
9:05 a.m. (5 min)	Slide 9 Project Management Knowledge • Project management practices, processes, tools, techniques, standards, and best practices • Project management methods	**Learning Content/Lecture and Discussion** **Project Management Knowledge** Explain that project management knowledge includes all the practices, processes, and activities—including project management methods—that the project manager undertakes in managing a project. PMI's *PMBOK® Guide* defines 47 project management processes, including knowledge of how to use the processes; their basic function; and key inputs, tools, and outputs associated with the processes. Here are other types of project management knowledge: • Best practices • New project management theories • Knowledge of shortcuts • Special types of project management considered acceptable and applicable to the type of project undertaken. Although they are the industry standard, PMI's 47 processes are not the only valid project management methods. Harold Kerzner (2013) of the International Institute of Learning takes a systems approach in his seminal book, *PM: A Systems Approach to Planning, Scheduling and Controlling*. True Solutions Inc. (TSI) takes a practical approach to project management. Each of these approaches provides a system of processes, templates, and methods to manage projects.

TIMING	SLIDES	ACTIVITIES/NOTES/CONSIDERATIONS
9:10 a.m. (5 min)	Slide 10 General Management Knowledge • Business management • Planning • Financial management • Organizational skills • People management	**Learning Content/Lecture** **General Management Knowledge** Because the purpose of the project is to meet business needs, knowledge of general management principles is also required to be a successful project manager. Briefly overview the general management points on the slide with the participants: • **Business management:** how to run a business • **Strategic planning:** how to ensure that the project meets the strategic goals of the organization • **Finance:** how to budget, control, and account for the budget • **Organizing:** how to manage the specific roles and responsibilities defined for the project team • **Human resource administration:** how to manage people and understand what is appropriate and legal when dealing with team members. Then spend a little more time on business management. Explain that the purpose of for-profit commercial businesses is to make a profit. So, the first question to ask about a proposed project is whether or not it has real value to the organization. In some cases, an organization undertakes a project for purposes other than profit—for example, because of a government regulatory requirement. Project managers need to have working knowledge of their organization's purpose, core products and services, marketing plans, resources, and enterprise environmental factors, among others.

TIMING	SLIDES	ACTIVITIES/NOTES/CONSIDERATIONS
9:15 a.m. (5 min)	Slide 11 General Management Knowledge: Planning • Strategic planning • Long-term planning • Operational or tactical Planning	**Learning Content/Discussion** **General Management Knowledge: Planning** Planning for the future in organizations involves three levels of planning: strategic, long term, and operational. **Strategic planning** looks three or more years out in the future to determine the direction of the enterprise. The project manager needs to be aware of the organization's strategic plan to determine whether or not the project meets that plan. **Long-term planning** looks one to three years out and seeks to make changes to the enterprise environment to fulfill the strategic plan. It focuses on the organization, services, and projects that enable the strategic goals. **Tactical or operational planning** is the kind of planning that project managers deal with most frequently. It focuses on fulfilling long-term and strategic plans with immediate tasks or activities geared to meet objectives. For project managers, tactical planning might include managing specific tasks or budgets to meet plans in the current calendar or fiscal year.
9:20 a.m. (5 min)	Slide 12 General Management Knowledge: Financial Management Operating Budgets - Revenue center - Cost center - Profit center Financial Budgets - Cash budgets - Capital expenditure budgets - Material budgets - Balance sheet budgets	**Learning Content /Discussion** **General Management Knowledge: Financial Management** Financial management knowledge involves knowing how to manage a budget and what type of budget is involved. A budget is a formalized statement of the goals of the organization in financial terms. It can also include future projections of revenues, expenses, and expected profits. Budgeting aids in basic management of planning, organizing, and controlling. Briefly overview the different types of budgets that project managers may need to understand. **Operating budgets** reflect operations and provide guidelines to managers: • **Revenue center:** projects profits produced by the business unit; does not take costs into account

TIMING	SLIDES	ACTIVITIES/NOTES/CONSIDERATIONS
	Slide 12, *continued*	• **Cost center:** projects all anticipated costs for a business unit over a time period; project managers are usually involved in this style of budget to track costs • **Profit center:** projects revenue versus costs to determine profits. **Financial budgets** are a projection of how a business intends to spend: • **Cash:** shows cash flow for the business • **Capital expenditure:** tracks capital investment in new physical resources • **Materials:** tracks direct and indirect costs of materials to support the business • **Balance sheet:** tracks assets, liabilities, and owner equity.
9:25 a.m. (5 min)	Slide 13 	**Learning Content/Lecture** **General Management Knowledge: Organizational Skills** "Organization" is the process of developing an orderly way to manage the physical and human elements needed to accomplish company goals. To organize, a project manager must have or ensure • Unity of purpose • Division of labor • Staff. When organizing the project team, project managers must first be aware of the type of organization they are working in: • **Functional organizations** focus on sustaining operations. • **Matrix organizations** share resources across functional areas. They are generally better than functional organizations at executing projects because authority is often shared or delegated to the project manager. • **Projectized organizations,** such as consultants, engineers, architects, or lawyers, are focused on the project. Project managers have the highest level of authority in projectized organizations.

TIMING	SLIDES	ACTIVITIES/NOTES/CONSIDERATIONS
9:30 a.m. (5 min)	Slide 14 General Management Knowledge: People Management	**Learning Content/Lecture** **General Management Knowledge: People Management** The final area of general management knowledge is people management. To accomplish a project, a project manager must manage a project team. Often the team is a diverse group of people with many different characteristics. The project manager must know • Human resource policies and procedures, as well as application laws and regulations • Interviewing, selection, hiring, and separation processes • Compensation and career growth opportunities to help motivate the team to achieve project goals. And because of today's global business environment, project managers must be knowledgeable about all of the above for *each* country and culture of people involved in the project or under their management.
9:35 a.m. (5 min)	Slide 15 Team Management Tips •Make sure your core project team is made up of people you trust •Don't expect team members to perform well if they are not comfortable with the role they are playing •Understand your team's capabilities, motivation and limitations.	**Learning Content/Discussion** **Team Management Tips** Use this slide to share tips for selecting and working with the project team. Conduct a quick brainstorming activity. Ask participants to share other team management tips from their experience in leading or working on teams. Record their ideas on a flipchart. Encourage participants to use their smartphones or tablets to take a photo of the chart as a reminder of tested team management tips.

TIMING	SLIDES	ACTIVITIES/NOTES/CONSIDERATIONS
9:40 a.m. (10 min)	Slide 16	**Learning Content/Discussion** **Specialized Knowledge** • **Handout 25: My Project Management Goal Plan** Explain that project managers do not need to be experts in their field, but they should understand the standards, regulations, processes, and practices for their industry. Specialized knowledge is used as a basis for decision making. The more application-specific knowledge project managers have, the better equipped they will be to reduce risk and improve project performance. Ask participants to give some examples of how specialized knowledge could make a difference on a project. Consider, for example, the specialized knowledge that might be needed for projects in construction, pharmaceutical research, software engineering, manufacturing, customer service, hospital administration, and so on. In many of these cases, project management or general business knowledge alone isn't enough. Encourage the participants to develop their knowledge of their industry and organization. To wrap up the project management knowledge section, introduce Handout 25: My Project Management Goal Plan. Explain that they will return to this goal planner throughout the day to capture ideas they may have for implementation or further learning back on the job. Explain that they should aim to make their next steps SMART—specific, measurable, achievable, realistic, and time-bound. Give participants 5 minutes to add notes from the knowledge requirements portion of the workshop.
9:50 a.m. (15 min)	Slide 17	**BREAK**

TIMING	SLIDES	ACTIVITIES/NOTES/CONSIDERATIONS
10:05 a.m. (15 min)	Slide 18 Interpersonal Skills Communicating Leading Motivating Problem Solving Decision Making Influencing	**Learning Activity 14: Interpersonal Skills Quick Assessment** • **Assessment 1: Interpersonal Skills Quick Assessment** Welcome the participants back from the break. Emphasize how necessary it is for project managers to have a wide range of interpersonal skills. Let them know that the rest of the day will be devoted to exploring some of the key interpersonal skills required to be a successful project manager: communicating, leading, motivating, problem solving, decision making, and influencing. Note that communicating is highlighted in red on the slide to emphasize that it is by far the most important of the interpersonal skills for project managers. Introduce the interpersonal skills module with a skills assessment. Follow the instructions in the learning activity to conduct the assessment.
10:20 a.m. (5 min)	Slide 19 Communication Skills • Effective communication is critical in project management. • Communication provides a vital connection between people, concepts, and information. • Communication involves speaking, writing, and listening. • Good project communications is easier with proper planning.	**Learning Content/Lecture** **Communication Skills** Explain that the first interpersonal skill set we will explore is communication, which provides vital connections among people, concepts, and information throughout the project environment. Effective communication enables all the other skills and is considered a critical success factor in project management. When troubled projects are evaluated, it is typical to find poor communication as a major source of the problems. Good communication ensures important information is generated, gathered, and stored in an appropriate and effective manner. It also confirms and verifies that everyone understands the concepts, terms, processes, and expectations. Communication skills include all the elements of communication: • formal and informal

TIMING	SLIDES	ACTIVITIES/NOTES/CONSIDERATIONS
	Slide 19, *continued*	• up and down the organization chart, including employees, peers, and executive leaders • across diverse cultural or ethnic backgrounds • with individuals of all dispositions—easygoing and difficult • involving speaking, writing, and listening In planning the project the project manager must set guidelines for acceptable and nonacceptable communication and who communicates with whom.
10:25 a.m. (10 min)	Slide 20 Communication Interference	**Learning Activity 5: Communication Interference** Use this activity to help participants explore the idea of communication "blockers"—things that can get in the way of effective communication. Because of time constraints, you will only facilitate Part 2 of the activity. Follow the instructions in the learning activity to complete Part 2 of this activity.
10:35 a.m. (5 min)	Slide 21 Communication Model Communicating involves three elements: sender, receiver, and information. Communication is a two-way activity.	**Learning Content /Lecture** **Communication Model** Walk through the communication model with the participants. It illustrates the communication process with a sender and receiver, a message, and a method of transmission. Start with the top left of the model. The information to be communicated must be encoded by the sender. The sender sends the encoded information to the receiver, who decodes it. This, is in its simplest form, is how communication takes place. Many times there are factors that slow the process, such as communications media, time, language, vocabulary, or even point of reference. It's important to understand that communication is not complete until the sender confirms or receives confirmation that the receiver has received and understood the intended message (the bottom row of the model).

TIMING	SLIDES	ACTIVITIES/NOTES/CONSIDERATIONS
10:40 a.m. (5 min)	Slide 22 Communication Types •Informal verbal •Formal verbal •Nonverbal •Informal written •Formal written	**Learning Content/Discussion** **Communication Types** How information is encoded is based on the media used to send the information. There are many forms in which information can be sent—verbal, nonverbal, and written, and both formal and informal. Ask participants for some examples of each of the five types of communication listed on the slide. Here are some examples you can use to get them started: • Informal verbal (hallway chat) • Formal verbal (presentation) • Nonverbal (body language) • Informal written (email, text message) • Formal written (report) Part of good communication is discerning which type of communication to use in a given situation. Ask participants about the role of social media. Which category would they put social media in? What kinds of special considerations are there for using social media with project management?
10:45 a.m. (5 min)	Slide 23 Communication Planning • Identify stakeholders • Determine appropriate interaction levels • Create and implement the communications management plan	**Learning Content/Lecture** **Communication Planning** Share again that when troubled projects are evaluated, it is typical to find poor communication at the heart of conflict and negative outcomes. It is a common rule of thumb that good project managers spend up to 90 percent of their time communicating. To ensure that project communication is effective, project managers need to plan communications. Here are the key tasks involved in communications planning: • **Identify stakeholders.** Stakeholders are the people affected by the project.

TIMING	SLIDES	ACTIVITIES/NOTES/CONSIDERATIONS
		• **Make a list of stakeholders.** In project management parlance, this is a stakeholder register.
		• **Identify the stakeholder's influence on what you intend to accomplish.** This can be positive or negative.
		• **Determine interaction levels.** How much interaction do they want, need, or can consume? What format? What frequency?
		• **Create and implement the communications plan.** Define what will be communicated to whom, how often, and in what format. It is required for projects or operations to determine how communications will be managed.
10:50 a.m. (5 min)	Slide 24 Identify Stakeholders	**Learning Content/Discussion** **Identify Stakeholders** • **Handout 4: Potential Stakeholders** Briefly explain that stakeholders are the people and organizations participating in the project or those who are directly or indirectly affected by the project. Stakeholders can be internal or external to the organization and can include the general public in some projects. The handout lists many potential stakeholders on projects. Give participants 2-3 minutes to think about who else could be considered a stakeholder in a project and then to share their ideas with the people at their tables. Ask table groups to share additional stakeholders with the whole group. Encourage participants to take notes to enhance the stakeholder list on the handout. Some examples of stakeholders *not* listed in the handout are clients, human resources, chief executive officers, chief technology officers, chief financial officers, procurement, and social media team.

TIMING	SLIDES	ACTIVITIES/NOTES/CONSIDERATIONS
10:55 a.m. (10 min)	Slide 25 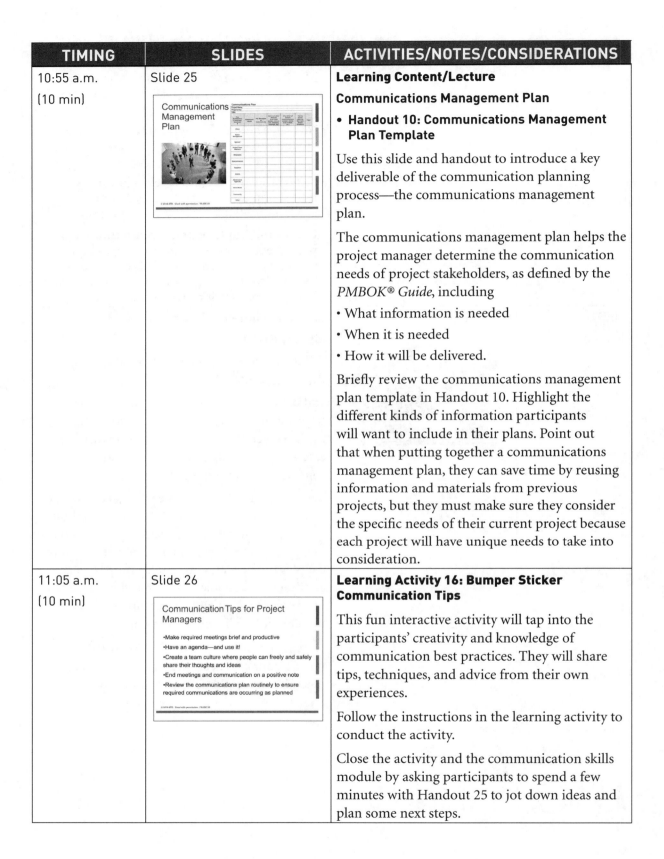	**Learning Content/Lecture** **Communications Management Plan** • **Handout 10: Communications Management Plan Template** Use this slide and handout to introduce a key deliverable of the communication planning process—the communications management plan. The communications management plan helps the project manager determine the communication needs of project stakeholders, as defined by the *PMBOK® Guide*, including • What information is needed • When it is needed • How it will be delivered. Briefly review the communications management plan template in Handout 10. Highlight the different kinds of information participants will want to include in their plans. Point out that when putting together a communications management plan, they can save time by reusing information and materials from previous projects, but they must make sure they consider the specific needs of their current project because each project will have unique needs to take into consideration.
11:05 a.m. (10 min)	Slide 26	**Learning Activity 16: Bumper Sticker Communication Tips** This fun interactive activity will tap into the participants' creativity and knowledge of communication best practices. They will share tips, techniques, and advice from their own experiences. Follow the instructions in the learning activity to conduct the activity. Close the activity and the communication skills module by asking participants to spend a few minutes with Handout 25 to jot down ideas and plan some next steps.

TIMING	SLIDES	ACTIVITIES/NOTES/CONSIDERATIONS
	Slide 26, *continued*	**Variation:** If you would rather give participants an opportunity to practice tailoring their communication styles to suit particular purposes and audiences, you could replace this activity with Learning Activity 12: Matrix Game: Communications 101 from the two-day workshop. To make Learning Activity 12 fit into the timing of this workshop, however, you would need to cut 10 minutes elsewhere in the agenda. An easy change would be to allow only 50 minutes for lunch instead of a full hour.
11:15 a.m. (60 min)	Slide 27 Lunch	**LUNCH**
12:15 p.m. (10 min)	Slide 28 Leadership Skills Exercise	**Learning Activity 17: Leadership Skills: Manager or Leader?** • **Handout 26: Manager or Leader?** For a change of pace, introduce leadership, the next interpersonal skills module, with a small group activity. The activity helps participants discern the difference between the roles of managers and leaders. They will be able to see that even though the word *manager* is in their job title, they must also develop leadership skills to be able to deliver successful projects. Follow the instructions in the learning activity to conduct this activity.

TIMING	SLIDES	ACTIVITIES/NOTES/CONSIDERATIONS
12:25 p.m. (5 min)	Slide 29	**Learning Content/Lecture** **Six Characteristics of Successful Leaders** Briefly overview six characteristics that successful leaders commonly share. Operating as project leaders, project managers must develop these characteristics: **Vision:** Leaders have a clear vision of the project intent and what goals and objectives must be accomplished to be successful. They also communicate that vision to their teams and the project stakeholders. **Responsibility and Accountability:** Leaders take responsibility for their actions and hold themselves and others accountable for fulfilling their roles and duties. **Desire to Lead:** Although this may seem obvious, leaders want to lead. They understand that they often need to make difficult decisions. To do that, they must own their leadership role. **Stamina and Perseverance:** If leaders require their teams to work long hours and put forth extraordinary effort to accomplish an objective, they must to be able to keep up and work as hard and as long as their teams. **Empathy:** Leaders have the ability to understand what others are feeling because they have experienced it themselves or they can put themselves in others' shoes. A leader who can empathize and participate with the team is more respected than one who dictates outcomes without regard for how others feel. **Credibility:** Leaders must do what they say and say what they do. Credibility and trust are the foundation of leading teams and collaborating effectively.

TIMING	SLIDES	ACTIVITIES/NOTES/CONSIDERATIONS
12:30 p.m. (5 min)	Slide 30 Project Managers as Leaders • Support their teams • Create synergy • Assign realistic tasks • Clearly define tasks, goals, objectives, roles, and responsibilities • Use checkpoint reviews to determine outcomes • Be consistent and build trust	**Learning Content/Lecture** **Project Managers as Leaders** Use this slide to share these powerful leadership behaviors for project managers: • **Support teams** with encouragement, resources, and guidance • **Create synergy,** including motivation and collaboration • **Assign realistic tasks,** with a clear understanding of team capabilities and constraints • **Clearly define tasks, goals, objectives, roles, and responsibilities,** and then communicate, communicate, communicate • **Use checkpoint reviews to determine outcomes,** monitoring and controlling the project's progress • **Be consistent and build trust** by keeping your word and doing what you say you will do.
12:35 p.m. (15 min)	Slide 31 Identify an Inspirational Leader	**Learning Activity 18: Inspirational Leader** • **Handout 27: Inspirational Leadership** This reflective small group activity enables participants to identify qualities of inspirational leaders and begin thinking about the type of leader they aspire to be. Follow the instructions in the learning activity to facilitate this activity.
12:50 p.m. (5 min)	Slide 32 Leadership Power •Reward Power • Title Power •Punishment Power • Information Power •Referent Power • Charismatic Power •Expert Power • Contacts Power	**Learning Content/Discussion** **Leadership Power** • **Handout 28: Leadership Power** Use this slide and handout to introduce the concept of leadership power. Power theories of leadership are based on the different ways leaders use power and influence to get things done. Briefly overview the different types of power found in the leadership role and then ask participants to answer the questions at the bottom of the handout. If time allows, have them discuss their answers with the people at their tables.

TIMING	SLIDES	ACTIVITIES/NOTES/CONSIDERATIONS
	Slide 32, *continued*	**Reward Power** is based on the leader's authority to reward desired behavior with salary increases, promotions, vacations, and other positive incentives.
		Punishment Power is based on the leader's authority to punish undesirable behavior with termination, pay docking, reprimands, and other negative incentives.
		Referent Power is earned power. Leaders, who are admired by others as a role model, for example, may elicit desired behavior from their people through this type of power.
		Expert Power is related to referent power but is earned when the leader is viewed as an expert and elicits desired behavior because people believe the leader knows best.
		Title Power is based the job title or position of the leader, as authorized by senior management.
		Information Power based on controlling the distribution of key information to people.
		Charismatic Power is based on extraordinary communication skills and can be used in environments where the leader has limited formal authority.
		Contacts Power is based on alliances and networks with influential people in the organization.
12:55 p.m. (10 min)	Slide 33	**Learning Content/ Lecture** **Leadership Wrap-Up** Wrap up the leadership topic by briefly reviewing the key learning points in the module. 1. Successful leaders share similar characteristics: • Vision • Responsibility and accountability • Desire to lead • Stamina • Empathy • Credibility

TIMING	SLIDES	ACTIVITIES/NOTES/CONSIDERATIONS
	Slide 33, *continued*	2. Project managers who lead effectively engage in these behaviors: • Support their teams • Create synergy • Assign realistic tasks • Clearly define tasks, goals, objectives, roles, and responsibilities • Use checkpoint reviews to determine outcomes • Are consistent. Ask participants to use the goal planner (Handout 25) to jot down some notes about what they've learned about leadership that they would like implement back on the job.
1:05 p.m. (5 min)	Slide 34 	**Learning Content/Lecture** **Motivation Skills** Introduce the next interpersonal skills topic: motivation. Because motivation influences productivity, project managers need to understand what motivates project team members to reach peak performance. Motivation is the set of processes that moves a person or team toward a goal. The project manager (the motivator) wants to influence the factors that motivate team members to higher levels of productivity. Some of these factors include: • Desire to stay and grow with the project • Desire to fulfill responsibilities and perform assigned tasks • Desire to go beyond average performance to demonstrate creativity and innovation. Tell participants that this section of the workshop will help participants explore many motivational techniques they can take back to their teams.

TIMING	SLIDES	ACTIVITIES/NOTES/CONSIDERATIONS
1:10 p.m. (15 min)	Slide 35 Motivating Learning Activity	**Learning Activity 19: MBWA Exercise** • **Handout 29: MBWA for Project Managers** In this small group activity, participants will practice a motivational technique based on the concept of management by walking around (MBWA). Follow the instructions in the learning activity to facilitate this activity. Close by encouraging participants to learn more about MBWA and to explore the six tips to make MBWA more effective provided in the handout.
1:25 p.m. (10 min)	Slide 36 Motivation Techniques •Management by walking around (MBWA) •Public opinion baths •Choosing battles •Sharing the "why" •Focusing on goals and objectives •Forgiving and forgetting •Coaching the team	**Learning Content/Lecture** **Motivation Techniques** • **Handout 30: Motivation Techniques** Use this slide and handout to present other motivational techniques that project managers can use to motivate their project teams. The project manager must use many ways to motivate the team and tailor techniques to individual team members. Here are some effective techniques they can develop for their motivation toolkit. **Management by walking around (MBWA):** As a leader, if you aren't walking around your organization, how can you know what is going on? Get out of your office or cubicle and find out what the project team is doing. **Public opinion baths:** To build understanding and rapport across all stakeholders, take a couple of "public opinion baths." While walking around, ask your team, customers, and sponsors for their opinions. **Choose your battles:** Not every situation is worthy of a fight. Choose your battles carefully to conserve your management time and resources and to promote the perception that you are a reasonable person.

TIMING	SLIDES	ACTIVITIES/NOTES/CONSIDERATIONS
	Slide 36, *continued*	**Focus on your goals and objectives:** And communicate them to your team. **Share the why:** Share the "why"—the value of the project—not just the "what." **Forgive and forget:** It is many times better to "forgive and forget" than to "review and retrieve." No one can stay motivated and productive if constantly reminded of failures. **Coach the team:** Great coaches provide positive input to their teams on how to achieve goals—not negative input on how they have failed.
1:35 p.m. (5 min)	Slide 37 Positive Motivation • Praise good performance openly • Handle poor performance discreetly • Help people identify problems • Show interest	**Learning Content/Lecture** **Positive Motivation** Use this slide to briefly overview these tips to positively motivate project teams: • **Praise good performance openly.** When an individual performs well, praise him or her in front of the team. • **Handle poor performance discreetly.** When an individual performs poorly, avoid de-motivating him or her with public criticism. • **Help people identify problems.** Empower team members to identify problems for themselves. This will increase ownership and buy-in. • **Show interest.** Being genuinely interested in people—and what's important to them—goes a long way in motivating performance. **Variation:** If time permits, you could turn this learning content into an interactive group activity. You could ask table teams to role-play what using these tips might look like in action. Depending on the group, they might have fun role-playing first how *not* to perform the tip and then how to do it right.

TIMING	SLIDES	ACTIVITIES/NOTES/CONSIDERATIONS
1:40 p.m. (5 min)	Slide 38 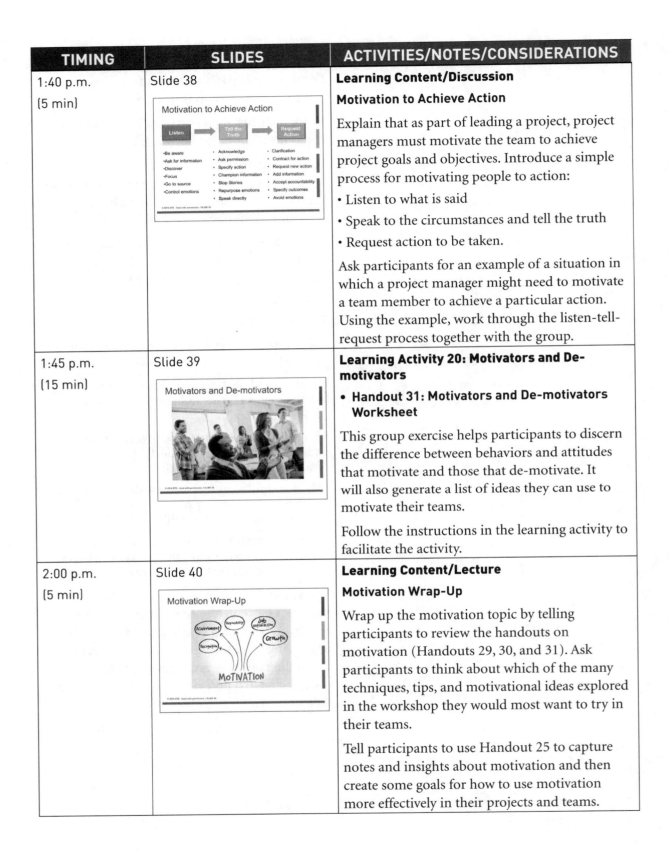	**Learning Content/Discussion** **Motivation to Achieve Action** Explain that as part of leading a project, project managers must motivate the team to achieve project goals and objectives. Introduce a simple process for motivating people to action: • Listen to what is said • Speak to the circumstances and tell the truth • Request action to be taken. Ask participants for an example of a situation in which a project manager might need to motivate a team member to achieve a particular action. Using the example, work through the listen-tell-request process together with the group.
1:45 p.m. (15 min)	Slide 39	**Learning Activity 20: Motivators and De-motivators** • **Handout 31: Motivators and De-motivators Worksheet** This group exercise helps participants to discern the difference between behaviors and attitudes that motivate and those that de-motivate. It will also generate a list of ideas they can use to motivate their teams. Follow the instructions in the learning activity to facilitate the activity.
2:00 p.m. (5 min)	Slide 40	**Learning Content/Lecture** **Motivation Wrap-Up** Wrap up the motivation topic by telling participants to review the handouts on motivation (Handouts 29, 30, and 31). Ask participants to think about which of the many techniques, tips, and motivational ideas explored in the workshop they would most want to try in their teams. Tell participants to use Handout 25 to capture notes and insights about motivation and then create some goals for how to use motivation more effectively in their projects and teams.

TIMING	SLIDES	ACTIVITIES/NOTES/CONSIDERATIONS
2:05 p.m. (5 min)	Slide 41 Problem-Solving Skills SOLUTION PROBLEM	**Learning Content/Lecture** **Problem-Solving Skills** Introduce the next interpersonal topic: problem solving. Point out that projects will inevitably run into problems, so project managers need to be prepared to deal with and resolve problems in a fair and responsive manner as they arise. Good planning on the part of the project manager can prevent some problems from happening altogether. But when they do happen, problem-solving skills can enable solutions that are based on facts and well-thought-out processes.
2:10 p.m. (5 min)	Slide 42 What Is a Problem?	**Learning Content/Lecture** **What Is a Problem?** Explain that a project manager must be on the alert to identify issues before they become problems. Issues and problems are not the same. An *issue* is a matter to be decided now but is not necessarily negative. A *problem*, however, is negative—an obstacle that makes achieving a desired goal, objective, or purpose difficult. Nor are *problems* and *risks* the same. A risk can be positive or negative, whereas problems are always negative. In addition, a risk is a condition that may or may not occur in the future, but a problem actually exists. No matter how well planned a project is, problems are inherent in the process. Share a few examples of problems that can arise as a project progresses: • A needed resource is unavailable or becomes unavailable. • A project action cannot be completed in the planned time. • A project action cannot be completed within the planned budget. • A stakeholder becomes unhappy with project execution or results. • A conflict arises between project stakeholders or team members.

TIMING	SLIDES	ACTIVITIES/NOTES/CONSIDERATIONS
2:15 p.m. (20 min)	Slide 43 Problem-Solving Activity **Four Steps to Problem Solving** •**Identify the problem:** what, why, how, where, who, when. •**Define potential solutions:** options a, b, c, d. •**Choose a solution to implement:** decide, act, implement. •**Verify the solution worked:** verify, validate, confirm.	**Learning Activity 21: Problem-Solving Exercise** • **Handout 32: Question Checklist Tool for Problem Solving** In this small group activity participants will practice identifying a problem using a checklist question tool and work together with a small group to use a four-step method to solve a problem. Briefly overview the simple four-step method to solve problems: 1. Identify the problem: answering what, why, how, where, who, and when. 2. Define potential solutions: options a, b, c, d. 3. Choose a solution to implement: decide, act, implement. 4. Verify that the solution worked: verify, validate, confirm. Explain that participants will be using a question checklist tool to help identify the problem (step 1). Using a set of structured questions encourages both broad and deep analysis of your situation or problem. The questions themselves may be simple, but when used as part of the checklist, they become a powerful management tool. Follow the instructions in the learning activity to complete the activity.

TIMING	SLIDES	ACTIVITIES/NOTES/CONSIDERATIONS
2:35 p.m. (5 min)	Slide 44 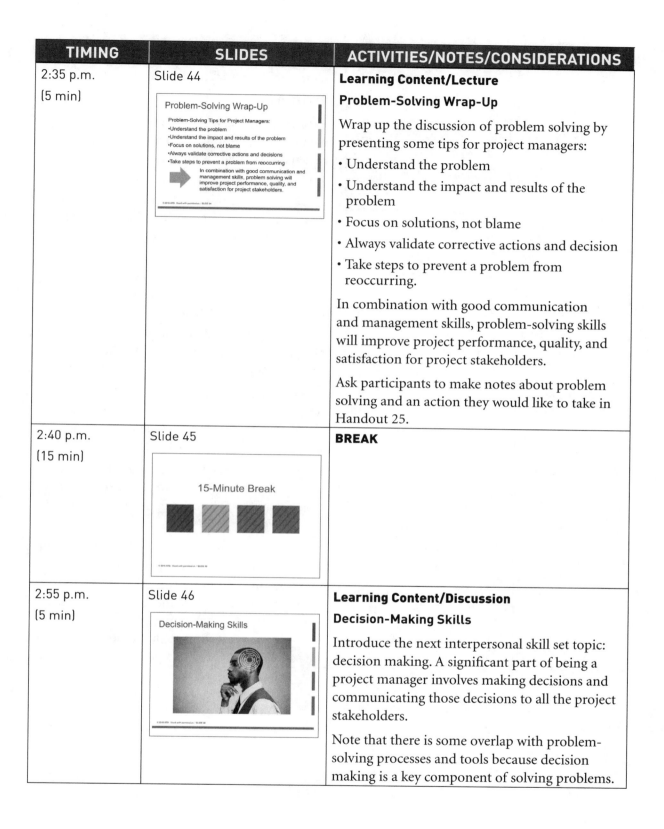	**Learning Content/Lecture** **Problem-Solving Wrap-Up** Wrap up the discussion of problem solving by presenting some tips for project managers: • Understand the problem • Understand the impact and results of the problem • Focus on solutions, not blame • Always validate corrective actions and decision • Take steps to prevent a problem from reoccurring. In combination with good communication and management skills, problem-solving skills will improve project performance, quality, and satisfaction for project stakeholders. Ask participants to make notes about problem solving and an action they would like to take in Handout 25.
2:40 p.m. (15 min)	Slide 45	**BREAK**
2:55 p.m. (5 min)	Slide 46	**Learning Content/Discussion** **Decision-Making Skills** Introduce the next interpersonal skill set topic: decision making. A significant part of being a project manager involves making decisions and communicating those decisions to all the project stakeholders. Note that there is some overlap with problem-solving processes and tools because decision making is a key component of solving problems.

TIMING	SLIDES	ACTIVITIES/NOTES/CONSIDERATIONS
3:00 p.m. (5 min)	Slide 47 Making a poor decision is often better for a project manager than making no decision at all.	**Learning Content/Discussion** **Decisions** Read aloud the statement on the slide: "Making a poor decision is often better for a project manager than making no decision at all." Ask participants whether they agree with this potentially controversial statement and to share why or not. How could *not* making a decision be more harmful to a project than making a poor decision? Once participants have shared their thoughts on the quote, explain that while making a poor decision could be harmful to a project, not making a decision can be worse from the perspective of stopping the project, holding up resources, and interrupting the project rhythm. In a sports match, such as golf, football, or tennis, when the rhythm of the event is interrupted, the game changes. Often the momentum changes, which in turn can change the outcome. Likewise, when the flow of a project begins, it will achieve a natural rhythm, flow, and cadence. When that flow is disrupted, the outcome could also change. Making a decision to start a day later rather than not deciding when to start a task introduces questions in the minds of team members and other stakeholders. Once the focus of project work moves to speculation, doubt, or concern, it requires a lot of effort to put things back on track.

TIMING	SLIDES	ACTIVITIES/NOTES/CONSIDERATIONS
3:05 p.m. (5 min)	**Slide 48** Gather Information • What—what is the situation? • Where—where did it occur or where will it occur? • When—when did it occur or when will it occur? • Who—who is affected? • Why—why is action required? the 5 Ws	**Learning Content/Lecture** **Gather Information** Explain that project managers facilitate decision making for the project by gathering and presenting the facts to inform decisions. In some cases, project managers have the authority to make the decisions themselves (after all, if the project manager cannot make decisions, why have one?). In other cases, they don't the authority to make decisions, but they are responsible for presenting the information to stakeholders who can make the decisions. Either way, a project manager should gather as much information as possible to enable the correct decision in a given set of circumstances. One tool that can help with information gathering is asking the five Ws—what, where, when, who, and why. Briefly present the five Ws and then discuss each in some detail. Use your own experiences to add some realism to this general discovery technique. Point out that the question checklist tool in Handout 32 works well for this information-gathering phase.
3:10 p.m. (5 min)	**Slide 49** Decision-Making Wrap-Up • Gather as much information as possible • Own the decisions • Involve those affected by the decision in the decision-making process • Acknowledge that making a poor decision often is better than making no decision	**Learning Content/Lecture** **Decision-Making Wrap-Up** Decision making is clearly critical to project management success. Wrap up the topic of decision making with a brief overview of the lessons learned: • **Gather information.** Information is king when it comes to being able to make good decisions. • **Own the decisions.** Project managers must accept responsibility and take ownership for decisions they make. Project managers who make decisive and educated decisions will find their project teams more apt to follow and respect them, regardless of the popularity of individual decisions.

TIMING	SLIDES	ACTIVITIES/NOTES/CONSIDERATIONS
	Slide 49, *continued*	• **Involve stakeholders.** Project managers should try to involve those affected by the decision. Don't wait until the decision has already been reached to involve the stakeholders or the project team. • **Acknowledge that making a poor decision can be better than making no decision at all.** Of course, a good decision is the goal, but maintaining forward movement is very important in project management. Ask participants to jot down notes on decision making in their goal planner (Handout 25) and add any goals they have in this area. Encourage them to create SMART goals that they can work on in their teams and projects.
3:15 p.m. (5 min)	Slide 50 Influencing Skills	**Learning Content/Lecture** **Influencing Skills** Introduce the next and final interpersonal skills topic for project managers: influence. A project manager's ability to influence stakeholders, project team members, and the organization is yet another a key factor in successful projects. The project manager uses influence to foster acceptance of decisions being made and to improve performance and ensure product quality. Influencing involves the project manager promoting the project, the project team, and the value they bring to the organization. In short, successful project managers do their best to ensure that the project management group provides value to the organization and works effectively to accomplish the objectives of the project.

TIMING	SLIDES	ACTIVITIES/NOTES/CONSIDERATIONS
3:20 p.m. (5 min)	Slide 51 Influencing Tactics and Responses Tactics Responses Join → Commitment Sell → Compliance Push → Resistance	**Learning Content/Lecture** **Influencing Tactics and Responses** Use this slide to briefly introduce the three general tactics used to influence others: • Join • Sell • Push These tactics typically result in three types of responses from those they seek to influence: • Commitment • Compliance • Resistance Walk the participants through the slide to elaborate on the tactics and their responses: • **Join:** convincing a person to buy in and actively join the group or event will most likely result in **commitment**. • **Sell:** convincing the person to buy in, but only after a significant "selling" process, may induce some level of reluctance but will most likely result in **compliance**. • **Push:** actively convincing and pressuring the person to buy in will most likely induce active resistance, either now or in the future. Point out that successful project managers learn to balance the tactics they use to ensure the most positive outcome.

TIMING	SLIDES	ACTIVITIES/NOTES/CONSIDERATIONS
3:25 p.m. (15 min)	**Slide 52** Influencing and Listening One of the most powerful, yet underused skills a project manager can develop to influence others is the ability to ask great questions . . . and then listen to the answers. Listening builds trust and credibility. Are you a good listener?	**Learning Activity 22: Are You a Good Listener?** • **Assessment 3: Listening Skills Quick Assessment** This self-assessment activity helps participants reflect on their listening skills and identify areas of strength and areas of potential development. Begin by emphasizing the integral link between influencing and listening skills. The ability to listen well is one of the most potent—and underused—skills a project manager can develop to influence others. Put simply, listening skills build trust and credibility. Then introduce the assessment and review the instructions with the participants. Follow the instructions in the learning activity to conduct this activity.
3:40 p.m. (5 min)	**Slide 53** Workshop Review Project management knowledge requirements include these key areas: •Project management knowledge •General management knowledge •Interpersonal skills •Knowledge of the project environment •Specialized knowledge	**Workshop Wrap-Up and Review** Wrap up the workshop with a brief review of the content you've covered in your time together. Participants have defined a project and project management. They have also identified the knowledge requirements for successful project management. (Slide 1 of 2)
	Slide 54 Interpersonal Skills Communicating Leading Motivating Problem Solving Decision Making Influencing	Review the critical interpersonal skills that they have discussed throughout the day, highlighting the importance of communication. Answer any questions participants might still have about the workshop topic. (Slide 2 of 2)

TIMING	SLIDES	ACTIVITIES/NOTES/CONSIDERATIONS
3:45 p.m. (10 min)	Slide 55 Action Planning ☑ What's your plan?	**Action Planning** Remind your participants that learning is a journey, not a destination. The learning and work that they have done in this workshop has given them a good start toward building the knowledge base and interpersonal skills needed to be a successful project manager. But it is only a start. They need to continue to build their project management knowledge and skills. Ask participants to take 5 minutes to review their goal planner (Handout 25) one last time to capture insights, notes, and goals for how they would like to continue their project management learning after the workshop. Encourage them to add details to make their learning goals SMART (specific, measurable, actionable, realistic, and timely). Gather everyone in a circle. Start by sharing a project management goal you are going to work on. Then toss a soft throwing object such as a Koosh ball to a participant and ask him or her to share one of his or her learning goals. Continue tossing the ball around the circle until everyone has shared.

TIMING	SLIDES	ACTIVITIES/NOTES/CONSIDERATIONS
3:55 p.m. (5 min) Ends at 4:00 p.m.	Slide 56 What do great project managers do?	**Workshop Wrap-Up: What Do Great Project Managers Do?** • **Handout 23: 10 Things Great Project Managers Do Every Day** • **Assessment 2: Workshop Evaluation** Ask participants to help you learn by completing the evaluation form. As participants are completing the evaluation, ask them to think about what they will do *every day* to be great project managers. Handout 23 gives 10 simple but profound ideas for habits they can cultivate to be great project managers. Be available to field questions about the workshop topics. Share plans for follow-up coaching if applicable (see Chapter 10 for ideas to follow up the training with support and activities.) Thank the participants for their contributions and wish them well. **Optional:** Because of time constraints of a one-day workshop, participants do not get a chance to explore the project management processes. To support their work back on the job, you may distribute the bonus Project Manager Toolkit (available in Chapter 14), which includes powerful templates for project management processes that they can implement in their projects and teams right away. You could give it to them as a parting gift now or send it as a digital document after the workshop as a follow-up support.

What to Do Next

If you have decided that the one-day workshop is the best choice for your participants, consider these next steps as you prepare for your workshop:

• Determine the schedule for workshops, reserve location, and order any catering you may wish to provide.

• Identify and invite participants.

PROJECT MANAGEMENT training

- Review the workshop objectives, activities, and handouts to plan the content you will use.

- Prepare copies of the participant materials and any activity-related materials you may need. Refer to Chapter 15 for information about how to access and use the supplemental materials provided for this workshop.

- Gather tactile items, such as Koosh balls, crayons, magnets, or Play-Doh, to place on the tables for tactile learners. See Chapter 8 for other ideas to enhance the learning environment of your workshop.

- Confirm that you have addressed scheduling and personal concerns so that you can be fully present to facilitate the class.

References

Fisher, A. (2013). "Management by Walking Around: 6 Tips to Make It Work." Ask Annie blog, August 23, 2013, www.fortune.com.

Hogson, P., and A. Sturgess. (2014). *Uncommon Leadership: How to Build Competitive Advantage by Thinking Differently*. Philadelphia: Kogan Page. Checklist and 5 Whys available online, at www.the-happy-manager.com.

Kerzner, H. R. (2013). *Project Management: A Systems Approach to Planning, Scheduling, and Controlling*, eleventh ed. Hoboken, NJ: Wiley.

Mulle, K. (2016). *Emotional Intelligence Training*. Alexandria, VA: ATD Press.

Peters, T., and R. Waterman. (1982). *In Search of Excellence: Lessons from America's Best-Run Companies*. New York: Harper and Row.

Peterson, D. (2016). "Listening Test: Are You a Good Listener?" www.adulted.about.com.

PMI. (2013). *A Guide to the Project Management Body of Knowledge: PMBOK® Guide*, fifth ed. Newtown Square, PA: PMI.

Chapter 3

Half-Day Project Management Workshop

What's in This Chapter

- Project management fundamentals and introduction
- Objectives of the half-day Project Management Workshop
- Half-day workshop agenda in detail

As the other workshop agendas in this book have shown, project management is a process-intensive practice that requires significant time and expertise to do well. Clearly, a half-day workshop cannot cover all the concepts required to learn project management. The question, then, is how to design a half-day workshop on the topic. The approach that this half-day workshop takes is to provide a broad framework of what project management is and an overview of the cycle of processes involved, with some tools and practice included for usefulness and variety. This half-day workshop can serve as a nice introduction to the two-day and one-day workshops as well. It will benefit anyone who must manage projects or who works on project teams.

Project Management: From the Beginning

Because formal project management theory, methods, and best practice standards have been employed in every conceivable governmental, military, and commercial organization and industry, the field of project management has evolved over time. This evolution (revolution even) continues as the profession is continually refined and gains more traction globally. Project management is a methodical approach and discipline that everyone knows about but may not realize they use.

Consider the case of doctors—they see patients, they diagnose their problems, they prescribe solutions, and then they discharge the patients with possible follow-up visits. Compare that to the definition of a project: distinctive, transitory, defined start and finish, and continuously advanced. Doctors see a unique problem (patient), for a temporary time with a start and finish, and throughout the process determine the problem through diagnoses. They complete projects: They are project managers!

Project management is in the business of delivering results. Its strategies and methodologies work as well for disaster relief, fighting fires, and emergency response as they do for business goals in for-profit and nonprofit organizations. It is a proven method that will consistently deliver the results the project defines.

The workshops in this book have been designed from the perspective of healthy project management, which simply means that you do not have to use every process, procedure, template, trick, tip, and technique on every project to achieve your desired results. But you should know what tools are available before you can decide which tools you don't need. Using just the right amount of project management is one of the keys to success.

The half-day workshop will introduce the topic of project management and give participants a good start toward building a solid foundation of project management processes and practices. The workshop materials provide templates for the participants to use during the workshop activities and as tools back on the job. You are welcome to use these templates or create your own that are more specific to the needs of your organization and participants. Keep in mind, however, that project management is not about filling in templates or using a particular project software. Such tools can help save time and make project management easier, but there is only one element that can deliver a project on time, within scope, and within budget—*the project manager*. You will want to stress this point with your participants to empower their project management success.

As you prepare to deliver the workshop, think about times you have used project management to facilitate a training session, create a product, deliver a service, convene a meeting, or even plan a vacation. That's right—you, too, are a project manager. Add your personal experiences and successes to this workshop to make it your own. (And don't forget that people learn as much from your failures as they do from your successes.) Be willing to share whatever will make the concepts real and doable. Just like we tell the project manager to own the project, as the facilitator you should own your role in this workshop. The more of "you" you put into the sessions, the more your participants will get out of them.

Managing projects requires the ability to set clear objectives, report, project plan, work collaboratively, navigate uncertainty, and monitor and control project outcomes. Everything you do to prepare for and deliver this workshop needs to model these skills. Spend time building your understanding of project management methods and practice them in your preparation, design, delivery, and follow-up of this workshop.

A Word About Pre-Work

The half-day workshop includes a pre-work assignment to help your participants think about project management in their own specific context. When you send a welcome or confirmation message to participants, ask them to think about a project they were involved in this past year. Ask your participants to answer these questions about the project:

- What role did you play?
- What was unique about the project?
- Did it come in on time, within budget, and within scope?
- Did your project follow any specific process?

This is a great way to begin the relationship with your participants. At the start of the workshop you will debrief their pre-work by encouraging them to share one or two of their answers to the questions with group. Not everyone has to share; you can ask everyone to keep the questions in mind as they experience the workshop.

A Word About the Slides, Notes, and Handouts

The slides for this workshop contain key learning concepts about project management. Additional and supporting information will be found in the notes column of the agenda. Because it is impossible to include every piece of information in the slide, you will need to be prepared to discuss points from your own experience to help answer participants' questions. Project management is a complex topic, so I encourage you to research and learn more about the concepts covered in the workshop. See Figure 1-1 in chapter 1 for resources that will help you sharpen your project management skills and build your project management acumen. The blogs and online resources noted in the figure will bolster the information presented in the workshop with cutting-edge expertise in project management topics. Also, if you are unsure about any topic in the agenda, send me an email with your questions at wes.balakian@truesolutions.com and I will be glad to help you.

The handouts provided in this volume are another source of information for you as the facilitator and for your participants. In some cases, the handouts provide templates to be used in the learning activities. In other cases, they include "must-know" concepts that summarize the key learning in the modules or they provide tips, examples, flowcharts, and so on. And still other handouts provide useful information you won't have time to present within the scope of this workshop but that will help participants once they are back in their workplaces. Encourage participants to review these valuable resources to increase their project management knowledge and skills.

Also included in this volume is a Project Manager Toolkit (Chapter 14) that includes all the templates from the two-day agenda plus additional templates, all created by True Solutions Inc. (TSI). You can distribute a print copy of the Project Manager Toolkit to your participants at the close of the workshop or send it to them digitally a week or two after the workshop is completed as follow-up support for their learning. (In addition, TSI publishes a set of more than 100 templates on a wide range of project management processes and tasks to help project managers.)

The agenda notes are not highly scripted. They are addressed to you, the facilitator, and crafted in a natural voice that you can make your own when you deliver the content. Avoid just reading the slides—or your participants will immediately see that you are not comfortable with the subject and begin a contest to uncover what you don't know.

As an instructor, author, consultant, and experienced corporate executive, I can talk for days about project management, but when I get in front of people they see my passion. Show them yours. If you are confident with project management principles and content, you will find navigating the agenda very easy. If you are more of a novice to the field, rely on the agendas to help guide you through the material but plan to spend some time broadening your knowledge base with the resources noted in Figure 1-1.

Half-Day Workshop Objectives

In the half-day workshop, participants will

- Define what a project is
- Develop a working definition of project management
- Learn the project process groups—initiate, plan, execute, control, and close
- Gain confidence to apply project management processes to a project as a project manager or project team member.

Half-Day Workshop Overview

TOPICS	TIMING
Welcome and Introductions	5 minutes
Learning Activity 1: My Project Management Story	10 minutes
Workshop Objectives	5 minutes
What Is Project Management?	
What Is a Project?	5 minutes
Continuous Advancement	5 minutes
What Is Project Management?	5 minutes
Manage Project Constraints	5 minutes
The Project Management Process	
Project Management Process Groups	5 minutes
Initiate the Project	
Initiate: Key Tasks	5 minutes
Initiate: Project Charter	5 minutes
Learning Activity 3: Create a Project Charter	10 minutes
Identify Stakeholders	5 minutes
Stakeholder Power–Interest Grid	5 minutes
BREAK	**15 minutes**
Plan the Project	
Plan: Key Tasks	5 minutes
Project Management Plan	5 minutes
Learning Activity 5: Communications Interference, Part 1	5 minutes
Communications Management	5 minutes
Scope Management	5 minutes
Product Scope vs. Project Scope	5 minutes
Quality Management	5 minutes
Impact of Poor Quality	5 minutes
Risk Management	5 minutes
Risk Management Processes	5 minutes
Identify Risks	5 minutes
Learning Activity 11: Risk Categorization Exercise	10 minutes
Risk Responses	5 minutes
Execute the Project	
Execute: Key Tasks	3 minutes
Execute: Purpose	2 minutes
Execute: Processes	5 minutes
Manage Communications	5 minutes

TOPICS	TIMING
Direct and Manage Project Work	5 minutes
Monitor and Control the Project	
Monitor and Control: Key Tasks	5 minutes
Monitor and Control: Purpose	5 minutes
Control Scope	5 minutes
Control Schedule	5 minutes
Control Costs	5 minutes
Close the Project	
Close: Key Tasks	5 minutes
Close Procurements	5 minutes
Close Contract and Close Project Interactions	5 minutes
Close Project or Phase	5 minutes
Workshop Wrap-Up	
Action Planning	10 minutes
What Do Great Project Managers Do?	5 minutes
TOTAL	**240 minutes (4 hours)**

Half-Day Workshop Agenda

Half-Day: (8:00 a.m. to 12:00 p.m.)

TIMING	SLIDES	ACTIVITIES/NOTES/CONSIDERATIONS
8:00 a.m. (5 min)	Slide 1 **ATD** Workshop Project Management Training Half-Day Workshop	**Welcome and Introductions** Welcome the participants as they enter the room and briefly introduce yourself. Make an effort to talk to each person, which will set the tone for the session and begin to model communication as a primary skill for successful project management. Note the usual housekeeping items such as restroom locations and breaks.

TIMING	SLIDES	ACTIVITIES/NOTES/CONSIDERATIONS
8:05 a.m. (10 min)	Slide 2 My Project Management Story 1. What is your name and current position? 2. What is your project management experience? 3. What do you hope to learn today? 4. How will you define success at the end of the workshop?	**Learning Activity 1: My Project Management Story** This icebreaker partner activity will help you get a sense of your participants' level of experience with project management and what their learning needs are. It will also help your participants get to know each other better. To help participants interact with each other, divide the group into pairs and have them interview each other using the same set of questions. Then have each pair introduce each other to the group. NOTE: To conduct this activity in the time allotted, follow the instructions in the learning activity, but skip steps 1 and 2 and start the activity at step 3.
8:15 a.m. (5 min)	Slide 3 Workshop Objectives • Define what a project is • Develop a working definition of project management • Learn the five project process groups: initiate, plan, execute, monitor and control, close • Gain confidence to apply project management processes to a project as a project manager or project team member	**Workshop Objectives** Introduce the topic of project management to the participants. Make the point that they use project management every day—even though they may not call it that. Just about everyone is a project manager based on the definition of a project (distinctive, transitory, defined start and finish, continuously advanced). Doctors, police officers, attorneys, veterinarians, and teachers all deliver and manage projects. Briefly present the workshop objectives at a high level. Let the participants know that although the workshop will cover a lot of information, there will be opportunities to practice the concepts they are learning with each other in small groups. Explain that the session will introduce them to basic project management terminology and processes and will help them develop several key project management skills they will need to lead a project or participate as a project team member. (Slide 1 of 2)

TIMING	SLIDES	ACTIVITIES/NOTES/CONSIDERATIONS
	Slide 4 **Pre-Work Assignment** Think of a project that you have been involved with recently: •What role did you play? •What was unique about the project? •Did it come in on time, budget, and within scope? •Did your project follow any specific process?	Wrap up your overview of the objectives by asking, by a show of hands, how many of the participants have had some experience with project management before, perhaps having attended other workshops, read books about it, or worked as team members on projects. Take a moment to review the pre-work assignment you gave the participants to identify a project they were involved in this year. Ask for a few volunteers to briefly share their project examples with the group. Ask them: • What role did you play? • What was unique about the project? • Did it come in on time, within budget, and within scope? • Did your project follow any specific process? (Slide 2 of 2)
8:20 a.m. (5 min)	Slide 5 **What is a Project?** Project Program Company	**Learning Content/Lecture and Discussion** **What Is a Project?** To understand what project management is, you have to start even farther back and ask what a project is. Ask participants: What is the difference between a project and a program? Use the slide to explain that a program is an ongoing set of activities, such as a car company that produces a fleet of vehicles. A project, however, has four specific characteristics: • Distinctive • Transitory • Defined start and finish • Continuously advanced. A project, using the example on the slide, would be the development of a single model of car in a single model year.

TIMING	SLIDES	ACTIVITIES/NOTES/CONSIDERATIONS
	Slide 5, *continued*	Briefly discuss the first three characteristics (distinctive, transitory, and defined start/finish), which are mostly self-explanatory.
		Then introduce the fourth characteristic: *continuous advancement*. Emphasize that it is a key element in defining a project. Open the discussion by asking participants what they think the term means. Once they have shared their ideas with the group, use the next slide to help explain it further.
8:25 a.m. (5 min)	Slide 6	**Learning Content/Lecture and Discussion** **Continuous Advancement** Continuous advancement works in a manner similar to the Plan-Do-Check-Act cycle made popular by W. Edward Deming. We *plan*, we *do*, we *check*, and we *act* the plan. As we move forward and go around the wheel, we get increasingly more detailed as we gather information. Walk the participants step by step through the Plan-Do-Check-Act cycle shown on the slide: • **Plan:** planning the project • **Do:** executing the project work • **Check:** the monitoring portion of the M&C (monitoring and control) process, checking to determine status • **Act:** the controlling portion of the M&C process, taking corrective or preventive action The entire model is built on a wheel, with communicating—the most critical interpersonal skill for a project manager—as the hub. Other interpersonal skills make up the various spokes of the wheel. Discuss the interpersonal skills listed in the diagram and point out that any interpersonal skill could be part of this wheel diagram. Explain that at the end of the cycle, there is a review, and the process starts over—representing the end-of-phase review.

TIMING	SLIDES	ACTIVITIES/NOTES/CONSIDERATIONS
8:30 a.m. (5 min)	Slide 7 **PROJECT MANAGEMENT** Project management is "the application of knowledge, skills, tools, and techniques to project activities in order to meet project requirements."	**Learning Content/Discussion** **What Is Project Management?** Use this slide to share the classic definition of *project management* as defined in the *PMBOK® Guide*. PMBOK stands for Project Management Body of Knowledge, which is created by the Project Management Institute. Discuss this definition with the participants by asking them to share other definitions they may have of project management. Ideally, this will spark some lively discussion that will reveal their views and thoughts about project management. For example, it has been suggested that project management is the art and science of getting things done. What do they think about that definition compared to the *PMBOK® Guide* definition?
8:35 a.m. (5 min)	Slide 8 Manage Project Constraints Scope Risk Time Cost	**Learning Content/Lecture** **Manage Project Constraints** Use this slide to present an alternate view of project management and to introduce the concept of the triple-triple constraint. Explain that the project manager is most often interested in managing project constraints to facilitate success. The triple constraint originally referred to "time-cost-scope" (as shown in the large triangle). If you change one of these parameters, then the others change. So, for example, if more work is to be performed (increase scope), then more time and money will be needed. Or, if you cut the budget, you will likely have to decrease project scope, which in turn may result in less time being used.

TIMING	SLIDES	ACTIVITIES/NOTES/CONSIDERATIONS
	Slide 8, *continued*	Over time, the definition of triple constraint has expanded to include risk, quality, and resources (as shown in the smaller inset triangle). This triple-triple constraint affects all the constraints. For example, changes to quality definitions can change the amount of work, time, and cost associated with the project; or changes to risk conditions may change work, time, cost, quality, and resource use. Share the bottom line takeaway from this slide: A change in one parameter may affect many or all of the other parameters.
8:40 a.m. (5 min)	Slide 9 	**Learning Content/Discussion** **Project Management Process Groups** Use this slide and Handout 1 to transition from defining projects and project management to learning about the process of managing projects. Explain that PMI and other key organizations in the field have developed global standards for project management and the process of project management. The model in the slide shows PMI's five project management process groups, which will be the focus of the next five learning modules. They include initiate, plan, execute, monitor and control, and close. Each process group contains multiple activities and processes.
8:45 a.m. (5 min)	Slide 10 	**Learning Content/Lecture** **Initiate: Key Tasks** Use this slide to briefly overview the following list of typical key tasks in the initiate process group, along with the definitions of key terms for the participants: • **Define high-level *scope,*** the sum of the deliverables of a project.

TIMING	SLIDES	ACTIVITIES/NOTES/CONSIDERATIONS
	Slide 10, *continued*	• **Identify and document high-level *risks, assumptions, and constraints.*** Risk is an uncertain event or consequence that may occur that has a measurable impact on the project. • **Develop the *project charter,*** which is essentially the project's "license to do business." It documents preliminary project characteristics, identifies and authorizes a project manager, and authorizes the project to begin. • **Obtain project charter *approval.*** • **Identify key *stakeholders,*** the people or organizations involved in the project. The two major outcomes of initiating the project are formally authorizing the project and identifying the stakeholders.
8:50 a.m. (5 min)	Slide 11 Project Charter	**Learning Content Lecture** **Project Charter** • **Handout 3: Project Charter Template** A key deliverable of the initiate process group is the project charter. The project charter documents and defines project information needed to officially start a project. It authorizes the project manager to begin the project and to use organizational resources. It also documents the initial vision of the project sponsor. The charter should be very concise, ideally completed in one page. Refer to the project charter template in Handout 3 to show the elements to include in the project charter. Other key considerations when creating a project charter include assumptions, constraints, and historical information. Encourage participants to use the handout as a tool in their projects back at their organizations. For simple projects, the initial paperwork or documentation in the project could be treated as a project charter.

TIMING	SLIDES	ACTIVITIES/NOTES/CONSIDERATIONS

8:55 a.m.
(10 min)
	Slide 12
	
	Create a Project Charter
	• Select a project:
	  – Make a cake
	  – Build a house
	  – Plan a vacation
	• Work through template with your group
	• Hint: Don't get bogged down in details
		Learning Activity 2: Create a Project Charter
		
		This small group activity gives participants practice creating a project charter. Working through the template together in a small group will help them identify and document a project's purpose, objectives, descriptions, budget, schedule, and more.
		
		Use this slide and the instructions in the learning activity to complete the activity.

9:05 a.m. (5 min)	Slide 13 Identify Stakeholders	**Learning Content/Lecture** **Identify Stakeholders** • **Handout 4: Potential Stakeholders** Briefly explain that stakeholders are the people and organizations participating in the project or those who are directly or indirectly affected by the project. Stakeholders can be internal or external to the organization and can include the general public in some projects. The handout lists many potential stakeholders on projects. Ask participants to think about who else could be considered a stakeholder. Some examples of stakeholders not listed in the handout are clients, human resources, chief executive officers, chief technology officers, chief financial officers, procurement, and social media team. A key deliverable of the initiating process group is a stakeholder register and stakeholder management strategy, which document relevant information for all identified stakeholders. This information may include the stakeholder's interests, involvement, expectations, importance, influence, and impact on the project's execution, as well as any specific communications requirements. It is important to note that all stakeholders must be identified even if they don't require any communications.

TIMING	SLIDES	ACTIVITIES/NOTES/CONSIDERATIONS
9:10 a.m. (5 min)	Slide 14 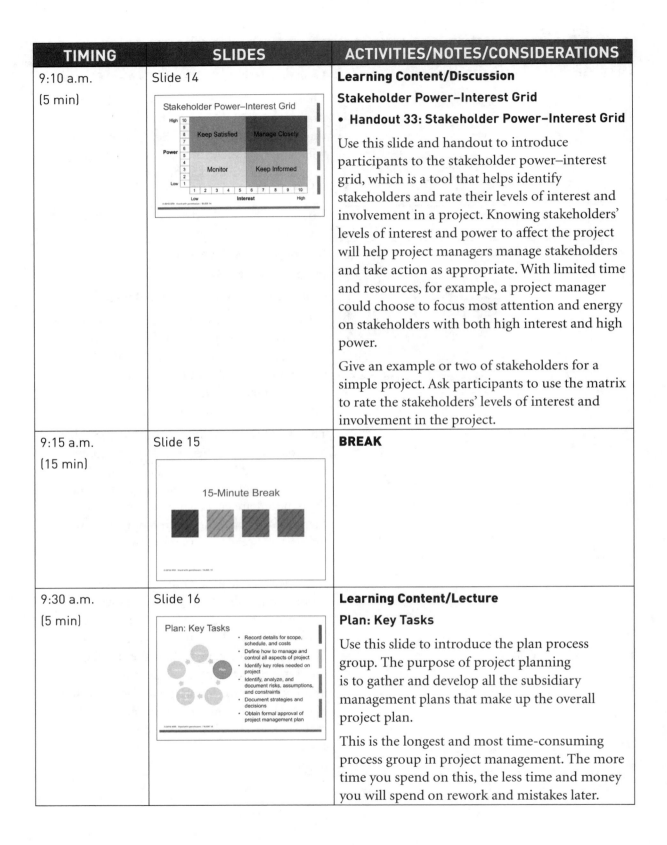	**Learning Content/Discussion** **Stakeholder Power–Interest Grid** • **Handout 33: Stakeholder Power–Interest Grid** Use this slide and handout to introduce participants to the stakeholder power–interest grid, which is a tool that helps identify stakeholders and rate their levels of interest and involvement in a project. Knowing stakeholders' levels of interest and power to affect the project will help project managers manage stakeholders and take action as appropriate. With limited time and resources, for example, a project manager could choose to focus most attention and energy on stakeholders with both high interest and high power. Give an example or two of stakeholders for a simple project. Ask participants to use the matrix to rate the stakeholders' levels of interest and involvement in the project.
9:15 a.m. (15 min)	Slide 15 15-Minute Break	**BREAK**
9:30 a.m. (5 min)	Slide 16 Plan: Key Tasks	**Learning Content/Lecture** **Plan: Key Tasks** Use this slide to introduce the plan process group. The purpose of project planning is to gather and develop all the subsidiary management plans that make up the overall project plan. This is the longest and most time-consuming process group in project management. The more time you spend on this, the less time and money you will spend on rework and mistakes later.

TIMING	SLIDES	ACTIVITIES/NOTES/CONSIDERATIONS
	Slide 16, *continued*	Briefly overview the key tasks associated with the plan process group: • Record detailed customer requirements, constraints, and assumptions with stakeholders to establish the project deliverables, using requirement gathering techniques (planning sessions, brainstorming, focus groups) and the project charter. • Identify key project team members, defining roles and responsibilities and creating a project organization chart to develop the human resource plan. • Create the work breakdown structure with the team, using tools and techniques to develop the cost, schedule, resource, and procurement plans. • Develop the change management plan by defining how changes will be handled to minimize risk. • Identify project risks by defining risk strategies and developing the risk management plan to reduce uncertainty throughout the project life cycle. • Obtain project plan approval from the customer or sponsor to formalize the project management approach.
9:35 a.m. (5 min)	Slide 17 Project Management Plan Planning the project produces one major outcome—the project management plan. Its components include – Subsidiary plans – Baselines – Project documents	**Learning Content/Lecture** **Project Management Plan** A key outcome of the plan process group is the *project management plan*, which is the formal, approved document that defines the project. Explain that many processes and plans go into creating the overall project plan (refer participants to Handout 1 for a complete list), but because of the time limitations, this workshop will focus on four areas: • Communications management • Scope management • Quality management • Risk management

TIMING	SLIDES	ACTIVITIES/NOTES/CONSIDERATIONS
9:40 a.m. (5 min)	Slide 18 Communication 	**Learning Activity 5: Communication Interference** Use Part 1 of this learning activity to underline the point that effective communication is a critical success factor in project management. You will not use Part 2 of the activity in this workshop. Lead participants in a simple listening exercise to demonstrate the importance of clear communication and good listening skills. Debrief the activity with the group using the following discussion questions: • What happened? Does everyone's product look the same? • The same instructions were given to everybody, so why are the resulting products so different? • What would have helped make the communication clearer in this activity? (For example, being able to ask questions, being able to see what others were doing, getting feedback from the person giving the instructions.) • How important is clear communication to the success of projects? NOTE: Follow the instructions in the learning activity to complete *only* Part 1 of this activity.
9:45 a.m. (5 min)	Slide 19 Communications Management Plan 	**Learning Content/Lecture** **Communications Management** • **Handout 10: Communications Management Plan Template** Share that when troubled projects are evaluated, poor communication is typically at the heart of the conflict and negative outcomes. A common rule of thumb is that good project managers spend up to 90 percent of their time communicating.

TIMING	SLIDES	ACTIVITIES/NOTES/CONSIDERATIONS
	Slide 19, *continued*	Communication provides vital connections between people, concepts, and information throughout the project environment. Good communications management ensures that important information is generated, gathered, disseminated, and stored in an appropriate and effective manner. It can facilitate success in projects, whereas the lack of it almost always contributes to project confusion, deficiencies, and failure.
		The communications management plan helps the project manager determine the communication needs of project stakeholders, including
		• What information is needed
		• When it is needed
		• How it will be delivered.
		Briefly review the communications management plan template in Handout 10. Highlight the different kinds of information they will want to include in their plans. Point out that they can save time and reuse information and materials from previous projects, but they must include the specific needs of their current project because each project will have unique needs that must to be taken into consideration. Encourage participants to use the template as a tool in their projects back in their teams and organizations.

TIMING	SLIDES	ACTIVITIES/NOTES/CONSIDERATIONS
9:50 a.m. (5 min)	Slide 20 **Scope Management** Developing a scope management plan documents how the project scope will be defined, validated, and controlled. It may also include – A scope statement – A work breakdown structure – Scope verification/validation	**Learning Content/ Lecture** **Scope Management** • **Handout 9: Scope Management Plan Template** Explain that scope equals work—the work that must be performed to deliver a product, service, or result with the specified features and functions. Use this slide and handout to briefly overview the scope management plan, which documents how the project scope will be defined, validated, and controlled. At a minimum, it will document • Project name • Approach to project scope changes • Who can request a scope change • Who can approve a scope change • Process description to request, consider, and implement a scope change. You will not have time to work through the scope management plan during the workshop, but a template is included in the handout that they can use for their projects back in their workplaces.
9:55 a.m. (5 min)	Slide 21 **Product Scope vs. Project Scope**	**Learning Content/Lecture** **Product Scope vs. Project Scope** Take a moment to discuss the differences between product scope and project scope. Share the *PMBOK® Guide* definitions of each: *Product* scope includes the features and functions that characterize the product, service, or other project deliverable. *Project* scope is work that must be done to deliver the product with the features and functions specified. The difference between the two is easy to see with the example on the slide. The bookcase is the product; its product scope is that it should have be 3' x 3' with three shelves, a light oak finish, and so on. The project scope is all the work that must be performed to deliver the bookcase as specified: buying materials, gathering tools, assembling components, and so on.

PROJECT MANAGEMENT training

TIMING	SLIDES	ACTIVITIES/NOTES/CONSIDERATIONS
	Slide 21, *continued*	Ask participants to think about this workshop and identify the product scope and project scope. Throughout the workshop they have been learning about project management—that is the product or deliverable, and its product scope could be the workshop objectives. The project scope is everything we must do to deliver that learning.
10:00 a.m. (5 min)	Slide 22 Quality Management • Quality must be "planned-in"—not "inspected in" • Quality means delivering precisely what is promised	**Learning Content/Lecture** **Quality Management** • **Handout 22: Quality Management Plan Template** Review the essentials of quality management with the participants. When a project team delivers on time, within budget, and satisfying all scope requirements, then quality has been achieved. The primary goals of quality management are to reduce or eliminate waste and to improve processes. Explain that quality management delivers many benefits: • Improved product quality • Greater customer satisfaction • Higher morale • Increased efficiency. To ensure that this happens, the project manager and team must define what quality means to the project and document it in the *quality management plan*. Have participants follow along on the template in Handout 22 as you briefly overview what the quality management plan identifies:

TIMING	SLIDES	ACTIVITIES/NOTES/CONSIDERATIONS
	Slide 22, *continued*	• Roles and responsibilities; specific subject matter expertise; and the who, when, and where of quality management
		• How the project will be measured and what outcomes will constitute acceptable quality
		• How the products of the project will be measured and what specific outcomes, functions, or specifications will qualify as acceptable quality
		• Organization-specific quality processes and procedures that must be applied to the project and product quality plans.
10:05 a.m. (5 min)	Slide 23	**Learning Content/Discussion** **Impact of Poor Quality** Good quality clearly has benefits associated with it, but what about the effects of poor quality? Briefly present this graph showing poor quality and its impact over time on a project. Ask your participants to share examples from their experiences of the negative impact of poor quality on projects. Be ready to share some of your own experiences as well. Here are some ideas to get you started: • **Rework during project:** Doing the same work a second time. • **Rework when products are delivered:** Failure to meet customer requirements and expectations. • **Rework after delivery:** Product recalls, warranty work, remedies after the fact; decreased reputation and credibility.

TIMING	SLIDES	ACTIVITIES/NOTES/CONSIDERATIONS
10:10 a.m. (5 min)	Slide 24 Risk Management • Risk management is one of the most important areas in project management. • Risk infiltrates into each and every aspect of a project.	**Learning Content/Lecture** **Risk Management** Define *project risk* as the risk of the project being unsuccessful. It is the degree of exposure to negative events and their probable consequences on the project objectives expressed in terms of scope, cost, time, and quality. Project risks can either be favorable (opportunities) or unfavorable (risks). Explain that risk management planning is used to decide how to approach, plan, and execute risk management activities. It is one of the most important aspects of project management, so we will spend time exploring it in greater depth.
10:15 a.m. (5 min)	Slide 25 Risk Management	**Learning Content/Lecture** **Risk Management Processes** Share the six processes that are closely associated with risk management, as identified by the *PMBOK® Guide*: 1. Plan risk management 2. Identify risk 3. Perform qualitative risk analysis 4. Perform quantitative risk analysis 5. Plan risk response 6. Control risks To identify risks, the project manager must start with interviewing the stakeholders—particularly the sponsors—for input. Based on the risks identified, this process also determines the degree of risk tolerance for the project. If you have a robust project methodology, this process is probably already documented for you.

TIMING	SLIDES	ACTIVITIES/NOTES/CONSIDERATIONS
10:20 a.m. (5 min)	Slide 26 Identify Risks This process determines which risks may affect the project and documents their characteristics. RISK!	**Learning Content/Discussion** **Identify Risks** • **Handout 18: Risk Identification and Diagramming Techniques** Overview the identify risks process with the participants. This process determines which risks may affect the project and then documents their characteristics. Its primary objective is to create a list of risks that includes indications that the risks have occurred or are about to occur. These indications are termed *triggers*, *risk symptoms*, or *warning signs*. Each identified risk will be analyzed during the application of subsequent risk management processes. To help identify as many risks as possible, include many knowledgeable people in the process. Several iterations are likely before an exhaustive list of risks is developed. Let the participants know that there are many techniques for identifying risk. Use the handout to share some of the most common: • Process flowcharting • Brainstorming • Delphi estimation • Nominal group • Checklist analysis • Assumptions analysis • Qualitative risk analysis • Documentation review. Remind participants that although most risk identification is done during planning, identifying risks should be encouraged frequently throughout the project life cycle. In many projects, new risks can surface daily.

TIMING	SLIDES	ACTIVITIES/NOTES/CONSIDERATIONS
10:25 a.m. (10 min)	Slide 27 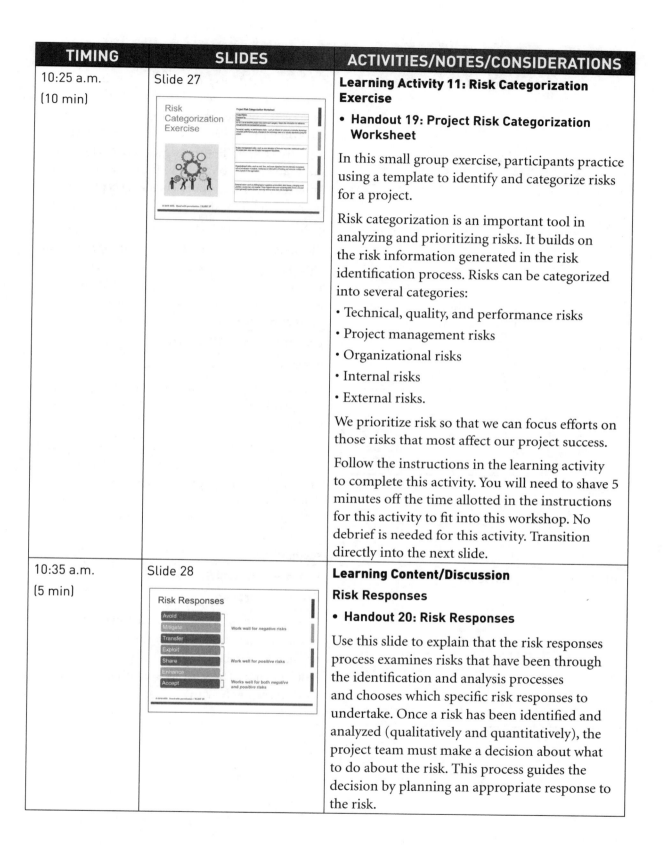	**Learning Activity 11: Risk Categorization Exercise** • **Handout 19: Project Risk Categorization Worksheet** In this small group exercise, participants practice using a template to identify and categorize risks for a project. Risk categorization is an important tool in analyzing and prioritizing risks. It builds on the risk information generated in the risk identification process. Risks can be categorized into several categories: • Technical, quality, and performance risks • Project management risks • Organizational risks • Internal risks • External risks. We prioritize risk so that we can focus efforts on those risks that most affect our project success. Follow the instructions in the learning activity to complete this activity. You will need to shave 5 minutes off the time allotted in the instructions for this activity to fit into this workshop. No debrief is needed for this activity. Transition directly into the next slide.
10:35 a.m. (5 min)	Slide 28	**Learning Content/Discussion** **Risk Responses** • **Handout 20: Risk Responses** Use this slide to explain that the risk responses process examines risks that have been through the identification and analysis processes and chooses which specific risk responses to undertake. Once a risk has been identified and analyzed (qualitatively and quantitatively), the project team must make a decision about what to do about the risk. This process guides the decision by planning an appropriate response to the risk.

TIMING	SLIDES	ACTIVITIES/NOTES/CONSIDERATIONS
	Slide 28, *continued*	A range of responses is available depending on whether the risk is negative or positive. Some responses, such as avoid, mitigate, and transfer, according to the *PMBOK® Guide,* work well for negative risks. Other responses, such as exploit, share, and enhance, work well for positive risks. And still other responses, such as accept, are appropriate for both negative and positive risks. Refer participants to the table in Handout 20, which lists advantages and disadvantages of each type of response. Give a few examples of risks and common responses to them. For example, with the risk involved in driving a car, you *transfer* the risk to the insurance company.
10:40 a.m. (3 min)	Slide 29 Execute: Key Tasks • Execute the project management plan • Resolve issues • Manage Resources • Implement procurement resources • Implement the quality management plan • Incorporate approved change requests • Improve team performance	**Learning Content/Lecture** **Execute: Key Tasks** Use this slide to introduce the next major process group: execute. Briefly overview the key tasks in the group. A key word that might characterize the executing process is *deliverables*. The most important output of the entire process group is the deliverables created for the project. In addition to deliverables, there are records of the deliverables that are distributed as information to project stakeholders.

10:43 a.m.
(2 min)
	Slide 30
	
	Execute: Purpose
	• Major outcome of execute process—deliverables
	• The project management plan will be used as the overall baseline of the project
	• The project manager manages the project work by
	  – Encouraging the project team to work together
	  – Managing communications with stakeholders
	  – Handling issues that may arise
		Learning Content/Lecture
		
		Execute: Purpose
		
		Use this slide to explain that the purpose of the execute phase is to produce the project deliverables as defined by the project requirements. The various executing processes work very closely with each other.

TIMING	SLIDES	ACTIVITIES/NOTES/CONSIDERATIONS
	Slide 30, *continued*	In addition, they also work closely with the processes in the monitoring and controlling process group. Executing processes focus on producing deliverables, whereas the monitoring and controlling processes concentrate on confirming that the planned deliverables are created and that these outputs meet the planned specifications and requirements. The project manager uses the project management plan as the overall baseline for the project and manages the project work by managing the project team, communications with stakeholders, and any issues that may arise.
10:45 a.m. (5 min)	Slide 31 Execute: Processes • Acquire Project Team • Develop Project Team • Manage Project Team • Perform Quality Assurance • Manage Communications • Manage Stakeholder Engagement • Conduct Procurements • Direct and Manage Project Work	**Learning Content/Lecture** **Execute: Processes** Use this slide and Handout 1 to overview the many tasks and processes associated with the executing project process, as identified in the *PMBOK® Guide*. Remind the participants that even though they have transitioned into the executing phase, planning does not stop if a need arises. Some of the processes are PMBOK based; others are practical. The processes of acquiring, developing, and managing the project team are self-explanatory and can be interpreted literally. The next two—manage stakeholder engagement and conduct procurements—are also easily understood and performed with a general understanding of business without extensive prior knowledge. In fact, the procurement function is often handled by the procurement or purchasing department in many organizations. Explain that for this workshop, you will focus on two of the remaining three processes in the execute group—communications and managing project work.

TIMING	SLIDES	ACTIVITIES/NOTES/CONSIDERATIONS
10:50 a.m. (5 min)	Slide 32 Manage Communications • Makes project information available to project stakeholders, as documented in the communications management plan • Creates, collects, distributes, stores, and retrieves project information • Requires orderly record keeping, distribution methods, information retrieval systems, and solid communications skills.	**Learning Content/Lecture** **Manage Communications** Managing communications requires orderly record keeping, distribution methods, and information retrieval systems, as well as excellent communication skills. Both the project manager and the stakeholders must possess solid communication skills. Following the communications plan (created in the project planning phase) is a key consideration for sharing information among project team members and stakeholders during the executing process. For example, if the communications plan calls for a Friday status report, the project manager must fulfill that requirement.
10:55 a.m. (5 min)	Slide 33 Direct and Manage Project Work • Coordinating and directing all project resources to carry out the project management plan • Typically, most project costs are expended during project execution	**Learning Content/Lecture** **Direct and Manage Project Work** This direct and manage project work process has one major goal: creating the deliverables defined in the project management plan. To successfully execute the project management plan, the project manager must manage the work performed; track scope, schedule, and budget baselines; and determine performance results. The project manager and team must continually monitor and measure performance against baselines so that timely corrective action can be taken when needed. They must also periodically update final cost and schedule forecasts. Typically, most project costs are expended during project execution. It is also when project managers most need general management skills. And because this process has a high degree of interpersonal activity, project managers also need to be skilled in conflict management, problem solving, and negotiation.

TIMING	SLIDES	ACTIVITIES/NOTES/CONSIDERATIONS
11:00 a.m. (5 min)	Slide 34 Monitor and Control: Key Tasks • Control scope • Control schedule • Control costs	**Learning Content/Lecture** **Monitor and Control: Key Tasks** Use this slide to introduce the next project management process group: monitor and control. A key word that might characterize this group is *check*. The most important element of monitoring and controlling is *checking* the project's progress against the plan to ensure that the project is on track. The monitoring and controlling process group includes 11 processes as defined in the *PMBOK® Guide* (refer participants to Handout 1 for a full listing). Because time is limited, this workshop will focus on three: controlling scope, controlling schedule, and controlling costs.

11:05 a.m.
(5 min)
	Slide 35
	
	Monitor and Control: Purpose
	• Ensures the work being performed is the planned work or is changed to meet the requirements of the project in a controlled manner
	• The project manager monitors and controls the project by
	  – Controlling changes
	  – Monitoring progress
		Learning Content/Lecture
		
		Monitor and Control: Purpose
		
		Explain that this process group focuses on controlling change in the project and measuring project performance. Its key deliverable is a controlled approach to managing change. The project manager will continue to manage the work on the project.
		
		Monitoring and controlling processes have a high degree of interaction with each other and also work closely with the processes in the executing process group. Executing processes focus on producing deliverables, whereas the monitoring and controlling processes concentrate on confirming that the right deliverables are created and that these outputs meet the planned specifications and requirements.
		
		When a change occurs in the project, the project manager will return to the planning processes to update affected project documents to ensure that the entire project is continually properly documented.

TIMING	SLIDES	ACTIVITIES/NOTES/CONSIDERATIONS
11:10 a.m. (5 min)	Slide 36 Control Scope • This process effectively manages changes in project scope and then integrates them across the entire project. • Scope changes are identified by using the variance analysis tool. • The project manager is responsible for discouraging unnecessary scope changes.	**Learning Content/Discussion** **Control Scope** Although it may seem obvious, ask participants why it is important to control the scope of a project and then let them share their ideas. Remind them that changes in scope, if not managed well, can lead to schedule delays, cost overruns, and scope creep (uncontrolled changes or growth of a project or product's scope). Change is a pervasive and unavoidable feature of our world, and in this environment, the project manager is responsible for minimizing unnecessary changes to the project using the control scope process, which manages necessary changes to the project work baseline. The process works closely with the other change control processes. If a change is approved, the project scope statement must be updated.
11:15 a.m. (5 min)	Slide 37 Control Schedule • Monitors the status of the project to update project progress • Manages changes to the schedule baseline	**Learning Content/Lecture** **Control Schedule** The control schedule process focuses on controlling changes to the schedule. As with scope control, the project manager is responsible for minimizing unnecessary changes to the project—in this case, the schedule. If a schedule change is approved, then the project schedule must be updated. Some organizations use a change control board (CCB) to evaluate and approve change requests.

PROJECT MANAGEMENT training

TIMING	SLIDES	ACTIVITIES/NOTES/CONSIDERATIONS
11:20 a.m. (5 min)	**Slide 38** Control Costs • Effectively manages changes to the project budget • Uses the earned value technique to measure project cost performance	**Learning Content/Lecture** **Control Costs** Briefly overview the control costs process, which manages necessary changes to the project cost baseline (budget) and measures project performance using earned value. The earned value technique is a tool that helps measure cost performance against the plan (earned value versus planned value). The control costs process works closely with the other change control processes. The project manager is responsible for minimizing unnecessary changes to the project. If a cost change is approved, the project manager updates the budget.
11:25 a.m. (5 min)	**Slide 39** Close: Key Tasks • Close project or phase • Release contracted and internal resources • Obtain stakeholder approval of final deliverables	**Learning Content/Lecture** **Close: Key Tasks** Use this slide to introduce the final project management process group: close. In closing the project, the project manager will carefully manage the closing and release contracted and internal resources. During the closure of a phase of a project, an end-of-phase review occurs to determine whether or not the project should continue. Two processes are used in closing projects: • Close procurements • Close project or phase.

TIMING	SLIDES	ACTIVITIES/NOTES/CONSIDERATIONS
11:30 a.m. (5 min)	Slide 40 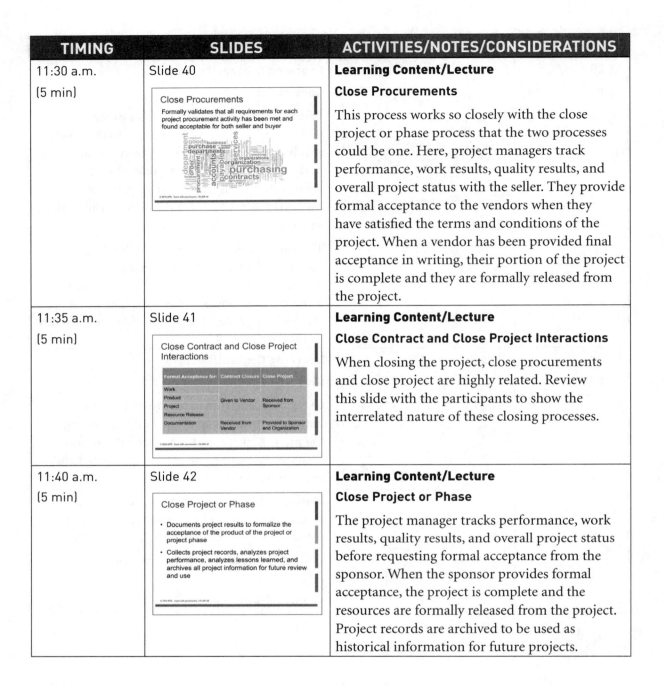	**Learning Content/Lecture** **Close Procurements** This process works so closely with the close project or phase process that the two processes could be one. Here, project managers track performance, work results, quality results, and overall project status with the seller. They provide formal acceptance to the vendors when they have satisfied the terms and conditions of the project. When a vendor has been provided final acceptance in writing, their portion of the project is complete and they are formally released from the project.
11:35 a.m. (5 min)	Slide 41	**Learning Content/Lecture** **Close Contract and Close Project Interactions** When closing the project, close procurements and close project are highly related. Review this slide with the participants to show the interrelated nature of these closing processes.
11:40 a.m. (5 min)	Slide 42	**Learning Content/Lecture** **Close Project or Phase** The project manager tracks performance, work results, quality results, and overall project status before requesting formal acceptance from the sponsor. When the sponsor provides formal acceptance, the project is complete and the resources are formally released from the project. Project records are archived to be used as historical information for future projects.

TIMING	SLIDES	ACTIVITIES/NOTES/CONSIDERATIONS
11:45 a.m. (10 min)	Slide 43 Action Planning ☑ What's your plan?	**Action Planning** • **Handout 34: My Project Management Development Plan** Remind your participants that learning is a journey, not a destination. The learning and work that they have done in this workshop has given them a good start toward building a solid foundation of management methods and best practices. But it is only a start. They need to continue to build their project management knowledge and skills. Ask participants to take 5 minutes to reflect on what they have learned about project management and its processes today and then to use the handout to write down insights, notes, and goals for how they would like to continue their project management learning after the workshop. Encourage them to add details to make their learning goals SMART (specific, measurable, actionable, realistic, and timely). Then gather everyone in a circle. Start by sharing a project management goal you are going to work on. Then toss a soft throwing object such as a Koosh ball to a participant and ask him or her to share a learning goal. Continue tossing the ball around the circle until everyone has shared.

TIMING	SLIDES	ACTIVITIES/NOTES/CONSIDERATIONS
11:55 a.m. (5 min) Ends at noon.	Slide 44 What do great project managers do?	**Workshop Wrap-Up: What Do Great Project Managers Do?** • **Handout 23: 10 Things Great Project Managers Do Every Day** • **Assessment 2: Workshop Evaluation** Ask participants to help you learn by completing the evaluation form. As participants are completing the evaluation, ask them to think about what they will do *every day* to be great project managers. Handout 23 gives 10 simple but profound ideas for habits they can cultivate to be great project managers. Be available to field questions about the workshop topics. Share plans for follow-up coaching if applicable (see Chapter 10 for ideas to follow up the training with support and activities). Thank the participants for their contributions and wish them well. **Optional:** Because of time constraints, participants in the half-day workshop do not get a chance to practice many of the tools or processes that they are learning about. To support their work back on the job, you may distribute the bonus Project Manager Toolkit (available in Chapter 14), which includes powerful templates for them to implement in their projects and teams right away. You could give it to them as parting gift now, send it as an digital document after the workshop as a follow-up support, or both.

What to Do Next

If you have decided that the half-day workshop is the best choice for your participants, consider these next steps as you prepare for your workshop:

- Determine the schedule for workshops, reserve location, and order any catering you may wish to provide.
- Identify and invite participants.
- Review the workshop objectives, activities, and handouts to plan the content you will use.

- Prepare copies of the participant materials and any activity-related materials you may need. Refer to Chapter 15 for information about how to access and use the supplemental materials provided for this workshop.

- Gather tactile items, such as Koosh balls, crayons, magnets, or Play-Doh, to place on the tables for tactile learners. See Chapter 8 for other ideas to enhance the learning environment of your workshop.

- Confirm that you have addressed scheduling and personal concerns so that you can be fully present to facilitate the class.

Reference

PMI. (2013). *A Guide to the Project Management Body of Knowledge: PMBOK™ Guide*, fifth ed. Newtown Square, PA: PMI.

Chapter 4

Customizing the Project Management Workshops

What's in This Chapter

- Ideas for creating new project management workshops
- Creative approaches for developing lunch-and-learn seminars
- Suggestions to design theme-based workshops

Many organizations find it difficult to have employees away from the workplace for an entire day or two, even if it is for professional development. As a result, you may need to adjust and adapt your workshop to the scheduling needs of the organization. Additionally, organizations often prefer to select content and topics to match the needs of the employees attending the training. Your training needs analysis will help you prioritize and select the content and activities of highest value for your participants. For more on needs analysis, see Chapter 5 in this book.

The materials in this ATD Workshop Series volume are designed to meet many training needs. They cover a range of topics related to project management skills training and can be offered in many timeframes and formats. Although lengthy immersion in a learning environment can enhance and increase the depth of learning experiences, the challenges of the workplace sometimes demand that training be done in short, small doses.

By using the expertly designed learning content and activities provided here as a foundation, you can modify and adapt the learning experience by customizing the content and activities, customizing the format, and customizing the delivery with technology.

Customizing the Content and Activities

Your level of expertise with training facilitation and project management skills will determine how much customization of the content you may want to do. If you are new to both training and the topic, you'll want to stick as closely as possible to the workshops as designed.

If you are a new trainer but an expert in project management, use the outline and materials as designed but feel free to include relevant materials you have developed. If you are an internal trainer or expert, take advantage of any actual documents, templates, or processes your organization uses. Many of the learning activities would be enhanced by introducing practice projects that are applicable to your organization or industry. The more actual content learners see, the better it will be.

Finally, if you are an expert facilitator, feel free to adapt the agenda and materials as you find necessary. Add new materials that you have developed to augment the learning. Or you can simply incorporate the learning activities, assessments, handouts, and tools into your own agenda.

As you become more confident with both the topic and facilitation, you will be able to introduce more of your own personal style into the workshop. You will also be better able to tailor the workshop to specific organizational needs and business imperatives.

Explore the variations in the learning activities. Many of the learning activities describe ideas for variations to a given activity. Try out some of these alternatives to see which ones resonate with your facilitation style and your participants' preferences.

What we know about the topic of project management is changing at a rapid pace. Stay on top of the research and new books in the field. Be sure to read those that are well researched and based in project management best practices.

Customizing the Workshop Format

Use the content from the workshops to adapt the workshop format to build a series of 90- to 120-minute workshops or one-hour lunchtime thematic seminars.

Project Management Skills Series

To address the need to provide learning in shorter segments, Table 4-1 breaks down the content into a series of ten 90- to 120-minute workshops. These workshops can be offered on a daily, weekly, biweekly, or monthly basis, depending on the scheduling needs of the organization. Note that the segments will require some additional connections to make them each a good session. Exploring the topics through additional debriefing questions or adding your organization's documents and examples will make them extremely valuable.

Use the project management process groups as a roadmap to help participants recognize the specific area they are addressing at each session.

Table 4-1. Project Management Skills Workshop Series

SESSION	90- TO 120-MINUTE WORKSHOP TOPICS	ACTIVITIES AND RESOURCES
1	Project Management Basics: What Is It and What Do I Need to Know?	• Half-Day Slides 2-16, 18, 29, 34, 39 • Learning Activities 1, 14 • Handouts 1, 24 • Assessment 1 • Plus, choose one learning activity to practice one of the process groups
2	Initiate Project Module	• Two-Day Slides 8-17 • Learning Activities 2, 3 • Handouts 1-5
3	Plan Project Module, Part I	• Two-Day Slides 8, 18-26, 28-29 • Learning Activities 4, 5 • Handouts 1, 2, 6-10
4	Plan Project Module, Part II	• Two-Day Slides 8, 30-35, 37-44, 47-49 • Learning Activities 6-8 • Handouts 1, 2, 11-15
5	Plan Project Module, Part III	• Two-Day Slides 8, 53-65 • Learning Activities 10, 11 • Handouts 1, 2, 18-20
6	Execute Project Module	• Two-Day Slides 8, 67-74 • Learning Activity 12 • Handouts 1, 2
7	Monitor and Control Project Module	• Two-Day Slides 8, 75-79, 81-91 • Learning Activity 13 • Handouts 1, 2, 22

Continued on next page

Table 4-1. Project Management Skills Workshop Series, *continued*

SESSION	90- TO 120-MINUTE WORKSHOP TOPICS	ACTIVITIES AND RESOURCES
8	Close Project Module and Process Action Planning	• Two-Day Slides 8, 93-98, 104-106 • Learning Activity 15 • Handouts 1, 2, 23
9	Two Key Interpersonal Skills for Project Management: Communicating and Leading	• One-Day Slides 18-19, 21-25, 28-31 • Learning Activities 12, 14, 17, 18 • Handouts 4, 10, 27, 28 • Assessment 1
10	Four More Key Interpersonal Skills for Project Management: Motivating, Problem Solving, Decision Making, and Influencing	• One-Day Slides 18, 34-40, 41-44, 46-49, 50-52 • Learning Activities 19-22 • Handouts 29-31 • Assessment 3

Small Bites—Lunch-and-Learn Seminars

Sometimes small means big impact. Table 4-2 shows topics that could be delivered effectively in one-hour sessions. The key to doing these bite-sized chunks successfully is to have a clear design with the right amount of content. Trying to cram in too much content can make a seminar seem shallow and rushed. Ask yourself an important question when creating a session of this size: What is the one key concept I would like the participants to remember after this workshop?

These topics could be used as stand-alone sessions or a series of lunchtime sessions that build on each other.

Customizing Delivery With Technology

Learning technologies can play an important role in adapting workshops to fit your organization. They have the potential to enhance learners' abilities to understand and apply workshop concepts. Examples include webinars, wikis, email groups, online surveys, and teleconferencing, to name just a few. Learn more about how to use technology to maximize learning in Chapter 7 of this book.

The Bare Minimum

With any of these customization options, always keep in mind the essentials of training design (Chapter 6) and delivery (Chapter 8). At a bare minimum, remember these basics:

Table 4-2. Lunch-and-Learn Seminars: Interpersonal Skills for Project Management

LUNCH-AND-LEARN TOPICS	ACTIVITIES AND RESOURCES
The Fundamentals: What Is Project Management?	• Half-Day Slides 2-10, 16, 29, 34, 39 • Learning Activity 1 • Handout 1 • Plus, choose one learning activity to practice one of the process groups
The Fundamentals: Project Management Knowledge Requirements	• One-Day Slides 8-16, 18 • Learning Activity 14 • Handout 24 • Assessment 1
Communicating Skills	• One-Day Slides 19-26 • Learning Activities 5, 16 • Handouts 4, 10
Leading Skills	• One-Day Slides 28-33 • Learning Activities 17, 18 • Handouts 26-28
Motivating Skills	• One-Day Slides 34-39 • Learning Activities 19, 20 • Handouts 29-31
Problem-Solving and Decision-Making Skills	• One-Day Slides 41-44, 46-49 • Learning Activity 21 • Handout 32
Influencing Skills	• One-Day Slides 50-52 • Learning Activity 22 • Assessment 3

- **Prepare, prepare, prepare.** Ready the room, the handouts, the equipment, and you. Familiarize yourself with the content, materials, and equipment. Practice can only make you a better facilitator. The more comfortable you feel, the more open and relaxed you will be for your participants. Many things can go wrong: Equipment can fail, the hotel can double-book your room, your Internet connection may not work, or 10 more participants may show up. You simply cannot control it all. You can, however, control 100 percent of how much you prepare.

- **Start with a bang.** The beginning of your session is crucial to the dynamics of the workshop. How participants respond to you can set the mood for the remainder of the workshop. Get to the training room at least an hour before the session begins. Be ready to welcome and greet the participants. Have everything ready so that you are available to learn something about them and their needs. Ask them simple questions to build rapport. After introducing yourself, introduce participants to each other or provide an activity in which participants can meet each other. The more time they spend getting to know you and each other, the more all of you will benefit when the session begins. Once the session starts, conduct an opening ice breaker that introduces the topic, ensures participants learn more about each other, and sets the stage for the rest of the seminar by letting participants know that this will be an active learning session. Try a provocative opening to get their attention.

- **Don't lecture without interaction.** Your learners like to have fun and participate in interactive learning opportunities. Be sure to vary the learning and teaching methods to maintain engagement. Yes, there will be times when you need to deliver information, but be sure to include participants by asking questions, posing critical incidents, incorporating a survey question, or in a dozen other ways.

- **End strong.** Providing time for participants to reflect and create an action plan at the end of a module or the session will help establish learning. Don't skip this opportunity to encourage participants to take action on something they have learned. Several of the activities in the workshop provide an opportunity to plan for next steps. Stress the importance of implementing what they learned upon returning to the workplace.

What to Do Next

- When customizing a workshop it is important to have a clear understanding of the learning objectives. Conduct a needs analysis to identify the gap between what the organization needs and what the employees are able to do and then determine how best to bridge the gap. At minimum, identify who wants the training, how the results will be defined, why the training is being requested now, and what the budget is. Chapter 5 provides more guidance on identifying training needs.

- Modify or add your own content to an existing agenda from Chapters 1-3 or create your own agenda using the learning support documents included in this book. There is no one way to flow project management content, but you must ensure that the topics build on one another and that you solidly connect the concepts and ideas together to make the most of the learning opportunity.

- Make sure to incorporate interactive practice activities into the design of the workshop.

- Compile and review all learning activities, handouts, and slides you will use for the session.

- Add your own slides or your own touches to the slides provided.

- Build a detailed plan for preparing for this session, including scheduling and room reservations, invitations, supply list, teaching notes, and time estimates.

SECTION II

ESSENTIALS OF EFFECTIVE PROJECT MANAGEMENT TRAINING

Chapter 5

Identifying Needs for Project Management Training

What's in This Chapter

- Discovering the purpose of needs analysis
- Introducing some data-gathering methods
- Determining the bare minimum needed to deliver training

Ideally, you should always carry out a needs analysis before designing and creating a workshop to address a performance gap. The cost of *not* identifying and carefully considering the performance requirement can be high: wasted training dollars, unhappy staff going to boring or useless sessions, increased disengagement of employees, and so forth. But the world of training is rarely ideal, and the existence of this book, which essentially provides a workshop in a box, is testament to that. This chapter describes the essential theory and techniques for a complete needs analysis to provide the fundamentals of the process and explain how it fits into designing learning. However, because the decision to train may already be out of your hands, the last part of this chapter provides a bare-bones list of things you need to know to train effectively even if someone just handed you this book and told you to put on a workshop.

Why Needs Analysis?

In short, as a trainer, learning professional, performance consultant, or whatever job title you hold, your role is to ensure that the employees of your organization know how to do the work that will make the organization succeed. That means you must first identify the skills, knowledge, and abilities that the employees need for optimal performance and then determine where these are lacking in the employee population to bridge that gap. However, the most important reason for needs assessment is that it is not your learning experience. You may deliver it, but the learning belongs to the learner. Making decisions for learners about what performance they need without working with them is inappropriate. If you are an experienced facilitator, you have a large repository of PowerPoint decks at your disposal. Resist the urge while talking with your customers to listen for words that allow you just to grab what you already have. Be open to the possibilities. A training needs analysis helps you do this (see Figure 5-1). Methods to identify this information include strategic needs analysis, structured interviews, focus groups, and surveys.

Strategic Needs Analysis

An analysis of future directions usually identifies emerging issues and trends with a major potential effect on a business and its customers over a two- to three-year period. The analysis

Figure 5-1. Introducing the ADDIE Model

> A needs analysis is the first step in the classic instructional design model called ADDIE, which is named after its steps: analysis, design, development, implementation, and evaluation. Roughly speaking, the tasks involved in ADDIE are
>
> 1. **Analysis:** Gather data about organizational and individual needs as well as the gap between the goals the organization means to accomplish and the skills and knowledge needed to accomplish those goals.
> 2. **Design:** Identify and plan the topics and sequence of learning to accomplish the desired learning.
> 3. **Development:** Create the components of the learning event, such as learning activities and materials.
> 4. **Implementation:** Put on the learning event or launch the learning materials.
> 5. **Evaluation:** Gather data to determine the outcome of the learning to improve future iterations of the learning, enhance materials and facilitation, and justify budget decisions.
>
> Instructional design models such as ADDIE are a systematic approach to developing learning and could also be viewed as a project management framework for the project phases involved in creating learning events.

helps a business develop goals and programs that proactively anticipate and position the organization to influence the future.

To conduct such an analysis, organizations look at issues such as expected changes within the business (for example, technology and professional requirements) and expected changes outside the company (for example, the economy, demographics, politics, and the environment).

Results of an analysis provide a rationale for developing company and departmental goals and for making policy and budgetary decisions. From the analysis comes a summary of key change dynamics that will affect the business.

These questions often are asked in strategic needs analysis:

- What information did previous organizational analyses impart?
- Are those issues and trends still relevant?
- Do the results point to what may need to be done differently in the future?
- How has the organization performed in achieving results?
- What is the present workforce like?
- How will it change or need to change?
- What does the organization know about future changes in customer needs?
- Are customer surveys conducted and, if so, what do they reveal?
- How might the organization have to change to serve customers better?
- Is the company's organizational structure working to achieve results?
- What are the strengths and limitations of the company?
- What are the opportunities for positive change?
- What do competitors do or say that might have implications for the organization?
- What are the most important opportunities for the future?
- What are the biggest problems?
- Is the organization in a competitive marketplace?
- How does the organization compare with competitors?

The results can be summarized in a SWOT analysis model (strengths, weaknesses, opportunities, threats—see Figure 5-2). Action plans are then developed to increase the strengths, overcome the weaknesses, plan for the opportunities, and decrease the threats.

Figure 5-2. SWOT Analysis Model

	STRENGTHS	WEAKNESSES
INTERNAL		
	OPPORTUNITIES	THREATS
EXTERNAL		

Structured Interviews

Start structured interviews as high up in the organization as you can go, with the CEO if possible. Make sure that you include input from human resource personnel and line or operations managers and supervisors. Managers and supervisors will want to tell you what they have seen and what they consider the most pressing issues in the organization.

Focus Groups

Focus groups can be set up to give people opportunities to brainstorm ideas about issues in the organization and to realize the potential of team involvement. One comment may spark another and so on. Focus groups should begin with questions that you prepare. It is important to record the responses and comments on a flipchart so everyone can see them. If that is not possible, you may simply take notes. Results of the sessions should be compiled.

Surveys

Surveys, whether paper or web based, gather information from a large or geographically dispersed group of employees. The advantages of surveys are speed of data collection, objectivity, repeatability, and ease of analysis.

Individual Learning Needs Analysis

While identifying organizational learning needs is critical to making the best use of an organization's training budget, analyzing individual learning needs is also important. Understanding the training group's current skills and knowledge can help to focus the training on those areas that require most work—this also helps to avoid going over what the individuals already know, thus wasting their time, or losing them by jumping in at too advanced a level. In addition, individual learning needs analysis can uncover unfavorable attitudes about training that trainers will be better able to address if they are prepared for them. For example, some learners may see the training as a waste of time, as an interruption to their normal work, or as a sign of potentially frightening organizational change.

Many of the same methods used to gather data for organizational learning needs are used for individual learning needs analysis. Analyzing employee learning needs should be carried out in a thoughtful, sensitive, and inclusive manner. Here are potential pitfalls to avoid:

- **Don't analyze needs you can't meet.** Training needs analysis raises expectations. It sends a message to employees that the organization expects them to be competent in particular areas.

- **Involve employees directly.** Sometimes employees don't see a value in participating in training. In assessing needs, trainers need to prepare employees to buy into the training. Asking useful questions and listening carefully to stated needs are excellent methods for accomplishing both of those goals. Ask these questions: "To what degree would you like to learn how to do [X] more effectively?" and "To what degree would you seriously consider participating in training to improve your competency in [X]?"

- **Make the identified needs an obvious part of your training design.** Participants should be able to see that they have influenced the content and emphasis of the training session. A good practice is briefly to summarize the local trends discovered in the training needs analysis when you introduce the goals of the session.

- **Don't think of training as a "magic bullet."** Sometimes a given employee needs coaching, counseling, or consulting, which is best carried out one on one and customized to the individual and the situation. Still other times, the problem is caused by equipment or processes that need upgrading, not people who need training.

The Bare Minimum

As noted, in an ideal world, you would have gathered all this data about the needs of the organization and the employees and determined that training was the right way to connect those dots.

However, even if the decision to put on this workshop has already been made, you still need a bare minimum of information to be successful:

- **Who is your project sponsor (who wants to do this, provides the budget, and so on)?** In fact, if you don't have a project sponsor, *stop* the project. Lack of a project sponsor indicates that the project isn't important to the business. Optimally, the project sponsor should come from the business side of the organization. If the project sponsor is the head of training, then the mentality behind the training—"build it and they will come"—is likely wrong. Even compliance training should have a functional sponsor.

- **What does the sponsor want the learners to be able to do when they are done with training?** How does the sponsor define measures of success? Answering these critical questions brings clarity to the sponsor's expectations and thus to the workshop design.

- **What are the objectives of the training?** What, specifically, do you want participants to be able to *do* after the workshop? Build clear, specific, and measurable learning objectives and then develop learning activities that directly support them. A good resource for writing objectives is Bloom's Taxonomy; if you use it, aim to create Application-level or higher objectives. Knowledge- and Comprehension-level objectives have their place, but learning events need to go beyond these levels of learning to effectively change behaviors in the workplace.

- **Why does the sponsor want this right now?** Is something going on in the organization of which you should be aware?

- **What is the budget?** How much time and money will be invested in the training?

Key Points

- Needs analysis identifies the gap between what the organization needs and what the employees are able to do and then determines how best to bridge that gap.

- Methods of data gathering for needs analysis include strategic needs analysis, structured interviews, surveys, focus groups, and others.

- Sometimes, needs analysis is not an option, but some minimum information is necessary, including who wants the training, how the results will be defined, why the training is being requested now, and what the budget is.

What to Do Next

- If you have the option, carry out a needs analysis to determine if this training is really what your organization requires to succeed. If it isn't, prepare to argue against wasting time, money, and effort on training that will not support the organization's goals.

- If you don't have the option of a needs analysis, make sure that you seek out at least the bare minimum information to conduct effective training.

- Prepare learning objectives that are measurable, clear, and specific.

- If you have little training background, read the next chapter (Chapter 6) to learn about the theories and concepts that are at the root of training design. If you are an experienced trainer, skim Chapter 6 on design theory or go straight to Chapters 7 and 8 for tips on leveraging technology and delivering training, respectively.

Additional Resources

Biech, E., ed. (2008). *ASTD Handbook for Workplace Learning Professionals*. Alexandria, VA: ASTD Press.

Biech, E., ed. (2014). *ASTD Handbook: The Definitive Reference for Training & Development*, 2nd edition. Alexandria, VA: ASTD Press.

McGoldrick, B., and D. Tobey. (2016). *Needs Assessment Basics*, 2nd edition. Alexandria, VA: ATD Press.

Russo, C. "Be a Better Needs Analyst." ASTD *Infoline* no. 258502. Alexandria, VA: ASTD Press.

Chapter 6

Understanding the Foundations of Training Design

What's in This Chapter

- Introducing adult learning theory
- Exploring multiple intelligences
- Incorporating whole brain learning
- Learning how theory enters into practice

Because this book provides fully designed workshops, you don't need to know all the details of designing a course—the design has already been done for you. However, understanding some of the principal design and learning theories that underpin these workshops is useful and helpful—especially if you are somewhat new to the field of workplace training and development. To effectively deliver training to learners requires a core understanding of how and why people learn. This gives you the flexibility to adapt a course to the unique learners in the room as needed.

When designing a project management workshop, paying attention to content flow is especially important. While there is no one right way to flow project management content, you must ensure that the topics build on one another and that you solidly connect the concepts and ideas together so you leverage the most of the learning opportunity. New skills require practice, so always include interactive practice sessions in the design of the workshop. Short but well-designed activities can have significant impact.

Basic Adult Learning Theory

The individual participant addressed in these workshops is typically an adult with learning needs that differ in many (but not all) ways from children. Much has been documented about how adults learn best. A key figure in adult education is Malcolm Knowles, who is often regarded as the father of adult learning. Knowles made several contributions to the field but is best known for popularizing the term *andragogy*, which refers to the art and science of teaching adults. Here are six assumptions about adult learners noted in *The Adult Learner: A Neglected Species* (Knowles 1984):

- Adults need to know why learning something is important before they learn it.
- Adults have a concept of self and do not like others imposing their will on them.
- Adults have a wealth of knowledge and experience and want that knowledge to be recognized.
- Adults open up to learning when they think that the learning will help them with real problems.
- Adults want to know how the learning will help them in their personal lives.
- Adults respond to internal motivations.

Given these principles of adult learning, designing sessions that are highly interactive and engaging is critical (see sidebar on the next page for more tips). Forcing anyone to learn anything is impossible, so the goal of effective training design is to provide every opportunity and encouragement to the potential learner. Involvement of the learner is the key. As an old Chinese proverb says, "Tell me and I will forget. Show me and I may remember. Involve me and I will understand." The designs in this book use several methods to convey information and engage participants. By incorporating varied training media—such as presentation media, discussion sessions, small-group work, structured exercises, and self-assessments—these designs maximize active participant involvement and offer something for every learning style.

In addition to engaging the interest of the learner, interactive training allows you to tap into another source of learning content: the participants themselves. In a group-learning situation, a good learning environment encourages participants to share with others in the group so the entire group's cumulative knowledge can be used.

More Theoretical Ideas Important to Learning

Research on how people learn and how the brain works occurs continuously. A few ideas that come up frequently in training design and delivery are multiple intelligences and whole brain learning.

Multiple Intelligences

Multiple intelligences reflect how people prefer to process information. Howard Gardner, from Harvard University, has been challenging the basic beliefs about intelligence since the early

1980s. Gardner initially described a list of seven intelligences. Later, he added three additional intelligences to his list, and he expects the list to continue to grow (Gardner 2011). The intelligences are

- **interpersonal:** aptitude for working with others
- **logical/mathematical:** aptitude for math, logic, and deduction
- **spatial/visual:** aptitude for picturing, seeing
- **musical:** aptitude for musical expression
- **linguistic/verbal:** aptitude for the written and spoken word
- **intrapersonal:** aptitude for working alone
- **bodily kinesthetic:** aptitude for being physical
- **emotional:** aptitude for identifying emotion
- **naturalist:** aptitude for being with nature
- **existential:** aptitude for understanding one's purpose.

How do multiple intelligences affect your learning? Gardner suggests that most people are comfortable in three or four of these intelligences and avoid the others. For example, if you are not comfortable working with other people, doing group case studies may interfere with your ability to process new material. Video-based instruction will not be good for people with lower spatial/visual aptitudes. People with strong bodily/kinesthetic aptitudes prefer to move around while they are learning.

Allowing your learners to use their own strengths and weaknesses helps them process and learn. Here's an example: Suppose you are debriefing one of the exercises in the material. The exercise has been highly interpersonal (team activity), linguistic (lots of talking), spatial/visual (the participants built an object), musical (music was playing), logical/mathematical (there were rules and structure), and kinesthetic (people moved around). You've honored all the processing styles except intrapersonal, so the people who process information in this manner probably need a return to their strength of working alone. Start the debriefing by asking people to quietly work on their own, writing down five observations of the activity. Then ask them to share as a group.

Whole Brain Learning

Ned Herrmann pioneered the concept of whole brain learning in the 1970s, developing the Herrmann Whole Brain Model, which divides the brain into four distinct types of thinking: analytical, sequential, interpersonal, and imaginative. Each individual tends to favor one type of thinking over another, and this thinking preference evolves continually throughout a person's life. In fact, the brain changes all the time with new input and new ways of thinking—a feature that is known as *plasticity*.

Although each person has a preferred thinking style, he or she may prefer it to varying degrees. To identify a person's thinking preference, Herrmann developed the Herrmann Brain Dominance Instrument in 1979. Learning about your own thinking and learning preferences can motivate you to learn new ways to learn and think. For trainers and facilitators, learning about your own preferences can help you identify where you may be neglecting other styles or preferences in your training design and delivery. As Ann Herrmann-Nehdi, daughter of Ned Herrmann and researcher in her own right, notes in the *ASTD Handbook for Workplace Learning Professionals*, "Effective learning is whole brained—designing, delivering, and evaluating the learning to best meet the varying needs of diverse learners" (2008, p. 215).

Herrmann-Nehdi continues, "Our knowledge of the brain and its inherent uniqueness shows that each individual is a unique learner with learning experiences, preferences, and avoidances that will be different from those of other learners. This means that learning designs must somehow factor in the uniqueness of the individual learner" (2008, p. 221). That is to say that effective facilitation must provide a blend of learning activities that addresses various thinking processes from analytical to sequential to interpersonal to imaginative. Because each individual has a unique combination of varying preferences for different types of learning, such a blend can engage most learners even when they are not directly learning in their preferred style. Engaging varied thinking styles ensures *whole brain learning*, rather than a narrow focus on one or two thinking styles.

Here are some tips for incorporating whole brain learning into your facilitation:

- Identify your own thinking preferences to avoid getting too one-sided in your presentation. Deliberately include styles you don't typically prefer.
- Recognize that your learners have unique brains that have continually changed as a result of a lifetime of experiences, learning, and ways of thinking.
- Address those variations in learning and thinking preferences by identifying different ways to deliver learning, including facts, case studies, metaphors, brainstorming, simulations, quizzes, outlines, procedures, group learning, role plays, and so on to engage their whole brains.
- Avoid diminishing learners' motivation to learn.
- Avoid overwhelming the brain or causing stress. Stick to need-to-know rather than nice-to-know.

Theory Into Practice

These theories (and more that are not addressed here) affect the way the content of the workshops are put together. Some examples of training features that derive from these theories include handouts, research references, and presentation media to read; quiet time to write notes and reflect; opportunities for listening and talking; and exercises for practicing skills. The workshop activities and materials for the programs in this book have taken these theories to heart in their design, providing content, activities, and tools that will appeal to and engage many learning and thinking styles. Additional ways to translate learning and design theory into practice include the following:

Establishing a Framework

For learners to understand the goals of training and how material relates to real work situations, a framework can be helpful. When presenting the training in the context of a framework, trainers should provide an overview of why the organization has decided to undertake the training and why it is important. This explanation should also highlight what the trainer hopes to accomplish and how the skills learned in this training will be useful back on the job.

Objectives and goals of the programs and learning activities are described in this workbook; share those objectives with the learners when discussing the purposes of specific exercises. Handouts will also help provide a framework for participants.

Identifying Behaviors

Within any training goal are many behaviors. For example, listening and giving clear directions are necessary behaviors for good customer service. Customer service does not improve simply because employees are told to do so—participants need to understand the reasons and see the relevant parts of the equation. For these reasons, facilitators should identify and discuss relevant behaviors throughout the program.

Training helps people identify the behaviors that are important, so that those behaviors can be targeted for improvement. Learning activities enable participants to analyze different skills and behaviors and to separate the parts from the whole. The learning activities in this book, with their clearly stated objectives, have been carefully crafted to take these considerations into account.

Practicing

Practice is crucial for learning because learning takes place by doing and by seeing. In the training designs included in this workbook, practice occurs in written exercises, verbal exercises, and role playing. Role playing helps participants actually practice the behaviors that are being addressed. Role-play exercises bring skills and behaviors to life for those acting out particular roles and for those observing the scenarios.

Learning a new skill takes a lot of practice. Some participants learn skills more quickly than others. Some people's attitudes might prevent them from being open to trying new behaviors. Your job is to facilitate the session to the best of your ability, taking different learning styles into account. The rest is up to the participants.

Providing Feedback

A key aspect of training is the feedback trainers give to participants. If delivered in a supportive and constructive manner, feedback helps learners develop a deeper understanding of the content you are presenting and the behaviors they are practicing. Feedback in role plays is especially powerful because this is where "the rubber hits the road." In role plays, observers can see if people are able to practice the behaviors that have been discussed, or whether habitual responses will prevail.

Making It Relevant

Throughout the program you will discuss how to use skills and new behaviors on the job. These discussions will help answer the question "So what?" Exercises and action plans help participants bring new skills back to actual work situations. This is also important in addressing the adult need for relevancy in learning.

The Bare Minimum

- **Keep the focus on self-reflection.** Be purposeful in designing content that encourages participants to analyze their own behaviors instead of what others do wrong.
- **Build practice into the design.** Provide your participants with hands-on, engaging opportunities to practice the correct skills.

Key Points

- Adults have specific learning needs that must be addressed in training to make it successful.

- People also have different intelligences; that is, different areas in which they are more comfortable and competent. Addressing different intelligences in the workshop keeps more people engaged in more ways.

- People take in new information in different ways; addressing a variety of different thinking styles can help everyone learn more effectively.

- Bring theory into practice by creating a framework, identifying behaviors, practicing, providing feedback, and making the learning relevant.

What to Do Next

- Look through the training materials to identify how they address the learning theories presented in this book. If you make modifications to the material, consider whether those modifications leave out an intelligence or a thinking style. Can you address more intelligences without making the material cumbersome?

- Read the next chapter to identify how to incorporate technology into the workshop to make it more effective.

Additional Resources

Biech, E., ed. (2008). *ASTD Handbook for Workplace Learning Professionals.* Alexandria, VA: ASTD Press.

Biech, E., ed. (2014). *ASTD Handbook: The Definitive Reference for Training & Development,* 2nd edition. Alexandria, VA: ASTD Press.

Gardner, H. (2006). *Multiple Intelligences: New Horizons in Theory and Practice.* New York: Basic Books.

Gardner, H. (2011). *Frames of Mind: The Theory of Multiple Intelligences.* New York: Basic Books.

Herrmann, N. (1988). *Creative Brain.* Lake Lure, NC: Brain Books.

Herrmann, N., and A. Herrmann-Nehdi. (2015). *Whole Brain Business Book,* 2nd edition. San Francisco: McGraw-Hill.

Herrmann-Nehdi, A. (2008). "The Learner: What We Need to Know." In E. Biech, ed., *ASTD Handbook for Workplace Learning Professionals.* Alexandria, VA: ASTD Press.

Jones, J.E., W.L. Bearley, and D.C. Watsabaugh. (1996). *The New Fieldbook for Trainers: Tips, Tools, and Techniques.* Amherst, MA: HRD Press.

Knowles, M.S. (1984). *The Adult Learner: A Neglected Species.* Houston, TX: Gulf Publishing.

Russell, L. (1999). *The Accelerated Learning Fieldbook: Making the Instructional Process Fast, Flexible, and Fun.* San Francisco: Jossey-Bass/Pfeiffer.

Chapter 7

Leveraging Technology to Maximize and Support Design and Delivery

What's in This Chapter

- Recognizing the importance of technology tools
- Determining when to use learning technologies
- Identifying types of learning technologies
- Enhancing learner engagement
- Deepening learner understanding
- Increasing learning application

The workshops offered in this book are designed to be facilitated in person. Even so, learning technologies can and should play a role in adapting workshops to fit your organization, reinforce learning, and measure effectiveness. Technology is an important learning component, but it can also become an expensive distraction. The key is whether and how well technology enhances learners' abilities to understand and apply workshop concepts.

Your use of technology should also align with your organization's culture and readiness. For example, using webinars and wikis in a high-tech environment where employees are familiar with these tools may be logical and welcome, but you might need to introduce these tools more slowly at another company where email is the primary technology used for communication (see Figure 7-1 for some dos and don'ts of recording webinars).

The most important factor to consider when deciding whether to use learning technologies is how they can best support your workshop's learning objectives. This is particularly critical (and not at all straightforward) when delivering these workshops' soft skills training because personal and interpersonal habits and skills tend to require participants to challenge their beliefs and shift their mindsets. This deeper level of self-reflection, though tougher to do in a virtual setting, can be done if you select the right tool and use it at the right time in the learning process.

In the previous chapter, you learned about the adult learning theories and learning styles that underpin the workshops in this volume. Keep these in mind as you assess and weigh opportunities to use learning technologies. In this chapter, you will explore where technology can augment learning transfer and application in your workshop. Please note that the information has been kept general for two reasons. First, each organization has access to specific and limited technologies, and you should learn about them and creatively use what you have. Second, recommendations for specific technologies are likely to become obsolete quickly; so instead, focus on the types of learning technologies that might best augment in-person workshops.

Figure 7-1. Dos and Don'ts of Recording Webinars

To increase your chances of a successful webinar, consider and incorporate these tips.

Do
- Introduce yourself and the topic.
- Keep recorded webinars short—ideally 20 minutes or less.
- Use a conversational voice to increase interest.
- Use adequate numbers of slides so that you do not stay on one slide for more than 30 or 45 seconds.
- Address simple, focused topics with five or fewer key points.
- Use pictures and minimal text on slides.

Don't
- Use your computer's microphone to record; instead, invest in a good headset.
- Use a recorded webinar that has poor audio quality; instead, re-record if needed.
- Use too much text or small fonts.
- Assume that participants are just watching the webinar; you have to keep their interest or they will get distracted.
- Try to cover a complex topic using a recorded webinar; the webinar should focus on one topic with a few main points.

Why Consider Learning Technologies?

You have decided to provide in-person workshops and will use the agendas offered in this book to plan and conduct the training. Learning technologies can be essential tools in your tool kit. Most behavior change does not occur in the classroom. The workshop is important, but it must be supported by strong pre- and post-course reinforcement. To learn something, learners need many points of contact with the new skills and concepts, such as presentation, reflection, discussion, practice, feedback, and exploration. Moreover, most of your participants are very busy and unable to attend multiple in-person pre- or post-course sessions. So to ensure learning transfer, you can augment in-person activities with technology-based engagement. The good news is that you can use technology in many ways to enhance learning, even of soft skills.

Opportunities to Use Learning Technologies

Whether you have many or few technology resources upon which to draw for learning, start by asking yourself this question: For this topic or series, how can I best use technology to increase learner engagement, understanding, and application? You will use these criteria to discover and evaluate potential ways technology might provide value in the learning process, including

- when designing the training
- before the training
- during the training
- after the training
- while building a learner community.

Note that this chapter offers ways to use technology to enhance traditional learning workshops (blended learning). It is important that you consult with a technology partner if you are considering a technology-driven training program—such as a workplace simulation or self-directed online learning. That said, the content found in this training series could be adapted for use in an online learning platform. For more information on how to use the online tools and downloads, see Chapter 15.

When Designing Training

The ATD Workshop Series offers fully designed training you can use with minimal preparation and solid facilitation skills. Even so, you will be creating a learning implementation plan that is an important part of the design process.

To increase engagement: You have to know your audience members to engage them, because engagement is a choice driven by interest, challenge, and relevance of the topic. Use learning technologies to ensure that you understand where your audience is coming from and the learning approaches they will most value. Email groups, online surveys, teleconferencing, and web meetings with polling can help you ascertain their wants and needs before you solidify your training plan.

To deepen understanding: When in the planning stage, make sure that you have not tried to cram too much presentation into the learning process and that you have planned sufficient time and attention to engaging participants. Flowcharting or mind-mapping software can help you visualize and communicate your learning plan and ensure that you allow for maximum engagement and practice.

To increase application: Increasing retention and application requires buy-in from sponsors and managers to ensure that what is learned is welcomed and applied on the job. Use email groups, online surveys, teleconferencing, and web meetings with polling to communicate with sponsors and managers about what they want out of the training and to identify ways to apply the learning back on the job. Having this information is also valuable in developing the training plan.

Before Training

You want to prime your participants' minds for the topic you will be presenting during the workshop. Pre-work does not have to be something arduous and unwelcome. In fact, a great pre-work assignment can help maximize precious time in the classroom and allow you to focus on the topics that require thorough discussion.

To increase engagement: Tap into the most fascinating aspects of the workshop topic and introduce these through video clips, blog posts, and online resources (see Figure 7-2 about the legal use of video clips, images, and so forth). Avoid boring participants with long "how-to" articles or book chapters before the workshop. In fact, do the opposite and ensure that the pre-work is interesting, provocative (even controversial), and brief. You might select a blog post or video clip that offers a counterpoint to the training or something that inspires your participants to think about the topic before attending training.

To deepen understanding: If you know that the workshop topic will be challenging to some of your participants, prepare and share a brief recorded webinar, video clip, or article that introduces the topic. For example, if your managers tend to tell versus coach, try sharing one or two external resources that discuss the value of service-oriented coaching conversations.

To increase application: You can improve the chances that your participants will apply what they learn by ensuring they identify real-world work challenges in which they can apply their new skills. Start with a one- or two-question pre-workshop survey (using Survey Monkey or similar) that requires they identify these opportunities and then use the responses to enhance your in-workshop discussions. If your organization has an internal social network or ways to create collaboration groups, use the pre-work questions to begin an online discussion of the topic. The conversations will help your participants think about the topic and will help you prepare for a great workshop (and will give you a beneficial "heads-up" on potential areas of conflict or disagreement).

During Training

Learning technologies can help make your workshops more interesting and can help enhance understanding of the material. Beware, however, that you always want to have a "Plan B" in case of technology glitches or breakdowns. Another critical point to make here is that technology does not change how people learn. Learning and performance drive the technology choice, not the other way around.

To increase engagement: The perennial favorite technology for spicing up a workshop is the use of a great video. Boring videos don't help! If you can find short video clips that reinforce your

Figure 7-2. Copyright Beware

Copyright law is a sticky, complex area that is beyond the scope of this book to address in detail. For legal advice, consult your legal department.

However, it's very important to note a few things about copyright, fair use, and intellectual property:

- Just because you found an image, article, music, or video online doesn't mean that you can use it in training without permission. Make sure you obtain permission from the copyright owner before you use it (sometimes the copyright owner is not obvious and you will need to do some research).

- Fair use is pretty limited. Although most fair use allows an educational exception, that does *not* include corporate or organizational training. Other exceptions relate to how much material relative to the original was used, the nature of the original work (creative work generally has more protection), and the effect on the market for the original (Swindling and Partridge 2008). Once again, your best bet is to get written permission.

- Just because something doesn't have a copyright notice on it doesn't mean that it isn't copyright protected. All original material is protected under copyright law as soon as it is published or created.

Don't despair. Plenty of online sources of images, videos, text, and so forth exist that you can use for free or for a minimal fee. Just search on the terms "copyright free" or "open source." Another place to look is Wikimedia Commons, which has millions of freely usable media files. For more information about how copyright law affects your use of materials in this volume, please see Chapter 14 on how to use the online materials and downloads.

most important points, please do so. In addition to adding contrast to the workshop flow, having other "experts" say what you want participants to hear is helpful. Another way to increase engagement is to use some kind of audience-response system or electronic polling. Although this might not be practical for small groups (the technology can be a bit pricey), some less expensive alternatives use texting schemas you might want to check out. Your participants will love seeing their collective responses instantly populate your PowerPoint charts. (For more on PowerPoint, see Figure 7-3 and Chapter 8.)

To deepen understanding: Videos can also help improve understanding. If your participants have access to computers during the workshop, consider short technology-based games and short simulations that reinforce the points. You can also ask participants to fill out worksheets and surveys online during the class. Share animated models, flowcharts, or mind maps to help explain key concepts or how they connect together.

To increase application: Learning simulations and practice sessions help prepare participants to apply new skills. You can do these in person, and you can use technology to facilitate practices. This depends a lot on the topic.

After Training

Your participants are busy, and the new skills and concepts they learned in the workshop will become a distant memory without follow-up. Just as you did before the training, you can and should use learning technologies to augment the learning that occurs during the workshop.

To increase engagement: Learners engage when they perceive something as interesting, relevant right now, or challenging. Use tools such as video, blogs, social networks, chat, websites, and email to increase interest in the topic and to provide challenge.

To deepen understanding: Use post-workshop surveys and polling tools to assess understanding so you can address any gap. Add to the participants' understanding of the topic by posting materials on a SharePoint site or through blog posts that you push to their email inboxes using an RSS feed.

To increase application: Provide a just-in-time online resource where participants find quick reference sheets and get application tips using a group site, social network, or SharePoint site. Request or require that participants report how they have used new skills through an online project management collaboration site, wiki, or email group.

While Building a Learning Community

Creating an ongoing network of learners is extremely valuable, especially for soft skills. The in-person workshop is just the beginning of the learning journey and so keeping learners engaged is helpful. In addition, you want to create a safe place where learners can discuss challenges, provide encouragement, and share their best practices. Learning technologies are particularly useful for building community among learners and teams.

To increase engagement: Busy people value community but often can't make the time to attend follow-up sessions or network with peers. They might, however, be able to take 10 minutes to check in on an internal social network, group site, or blog to learn from and share with others. If your organization does not have social networking or collaboration software, you might need to get creative. Talk to your technology department about the tools you do have—whether they are SharePoint, blog software, internal messaging, a wiki-type project management collaboration tool, or other. You can even use email groups to connect learners. Look for ways you can create pull (they choose when to engage) and push (they get updates), such as using RSS feeds.

To deepen understanding: After the workshop, use web meetings, teleconferencing, and messaging to connect learning partners or mentors and facilitate their sharing real-time application stories. Periodically facilitate online discussion groups to reinforce the learning and bring participants back together.

To increase application: Use a collaborative online project site or social network to set expectations about post-workshop peer discussions and reinforce engagement. Poll participants and assign sub-teams to lead a portion of each web meeting.

Figure 7-3. PowerPoint or Prezi or Other?

Although PowerPoint is the most common presentation software, other platforms you might want to consider include Prezi, GoAnimate, Google Docs, mind-mapping programs, or others. Here are a few key considerations that will help you choose:

- Aside from the in-class workshop, where will you want to share the presentation?
- If you will be sharing the presentation with others, consider whether new software will be required.
- Which presentation platform is best for the content you are presenting, or does it matter?
- What are the costs and resources required for each platform?
- Which platform will partner well with the technology tools you will use to reinforce the learning?
- What might be the advantage of using two or more platforms throughout the learning process?

The Bare Minimum

- **Know what resources you have available.** Many organizations have widely varying resources; don't assume that you know everything that is available.

- **Stretch yourself.** Be willing to try something new; develop your skills to use technology in innovative ways to facilitate learning.

- **Know your participants.** They may be far ahead of you in their skills with technology or they may be far behind. If you plan to use learning technologies, do your best to assess their skill level before designing the workshop.

- **Be prepared for challenges.** No matter the skill level of the group, technology glitches are unavoidable. Be sure to cultivate good working relationships with technology support staff.

Key Points

- Most behavior change does not happen in a classroom but through multiple points of reinforcement. Learning technologies are an efficient way to augment learning.

- You can use learning technologies your organization already has if you are creative and partner with your technology team.

- Use learning technologies throughout the learning process to increase engagement, understanding, and application.

What to Do Next

- **Highlight the portions of this chapter that seem most relevant to your learning plan.** Meet with your technology team and get its input on the most applicable tools you might use.

- **Create a plan for how you will use learning technologies to reinforce your workshop.** Ensure that you select only those tools and activities that will enhance the overall learning objectives and be mindful of your organization's culture and comfort level with technology.

- **Test, test, test!** Practice using technology tools to ensure they will deliver what you hope.

- **Read the next chapter to learn ways you can improve your facilitation skills.** Many of these skills will also be useful when using learning technologies, especially collaboration tools.

Additional Resources

Bozarth, J. (2014). "Effective Social Media for Learning." In E. Biech, ed., *ASTD Handbook: The Definitive Reference for Training & Development,* 2nd edition. Alexandria, VA: ASTD Press.

Chen, J. (2012). *50 Digital Team-Building Games: Fast, Fun Meeting Openers, Group Activities and Adventures Using Social Media, Smart Phones, GPS, Tablets, and More.* Hoboken, NJ: Wiley.

Halls, J. (2012). *Rapid Video Development for Trainers: How to Create Learning Videos Fast and Affordably.* Alexandria, VA: ASTD Press.

Kapp, K. (2013). *The Gamification of Learning and Instruction Fieldbook: Ideas Into Practice.* San Francisco: Wiley.

Palloff, R.M., and K. Pratt. (2009). *Building Online Learning Communities: Effective Strategies for the Virtual Classroom.* San Francisco: Jossey-Bass.

Quinn, C. (2014). "M-Thinking: There's an App for That." In E. Biech, ed., *ASTD Handbook: The Definitive Reference for Training & Development,* 2nd edition. Alexandria, VA: ASTD Press.

Swindling, L.B., and M.V.B. Partridge. (2008). "Intellectual Property: Protect What Is Yours and Avoid Taking What Belongs to Someone Else." In E. Biech, *ASTD Handbook for Workplace Learning Professionals.* Alexandria, VA: ASTD Press.

Toth, T. (2006). *Technology for Trainers.* Alexandria, VA: ASTD Press.

Udell, C. (2012). *Learning Everywhere: How Mobile Content Strategies Are Transforming Training.* Nashville, TN: Rockbench Publishing.

Chapter 8

Delivering Your Project Management Workshop: Be a Great Facilitator

What's in This Chapter

- Defining the facilitator's role
- Creating an effective learning environment
- Preparing participant materials
- Using program preparation checklists
- Starting and ending on a strong note
- Managing participant behaviors

Let's get one thing clear from the get-go: Facilitating a workshop—facilitating learning—is *not* lecturing. The title of ATD's bestselling book says it all: *Telling Ain't Training* (Stolovitch and Keeps 2011). A facilitator is the person who helps learners open themselves to new learning and makes the process easier. The role requires that you avoid projecting yourself as a subject matter expert (SME) and that you prepare activities that foster learning through "hands-on" experience and interaction.

Before you can help someone else learn, you must understand the roles you will embody when you deliver training: trainer, facilitator, and learner. When a workshop begins, you are the trainer, bringing to the learning event a plan, structure, experience, and objectives. This is only possible because you have a strong, repeatable logistics process. As you ask the learners to prioritize the learning objectives, you slowly release control, inviting them to become partners in their own learning. As you move from the trainer role into the facilitator role, the objectives are the contract between the learners and the facilitator. All great facilitators also have a third role in the classroom—the role of learner. If you are open, you can learn many new things when you are in class. If you believe you must be the expert as a learning facilitator, you will not be very effective.

To be most successful as a learning facilitator, consider this checklist:

- ☐ Identify the beliefs that limit your ability to learn and, therefore, to teach.
- ☐ Learning is a gift for you and from you to others.
- ☐ Choose carefully what you call yourself and what you call your outcomes.
- ☐ Clarify your purpose to better honor your roles at a learning event.
- ☐ If you can't teach with passion, don't do it.

This last point is especially important. Not everyone is destined to be a great facilitator and teacher, but you can still have enormous impact if you are passionate about the topic, about the process, and about helping people improve their working lives. If you are serious about becoming a great facilitator, Chapter 12 provides a comprehensive assessment instrument to help you manage your personal development and increase the effectiveness of your training (see Assessment 4). You can use this instrument for self-assessment, end-of-course feedback, observer feedback, or as a professional growth tracker.

With these points firmly in mind—facilitating is not lecturing and passion can get you past many facilitator deficiencies—let's look at some other important aspects of facilitating, starting with how to create an engaging and effective learning environment.

The Learning Environment

Colors, seating, tools, environmental considerations (such as temperature, ventilation, lighting), and your attitude, dress, preparation, and passion all enhance—or detract from—an effective and positive learning environment. This section describes some ways to maximize learning through environmental factors.

Color. Research has shown that bland, neutral environments are so unlike the real world that learning achieved in these "sensory deprivation chambers" cannot be transferred to the job. Color can be a powerful way to engage the limbic part of the brain and create long-term retention. It can align the right and left brains. Ways to incorporate color include artwork, plants, and pictures that help people feel comfortable and visually stimulated. Consider printing your handouts and assessments in color. The training support materials provided in this book are designed in color but can be printed in either color or grayscale (to reduce reproduction costs).

Room Setup. Because much learning requires both individual reflection and role playing, consider seating that promotes personal thought and group sharing. One way to accomplish this is to set up groups of three to five at round or square tables, with each chair positioned so the projection screen can easily be seen. Leave plenty of room for each person so that when he or she does need to reflect, there is a feeling of privacy. Keep in mind that comfortable chairs and places to write help people relax to learn. Figure 8-1 details more room configurations that you can use to accomplish specific tasks or purposes in training.

Tools of the Trade. Lots of flipcharts (one per table is optimal) with brightly colored markers create an interactive environment. Flipcharts are about as basic and low tech as tools get, but they are also low cost and do the trick. Consider putting colorful hard candy on the tables (include sugar-free options), with bright cups of markers, pencils, and pens. Gather pads of colorful sticky notes and "fidgets" (quiet toys such as chenille stems, Koosh balls, and others) to place on the table as well. For the right level of trust to exist, your learners must feel welcome.

Your Secret Weapon. Finally, the key to establishing the optimal learning environment is *you*. You set the tone by your attitude, the way you greet people, the clothes you wear, your passion, and your interest and care for the participants. You set the stage for learning with four conditions that only you as the facilitator can create to maximize learning:

1. **Confidentiality.** Establish the expectation that anything shared during the training program will remain confidential among participants and that as the facilitator you are committed to creating a safe environment. An important step in learning is first admitting ignorance, which has some inherent risk. Adult learners may resist admitting their learning needs because they fear the repercussions of showing their weaknesses. You can alleviate these concerns by assuring participants that the sole purpose of the training is to build their skills, and that no evaluations will take place. Your workshop must be a safe place to learn and take risks.

Figure 8-1. Seating Configurations

Select a room setup that will best support the needs of your learners:

- **Rounds.** Circular tables are particularly useful for small-group work when you have 16 to 24 participants.
- **U-Shaped.** This setup features three long rectangular tables set up to form a U, with you at the open end. It is good for overall group interaction and small-group work (two to three people). This setup also helps you establish rapport with your learners.
- **Classroom.** This setup is a traditional grade-school format characterized by rows of tables with all the participants facing forward toward the trainer. Avoid this setup as much as possible because you become the focal point rather than the learners, and your ability to interact with learners is extremely limited. Problems of visibility also occur when rows in the back are blocked by rows in the front.
- **Chevron.** Chevron setup features rows of tables as in the classroom setup but the tables are angled to form a V-shape. This opens up the room to allow you to interact more with the learners and accommodates a larger group of learners without sacrificing visibility. However, it shares many of the drawbacks of the classroom setup.
- **Hybrid or Fishbone.** This setup combines a U-shaped configuration with that of a chevron. It is useful when there are too many learners to form a good U and there is room enough to broaden the U to allow tables to be set up as chevrons in the center of the U. This hybrid approach allows for interaction and enables the trainer to move around.

Source: Drawn from McCain (2015).

2. **Freedom from distractions.** Work and personal demands cannot be ignored during training, but to maximize each participant's learning, and as a courtesy to others, outside demands should be minimized:

   a. Select a training site away from the workplace to help reduce distractions.

   b. Acknowledge that participants probably feel they shouldn't be away from work; remind them that the purpose of the training is to improve their work lives.

   c. Ask that mobile devices be turned off or set to silent alerts.

   d. Emphasize that because they are spending this time in training, trainees should immerse themselves in the learning experience and thereby maximize the value of their time, because far from being time "away from work responsibilities," it *is* a work responsibility.

3. **Personal responsibility for learning.** A facilitator can only create the *opportunity* for learning. Experiential learning requires that participants actively engage with and commit to learning—they cannot sit back and soak up information like sponges.

4. **Group participation.** Each participant brings relevant knowledge to the training program. Through discussion and sharing of information, a successful training session will

tap into the knowledge of each participant. Encourage all participants to accept responsibility for helping others learn.

Program Preparation Checklist

Preparation is power when it comes to facilitating a successful workshop, and a checklist is a powerful tool for effective preparation. This checklist of activities will help you prepare your workshop:

- ☐ Write down all location and workshop details when scheduling the workshop.
- ☐ Make travel reservations early (to save money, too), if applicable.
- ☐ Send a contract to the client to confirm details, or if you are an internal facilitator, develop guidelines and a workshop structure in conjunction with appropriate supervisors and managers.
- ☐ Specify room and equipment details in writing and then confirm by telephone.
- ☐ Define goals and expectations for the workshop.
- ☐ Get a list of participants, titles, roles, and responsibilities.
- ☐ Send participants a questionnaire that requires them to confirm their goals for the workshop.
- ☐ Send the client (or the participants, if you are an internal facilitator) an agenda for the workshop, with times for breaks and meals.
- ☐ Recommend that lunch or dinner be offered in-house, with nutritious food provided.
- ☐ Make a list of materials that you will need in the room (pads of paper, pens, pencils, markers, flipcharts, and so forth). Make sure to plan for some extras.
- ☐ Design the room layout (for example, rounds, U-shaped, classroom, chevron, or hybrid).
- ☐ Confirm whether you or your internal/external client will prepare copies of the workshop handouts. The workshop handouts should include all tools, training instruments, assessments, and worksheets. You may choose also to include copies of the presentation slides as part of the participant guide. All the supplemental materials you need to conduct the workshops in this book are available for download (see Chapter 14 for instructions).
- ☐ Find out if participants would like to receive pre-reading materials electronically before the session.
- ☐ Prepare assessments, tools, training instruments, and workshop materials at least one week before the workshop so that you have time to peruse and check them and assemble any equipment you may need (see the next two sections).

Participant Materials

Participant materials support participant learning throughout the workshop and provide continuing references after the workshop has ended. There are several kinds of participant materials. Here are some options:

Handouts

The development and "look" of your handouts are vital to help participants understand the information they convey. To compile the handouts properly, first gather all assessments, tools, training instruments, activities, and presentation slides and arrange them in the order they appear in the workshop. Then bind them together in some fashion. There are several options for compiling your material, ranging from inexpensive to deluxe. The kind of binding is your choice—materials can be stapled, spiral bound, or gathered in a ring binder—but remember that a professional look supports success. Your choice of binding will depend on your budget for the project. Because first appearances count, provide a cover with eye-catching colors and appropriate graphics.

Using the agendas in Chapters 1–3, select the presentation slides, learning activities, handouts, tools, and assessments appropriate to your workshop (see Chapter 15). If you choose to print out the presentation slides for your participants, consider printing no more than three slides per handout page to keep your content simple with sufficient white space for the participants to write their own notes. Use the learning objectives for each workshop to provide clarity for the participants at the outset. Remember to number the pages, to add graphics for interest (and humor), and to include tabs for easy reference if the packet of materials has multiple sections.

Some participants like to receive the handouts before the workshop begins. You may want to email participants to determine if they would like to receive the handouts electronically.

Presentation Slides

This ATD Workshop Series book includes presentation slides to support the two-day, one-day, and half-day agendas. They have been crafted to adhere to presentation best practices. If you choose to reorder or otherwise modify the slides, keep in mind these important concepts.

When you use PowerPoint software as a teaching tool, be judicious in the number of slides that you prepare. In a scientific lecture, slides are usually a necessity for explaining formulas or results, but a workshop relies on interaction so keep the slide information simple. Also, do not include more than five or six bullet points per slide. See more tips for effective PowerPoint slides in Figure 8-2.

A message can be conveyed quickly through the use of simple graphics. For example, an illustration of two people in conversation may highlight interpersonal communication, whereas a photo of a boardroom-style meeting may illustrate a group engaged in negotiation. Please note that any use of the images in the presentation slides provided with this book other than as part of your presentation is strictly prohibited by law.

When you use presentation slides ask yourself: What will a slide add to my presentation? Ensure that the answer that comes back is "it will enhance the message." If slides are simply used to make the workshop look more sophisticated or technical, the process may not achieve the desired results.

It can be frustrating when a facilitator shows a slide for every page that the participants have in front of them. The dynamics of the class are likely to disconnect. If the information you are teaching is in the handouts or workbook, work from those media alone and keep the workshop personally interactive.

Workbooks and Journals

A participant journal can be included in the binder with your handouts, or it may be a separate entity. Throughout the workshop participants can assess their progress and advance their development by entering details of their personal learning in the journal. The benefit of this journal to participants is that they can separate their personal discoveries and development from the main workshop handouts and use this journal as an action plan if desired.

Videos

If you show a video in your workshop, ensure that the skills it contains are up to date and that the video is less than 20 minutes long. Provide questions that will lead to a discussion of the information viewed. Short video clips can be effective learning tools.

Toys, Noisemakers, and Other Props

Experienced facilitators understand the value of gadgets and games that advance the learning, provide a break from learning, or both.

Figure 8-2. Tips for Effective PowerPoint Slides

Presentation slides can enhance your presentation. They can also detract from it by being too cluttered, monotonous, or hard to read. Here are some tips for clear, effective slides:

Fonts
- Use sans-serif fonts such as Arial, Calibri, or Helvetica; other fonts are blurry when viewed from 20 feet or more and are more easily read on LCD screens and in video/web presentations.
- Use the same sans-serif font for most (if not all) of the presentation.
- Use a font size no smaller than 24 points. (This will also help keep the number of bullets per slide down.)
- Consider using a 32-point font—this is the easiest for web/video transmission.
- Limit yourself to one font size per slide.

Colors
- Font colors should be black or dark blue for light backgrounds and white or yellow on dark backgrounds. Think high contrast for clarity and visual impact.
- Avoid using red or green. It doesn't project well, doesn't transfer well when used in a webinar, and causes issues for people who suffer color blindness.

Text and Paragraphs
- Align text left or right, not centered.
- Avoid cluttering a slide—use a single headline and a few bullet points.
- Use no more than six words to a line; avoid long sentences.
- Use sentence case—ALL CAPS ARE DIFFICULT TO READ AND CAN FEEL LIKE YELLING.
- Avoid abbreviations and acronyms.
- Limit use of punctuation marks.

Source: Developed by Cat Russo.

Adults love to play. When their minds are open they learn quickly and effectively. Something as simple as tossing a rubber ball from person to person as questions are asked about topics studied can liven up the workshop and help people remember what they've learned.

Case studies and lively exercises accelerate learning. Bells and whistles are forms of communication; use them when you pit two teams against each other or to indicate the end of an activity.

Facilitator Equipment and Materials

When all details for the workshop have been confirmed, it is time to prepare for the actual facilitation of the workshop at the site. You may know the site well because you are providing in-house facilitation. If, however, you are traveling off site to facilitate, important elements enter the planning. Here's a checklist of things to consider:

- ☐ Pack a data-storage device that contains your handouts and all relevant workshop materials. In the event that your printed materials do not reach the workshop location, you will have the electronic files to reprint on site.

- ☐ Pack the proper power cords, a spare battery for the laptop, and a bulb for the LCD or overhead projector in the event that these items are not available at the workshop location. This requires obtaining the make and model of all audiovisual and electronic equipment from the client or the training facility during your planning process.

- ☐ Bring an extension cord.

- ☐ Bring reference materials, books, article reprints, and ancillary content. Take advantage of all technology options, such as tablets or other readers to store reference materials. As a facilitator, you will occasionally need to refer to materials other than your own for additional information. Having the materials with you not only provides correct information about authors and articles, but it also positively reinforces participants' impressions of your knowledge, training, openness to learning, and preparedness.

- ☐ Bring flipcharts, painter's tape, and sticky notes.

- ☐ Pack toys and games for the workshop, a timer or bell, and extra marking pens.

- ☐ Bring duct tape. You may need it to tape extension cords to the floor as a safety precaution. The strength of duct tape also ensures that any flipchart pages hung on walls (with permission) will hold fast.

You can ship these items to the workshop in advance, but recognize that the shipment may not arrive in time, and that even if it does arrive on time, you may have to track it down at the venue. Also, take some time identifying backups or alternatives in case the materials, technology, and so on do not conform to plan. What are the worst-case scenarios? How could you manage such situations? Prepare to be flexible and creative.

A Strong Start: Introduction, Icebreakers, and Openers

The start of a session is a crucial time in the workshop dynamic. How the participants respond to you, the facilitator, can set the mood for the remainder of the workshop. To get things off on the right foot, get to the training room early, at least 30 to 60 minutes before the workshop. This gives you time not only to set up the room if that has not already been done, but also to test the environment, the seating plan, the equipment, and your place in the room. Find out where the restrooms are. When participants begin to arrive (and some of them come very early), be ready to welcome them. Don't be distracted with problems or issues; be free and available to your participants.

While they are settling in, engage them with simple questions:

- How was your commute?
- Have you traveled far for this workshop?
- Was it easy to find this room?
- May I help you with anything?

When the participants have arrived and settled, introduce yourself. Write a humorous introduction, if that's your style, because this will help you be more approachable. Talk more about what you want to accomplish in the workshop than about your accomplishments. If you have a short biographical piece included in the handouts or in the workbook, it may serve as your personal introduction.

At the conclusion of your introduction, provide an activity in which participants can meet each other (often called an icebreaker). Because participants sometimes come into a training session feeling inexperienced, skeptical, reluctant, or scared, using icebreaker activities to open training enables participants to interact in a fun and nonthreatening way and to warm up the group before approaching more serious content. Don't limit the time on this too much unless you have an extremely tight schedule. The more time participants spend getting to know each other at the beginning of the workshop, the more all of you will benefit as the session proceeds.

Feedback

Feedback is the quickest, surest way for you, the facilitator, to learn if the messages and instruction are reaching the participants and if the participants are absorbing the content. It is also important for you to evaluate the participants' rate of progress and learning. Answers to the questions you ask throughout the workshop will help you identify much of the progress, but these answers come from only a few of the participants at a time. They're not a global snapshot of the entire group's comprehension and skills mastery.

When you lead a workshop, the participants walk a fine line between retention and deflection of knowledge. Continuing evaluations ensure that learning is taking root. Three levels of questions—learning comprehension, skills mastery, and skills application—help you determine where the training may not be achieving the intended results.

- Learning comprehension checks that the participants understand and grasp the skills being taught (see Figure 8-3).

- Skills mastery means that the participants are able to demonstrate their newly acquired knowledge by some activity, such as teaching a portion of a module to their fellow participants or delivering their interpretation of topic specifics to the class (see Figure 8-4).

- Skills application is the real test. You may choose to substantiate this through role plays or group case studies. When the participants have the opportunity to verbally communicate the skills learned and to reach desired results through such application, then skills application is established (see Figure 8-5).

The questions in Figures 8-3 to 8-5 are designed for written answers so you can incorporate them into the takeaway workbook you create. The questions concerning skills mastery and skills application could be used as a job-based assignment if the workshop is longer than one day. Keep in mind that you will also reevaluate after each day of a multiday session.

Let's now look at other forms of in-class learning assessments: role plays, participant presentations, ball toss, and journaling.

Role Plays

Role plays are an effective tool for assessing learning comprehension. If two or more participants conduct a role play that reveals their understanding of the information, with an outcome that reflects that understanding, then it becomes a "live feed," instantaneous learning for all.

You must set up the role play carefully. It is often wise for you to be a part of the first role-play experience to show participants how it's done and to make them more comfortable with the activity. Ensure that you explain all the steps of the role play and the desired outcome. It is insightful to role-play a negative version first, followed by participant discussion; then role-play a positive aspect the second time. For example, if confrontational communication is the topic

Figure 8-3. Learning Comprehension Questions

Here are some questions that can be asked to determine each participant's level of *learning comprehension*:
• Give a brief overview of your learning in this workshop. Begin your phrases with "I have learned. . . ." This will assist you in focusing your responses.
• How/where will you apply this knowledge in your workplace?
• Did you acquire this knowledge through lectures/practice/discussion or a combination of all methods?
• Do you feel sufficiently confident to pass on this knowledge to your colleagues?
• Are there any areas that will require additional learning for you to feel sufficiently confident?

Figure 8-4. Skills Mastery Questions

Now let's look at some questions you can use to evaluate your participants' *skills mastery*:

- If you were asked to teach one skill in this workshop, which skill would it be?
- What would your three key message points be for that skill?
- Describe the steps you would take to instruct each message point (for example, lecture, group discussion, PowerPoint presentation, and so forth).
- What methods would you use to ensure that your participants comprehend your instruction?
- Would feedback from your participants, both positive and negative, affect the development of your skills mastery? If yes, illustrate your response and the changes you would make.

Figure 8-5. Skills Application Questions

And finally, let's consider some questions that identify participants' *ability to apply the skills* they've learned in the workshop:

- Please describe a situation at your workplace where you could employ one specific skill from this workshop.
- How would you introduce this skill to your colleagues?
- How would you set goals to measure the improvement in this skill?
- Describe the input and participation you would expect from your colleagues.
- How would you exemplify mastery of the skill?

and the situation under discussion involves a line manager and his or her supervisor, first enact the role play using the verbal and body language that is causing the negative result. Discuss this as a class to identify the specific language that needs improvement. Then enact the role play again, this time using positive language.

Frequently it is helpful for a participant who has been on the receiving end of negative communication in his or her workplace to adopt the role of deliverer. Walking in the other person's shoes leads to a quicker understanding of the transaction. This positive role play should also be followed by whole-group discussion of the elements that worked. Participants can be invited to write about the process and its results to give them a real-life example to take back to the workplace.

Participant Presentations

You might ask a participant to present a module of learning to the group. This allows you to observe the participants from a different perspective—both as a contributor to the conversation and as a presenter leading the discussion. Be ready to assist or to answer questions. For example, a participant may choose assertive communication as his or her module, and the specific issue on return to the workplace may be a request for promotion. The participant defines and delivers the steps required to ask for the promotion while the facilitator and other participants observe and evaluate the success of the approach and demonstration of confidence and assertiveness.

Ball Toss

A quick method for evaluating a class's knowledge of the material presented is to ask the participants to form a standing circle. The facilitator throws out a soft rubber ball to an individual and asks a question about the previous learning activity. When the catcher gives the right answer, he or she throws the ball to another participant who answers another question. The facilitator can step out of this circle and let the participants ask as well as answer questions to review the skills as a group. Candy for all as a reward for contributions is always enjoyed by the participants (consider keeping some sugar-free treats on hand as well).

Journaling

Keeping a journal is a quiet, introspective way for participants to get a grip on their learning. When you complete an activity, have everyone take five minutes to write a summary of the skill just learned and then ask them to share what they've written with a partner. Invite the partner to correct and improve the material if necessary or appropriate.

Responding to Questions

When participants are asking questions, they are engaged and interested. Your responses to questions will augment the learning atmosphere. The way in which you respond is extremely important. Answers that are evasive can disturb a class because they cast doubts on your credibility. Glib or curt answers are insulting. Lengthy responses break the rhythm of the class and often go off track. When dealing with questions, the value of effective communication is in hearing the question, answering the question asked, and moving on. Repeat questions so that all participants hear them. In addition, this can ensure that you have heard the question correctly.

However, don't rush to answer. Take time to let everyone absorb the information. When time is of the essence, don't be tempted to give long, complicated answers that embrace additional topics. Be courteous and clear. Check that your answer has been understood. When a question comes up that could possibly derail the session or that is beyond the scope of the topic, you can choose to record it on a "parking lot" list and then revisit it later at an assigned time. A parking lot can be as simple as a list on a flipchart. However, whenever possible, answer a question at the time it is asked. Consider answering with analogies when they are appropriate because these often help elucidate challenging concepts.

You are likely aware that effective questions that prompt answers are open ended. Here are some that you might ask:

- What have you learned so far?
- How do you feel about this concept?
- How would you handle this situation?

Any question that begins with "what" or "how" promotes a more extensive answer. Do you also know, though, that questions that begin with "why"—as in "why do you think that way?"—can promote defensiveness? So what is a facilitator to do when asked a "why" question?

When a participant asks a confrontational or negative question, handle it with dignity and do not become aggressive. It's helpful to ask open-ended questions of the participant to try to clarify the original question. For example, ask, "What do you mean by . . . ?" or "Which part of the activity do you find challenging?" This form of open-ended questioning requires additional accountability from the participant. The reason for the confrontation may have arisen from confusion about the information or the need to hear his or her own thoughts aloud. When you are calm and patient, the altercation is more likely to be resolved. If the participant persists, you may wish to ask him or her to discuss the specifics in a private setting. More ideas for dealing with difficult participants are provided later in this chapter.

Some participants enjoy being questioned because it gives them an opportunity to show their knowledge. Others are reticent for fear of looking foolish if they don't know the answer. Because your participants have unique styles and personalities, always have a purpose for asking questions: Will these questions test the participants' knowledge? Are these questions appropriate? Are you asking them in the style that suits the participant?

Training Room and Participant Management

When everything is in place and ready for the session, it's time to review the "soft skills" portion of your responsibilities—that is, how you conduct the workshop and interact with participants. Here are some things to consider:

- **"Respect and respond" should be a facilitator's mantra.** At all times respect the participants and respond in a timely manner.

- **Learn participants' names at the beginning of the workshop.** Focus on each participant, give a firm handshake, and repeat the name in your greeting. Paying attention to the details they share during your greeting, and thereby getting to know them on a personal level, makes learning names much easier. When you have time, survey the room and write down every name without looking at nametags or name tents on the tables.

- **Manage workshop program time.** This is vital because it ensures that the goals will be met in the time allotted.

- **Read the participants' body language.** This will help you know when to pause and ask questions or to give them a stretch break.

- **Answer questions fully and effectively.** If you don't know an answer, open the question up to the participants or offer to get back to the questioner. Make a note to remind yourself to do so.

- **Add a "parking lot" to the room**—a large sheet of paper taped to one of the walls (use your own artistic prowess to draw a vehicle of some sort). When questions arise that are out of step with the current activity, ask the participant to write the question on a sticky note and put it in the parking lot. When the current activity is completed, you can address the questions parked there.

- **Control unruly participants through assertiveness of vocal tone and message.** When appropriate, invite them to help you with tasks because frequently they just need to be more physically involved. If the unruliness gets out of hand, accompany the person out of the room to discuss the situation.

- **Be sure to monitor a participant who is slower to assimilate the information.** If time permits, give that person some one-on-one time with you.

- **Keep your energy high.** Inject humor wherever possible. Ensure the learning is taking root.

A Word About Dealing With Difficult Participants

Much of the preparation you do before a training session will help you minimize disruptive behavior in your training session. But, sadly, you are still likely at some point to have difficult participants in your training room. Beyond preparation, you may need some specific strategies to help you manage disruptions and keep the learning on track. Figure 8-6, drawn from McCain's second edition of *Facilitation Basics* (2015), identifies many of these behaviors and gives strategies for nipping them in the bud.

Figure 8-6. Managing Difficult Participants

THE PROBLEM	THE SOLUTION
Carrying on a Side Conversation	• Don't assume the talkers are being disrespectful; depersonalize the behavior by thinking: "Maybe they are unclear about a point in the material, or the material is not relevant to their needs." • Ask the talkers if they don't understand something. • Walk toward the talkers as you continue to make your point; this stops many conversations dead in their tracks.
Monopolizing the Discussion	• Some participants tend to take over the conversation; while the enthusiasm is great, you don't want to leave other learners out. • Tell the monopolizer that her comments are valuable and interesting and that you would like to open up the discussion to others in the group. Then call on another person by name. • Enlist the monopolizer to help you by being a gatekeeper and ensuring that no one monopolizes the conversation.
Complaining	• Don't assume someone who complains doesn't have a valid reason to do so. • Ask the rest of the group if they feel the same way. If they do, try to address the issue as appropriate. If they don't, talk to the individual in the hallway during the break.
Challenging Your Knowledge	• Determine if this person really knows more than you do, or is just trying to act as though he does. • If he does know more, try to enlist his help in the training. If he doesn't, ask him to provide expertise, and he will usually realize he can't and back down.
Daydreaming	• Use the person's name in an example to get her attention. • Switch to something more active. • If behavior affects more than just one person, try to find out if something work related is causing it and have a brief discussion about it.
Heckling	• Don't get upset or start volleying remarks. • Try giving the person learning-oriented attention: "John, you clearly have some background in this area; would you care to share your thoughts with the rest of the group?" • Get the attention off you by switching to a group-oriented activity.
Clowning Around	• Give the person attention in a learning-oriented way by calling on her to answer a question or be a team leader. • If a joke is intended to relieve tension in the room and others seem to be experiencing it, deal with the tension head on by bringing it up. • If it is just a joke, and it's funny and appropriate, laugh!

PROJECT MANAGEMENT training

THE PROBLEM	THE SOLUTION
Making an Insensitive Remark	• Remember that if the person truly didn't intend offense, you don't want to humiliate him. But you do need to ensure that the person and everyone else in the room know that you will not tolerate bigoted or otherwise inappropriate remarks. • Give the person a chance to retract what he said by asking if that is what he meant to say. If it wasn't, then move on. If it was, you need to let the person know that the comment is not in line with the values of your organization and it can't be allowed to continue. • If the person persists, speak to him in the hallway, or as a last resort, ask him to leave.
Doing Other Work	• Talk to the person at a break to find out if the workshop is meeting her needs. • If the person is truly under too much pressure, offer to have her come to another session.
Not Talking	• If you can tell the person is engaged because he is taking notes, maintaining eye contact, or leaning forward, let him alone. • Give the person opportunities to interact at a greater comfort level by participating in small groups or in pairs.
Withdrawing	• Talk to the person at break to find out if something is going on. Deal with the issue as appropriate. • If the person feels excluded, have her act as a team leader for a turn, or ensure that all members of teams are given opportunities to participate.
Missing the Point	• If someone misses the point, be sensitive in dealing with him. Try to find something to agree with in his point. • Try to identify what the person is having trouble grasping and clear up the point with an analogy or an example. • Never laugh at the person or otherwise humiliate him.
Playing With Technology	• Minimize distractions by setting specific ground rules for technology use in the training room. (See Chapter 7 for creative ways to use technology to enhance training.) • Direct a training-related question to the person. • If the behavior persists, talk to the person at break to determine if there is an issue with which you can help.

Source: McCain (2015).

When all else fails, you have a few last resorts, although you would clearly rather not get to that point. One option is to simply pull aside the individual who is disrupting the class and talk to her privately. Dick Grote (1998) suggests in "Dealing With Miscreants, Snivelers, and Adversaries" that you can often catch someone off guard by asking: "Is it personal?" The direct question will usually cause the individual to deny that it is personal. Next, you tell the person that the behavior is unacceptable and that you will speak to a supervisor or training sponsor if it continues. This often works.

However, if it does not work, you can ask to have the person removed or cancel the program and speak to the person's supervisor. Clearly, these options are not to be taken lightly, but realize that they are available when you are faced with truly recalcitrant behavior.

Follow up when you have faced a difficult situation. Take some time to reflect on the event and write down the details of what happened. If possible, get perspectives and feedback from participants who witnessed it. If outside perspectives are not an option, think about the event from the points of view of the disruptive individual and other participants and ask yourself: What went wrong? What went well? How could I manage the situation better next time?

An Unforgettable End

In Biech (2008), contributor Mel Silberman explains that

> [m]any training programs run out of steam in the end. In some cases, participants are marking time until the close is near. In other cases, facilitators are valiantly trying to cover what they haven't got to before time runs out. How unfortunate! What happens at the end needs to be "unforgettable." You want participants to remember what they've learned. You also want participants to think what they've learned has been special. (p. 315)

Silberman suggests considering four areas when preparing to end your workshop:

- How will participants review what you've taught them?
- How will participants assess what they have learned?
- What will participants do about what they have learned?
- How will participants celebrate their accomplishments?

For example, consider what you've learned in this chapter. You've developed a well-rounded picture of what it takes to create an optimal, effective learning environment, from creating an inviting and engaging space to preparing and gathering materials that will make you feel like an organizational champ. You're ready to get the training off to a productive start, to manage difficult participants and situations, and to pull it all together in a powerful way. Now review the bullet points that follow to determine what the next steps are and take pride in the preparation that will enable you to adapt and thrive in the training room.

The Bare Minimum

- **Keep things moving.** Create an engaging, interactive environment.

- **Pay attention to the energy in the room.** Be prepared to adjust the activities as needed. Build in content that can be delivered standing or through networking activities to get participants out of their seats when needed.

- **Have fun!** If you create an upbeat tone and enjoy yourself, the participants are likely to have fun as well.

Key Points

- Facilitation is not lecturing. It's providing learning activities and support to make learning easier for the participant.

- Facilitation is not about the facilitator—it's about the learner.

- An inviting space and a safe, collaborative environment are necessary for learning to occur.

- Good facilitation starts with passion and significant attention to preparation.

- A good start sets the tone for the whole training session.

- A strong ending helps learners to remember the training and carry lessons forward into their work.

What to Do Next

- Prepare, modify, and review the training agenda. Use one of the agendas in Section I as a starting point.

- Review the program preparation checklist and work through it step by step.

- Make a list of required participant materials and facilitator equipment and begin assembling them.

- Review all learning activities included in the agenda and start preparing for your delivery.

Additional Resources

Biech, E. (2006). *90 World-Class Activities by 90 World-Class Trainers.* San Francisco: John Wiley/Pfeiffer.

Biech, E. (2008). *10 Steps to Successful Training.* Alexandria, VA: ASTD Press.

Biech, E., ed. (2008). *ASTD Handbook for Workplace Learning Professionals.* Alexandria, VA: ASTD Press.

Biech, E., ed. (2014). *ASTD Handbook: The Definitive Reference for Training & Development,* 2nd edition. Alexandria, VA: ASTD Press.

Biech, E. (2015). *Training and Development for Dummies.* Hoboken, NJ: Wiley.

Duarte, N. (2010). *Resonate: Present Visual Stories That Transform Audiences.* Hoboken, NJ: Wiley.

Grote, D. (1998). "Dealing With Miscreants, Snivelers, and Adversaries," *Training & Development,* 52(10), October.

McCain, D.V. (2015). *Facilitation Basics,* 2nd edition. Alexandria, VA: ATD Press.

Stolovitch, H.D., and E.J. Keeps. (2011). *Telling Ain't Training,* 2nd edition. Alexandria, VA: ASTD Press.

Thiagarajan, S. (2005). *Thiagi's Interactive Lectures: Power Up Your Training With Interactive Games and Exercises.* Alexandria, VA: ASTD Press.

Thiagarajan, S. (2006). *Thiagi's 100 Favorite Games.* San Francisco: John Wiley/Pfeiffer.

Chapter 9
Evaluating Workshop Results

What's in This Chapter

- Exploring the reasons to evaluate your program
- Introducing the levels of measurement and what they measure

---

Evaluation represents the last letter of the ADDIE cycle of instructional design (analysis, design, development, implementation, and evaluation). Although evaluation is placed at the end of the model, an argument could be made for including it far earlier, as early as the design and development phase and perhaps even in the analysis phase. Why? Because the goals of the training, or the learning objectives (see Chapter 5), provide insight into what the purpose of the evaluation should be. In fact, business goals, learning goals, and evaluation of those goals are useful subjects to address with organizational leaders or the training sponsor. Trainers often begin a program without thinking about how the program fits into a strategic plan or how it supports and promotes specific business goals, but these are critical to consider before implementing the program.

However, this chapter is not about that upfront evaluation of the program design and materials; it is about evaluating the program after it has been delivered and reporting the results back to the training sponsor. This form of evaluation allows you to determine whether the program objectives were achieved and whether the learning was applied on the job and had an impact on the business. Evaluation can also serve as the basis for future program and budget discussions with training sponsors.

Levels of Measurement

No discussion of measurement would be complete without an introduction to the concepts that underpin the field of evaluation. The following is a brief primer on a very large and detailed subject that can be somewhat overwhelming. If your organization is committed to measuring beyond Level 2, take some time to read the classics of evaluation.

In 1956–57, Donald Kirkpatrick, one of the leading experts in measuring training results, identified four levels of measurement and evaluation. These four levels build successively from the simplest (Level 1) to the most complex (Level 4) and are based on information gathered at previous levels. For that reason, determining upfront at what level to evaluate a program is important. A general rule of thumb is that the more important or fundamental the training is and the greater the investment in it, the higher the level of evaluation to use. The four basic levels of evaluation are

- **Level 1—Reaction:** Measures how participants react to the workshop.
- **Level 2—Learning:** Measures whether participants have learned and understood the content of the workshop.
- **Level 3—Behavior (also referred to as application):** Measures on-the-job changes that have occurred because of the learning.
- **Level 4—Results:** Measures the impact of training on the bottom line.

These four levels correspond with the evaluation methods described below.

Level 1: Measuring Participant Reactions

One of the most common ways trainers measure participants' reactions is by administering end-of-session evaluation forms, often called "smile sheets" (for a sample, see Assessment 2). The main benefit of using smile sheets is that they are easy to create and administer. If you choose this method, consider the following suggestions, but first decide the purpose of evaluating. Do you want to know if the participants enjoyed the presentation? How they felt about the facilities? Or how they reacted to the content?

Here are a few suggestions for creating evaluation forms:

- Limit the form to one page.
- Make your questions brief.
- Leave adequate space for comments.

- Group types of questions into categories (for example, cluster questions about content, questions about the instructor, and questions about materials).

- Provide variety in types of questions (include multiple-choice, true-false, short-answer, and open-ended items).

- Include relevant decision makers in your questionnaire design.

- Plan how you will use and analyze the data and create a design that will facilitate your analysis.

- Use positively worded items (such as "I listen to others," instead of "I don't listen to others").

You can find additional tips for creating evaluation sheets and evaluating their results in the *Infoline* "Making Smile Sheets Count" by Nancy S. Kristiansen (2004).

Although evaluation sheets are used frequently, they have some inherent limitations. For example, participants cannot judge the *effectiveness* of training techniques. In addition, results can be overly influenced by the personality of the facilitator or participants' feelings about having to attend training. Be cautious of relying solely on Level 1 evaluations.

Level 2: Measuring the Extent to Which Participants Have Learned

If you want to determine the extent to which participants have understood the content of your workshop, testing is an option. Comparing pre-training and post-training test results indicates the amount of knowledge gained. Or you can give a quiz that tests conceptual information 30 to 60 days after the training to see if people remember the concepts. Because most adult learners do not generally like the idea of tests, you might want to refer to these evaluations as "assessments."

Another model of testing is criterion-referenced testing (CRT), which tests the learner's performance against a given standard, such as "greets the customer and offers assistance within one minute of entering the store" or "initiates the landing gear at the proper time and altitude." Such testing can be important in determining whether a learner can carry out the task, determining the efficacy of the training materials, and providing a foundation for further levels of evaluation. Coscarelli and Shrock (2008) describe a five-step method for developing CRTs that includes

1. Determining what to test (analysis)

2. Determining if the test measures what it purports to measure (validity)

3. Writing test items

4. Establishing a cut-off or mastery score

5. Showing that the test provides consistent results (reliability).

Level 3: Measuring the Results of Training Back on the Job

The next level of evaluation identifies whether the learning was actually used back on the job. It is important to recognize that application on the job is where learning begins to have real-world effects and that application is not solely up to the learner. Many elements affect transfer and application, including follow-up, manager support, and so forth. For example, consider a sales training attendee who attends training and learns a new, more efficient way to identify sales leads. However, upon returning to work, the attendee's manager does not allow the time for the attendee to practice applying those new skills in the workplace. Over time, the training is forgotten, and any value it may have had does not accrue.

Methods for collecting data regarding performance back on the job include reports by people who manage participants, reports from staff and peers, observations, quality monitors, and other quality and efficiency measures. In "The Four Levels of Evaluation," Kirkpatrick (2007) provides some guidelines for carrying out Level 3 evaluations:

- Use a control group, if practical.

- Allow time for behavior change to take place.

- Evaluate before and after the program, if possible.

- Interview learners, their immediate managers, and possibly their subordinates and anyone else who observes their work or behavior.

- Repeat the evaluation at appropriate times.

Level 4: Measuring the Organizational Impact of Training

Level 4 identifies how learning affects business measures. Consider an example related to management training. Let's say a manager attends management training and learns several new and valuable techniques to engage employees and help keep them on track. Upon return, the manager gets support in applying the new skills and behaviors. As time passes, the learning starts to have measurable results: Retention has increased, employees are demonstrably more engaged and are producing better-quality goods, and sales increase because the quality has increased. Retention, engagement, quality, and sales are all measurable business results improved as a result of the training.

Measuring such organizational impact requires working with leaders to create and implement a plan to collect the data you need. Possible methods include customer surveys, measurements of sales, studies of customer retention or turnover, employee satisfaction surveys, and other measurements of issues pertinent to the organization.

Robert Brinkerhoff, well-known author and researcher of evaluation methods, has suggested the following method to obtain information relevant to results:

- Send out questionnaires to people who have gone through training, asking: To what extent have you used your training in a way that has made a significant business impact? (This question can elicit information that will point to business benefits and ways to use other data to measure accomplishments.)
- When you get responses back, conduct interviews to get more information.

Return on Investment

Measuring return on investment (ROI)—sometimes referred to as Level 5 evaluation—is useful and can help "sell" training to leaders. ROI measures the monetary value of business benefits such as those noted in the discussion about Level 4 and compares them with the fully loaded costs of training to provide a percentage return on training investment. Hard numbers such as these can be helpful in discussions with organizational executives about conducting further training and raise the profile of training.

ROI was popularized by Jack Phillips. More in-depth information can be found in the *ASTD Handbook of Measuring and Evaluating Training* (Phillips 2010).

Reporting Results

An important and often under-considered component of both ROI and Level 4 evaluations is reporting results. Results from these types of evaluation studies have several different audiences, and it is important to take time to plan the layout of the evaluation report and the method of delivery with the audience in question. Consider the following factors in preparing communications:

- **Purpose:** The purposes for communicating program results depend on the specific program, the setting, and unique organizational needs.
- **Audience:** For each target audience, understand the audience and find out what information is needed and why. Take into account audience bias, and then tailor the communication to each group.

- **Timing:** Lay the groundwork for communication before program implementation. Avoid delivering a message, particularly a negative message, to an audience unprepared to hear the story and unaware of the methods that generated the results.

- **Reporting format:** The type of formal evaluation report depends on how much detailed information is presented to target audiences. Brief summaries may be sufficient for some communication efforts. In other cases, particularly those programs that require significant funding, more detail may be important.

The Bare Minimum

- If formal measurement techniques are not possible, consider using simple, interactive, informal measurement activities such as a quick pulse-check during the workshop.

- Empower the participants to create an action plan to capture the new skills and ideas they plan to use. Ultimately, the success of any training event will rest on lasting positive change in participants' behavior.

Key Points

- The four basic levels of evaluation cover reaction, learning, application, and organizational impact.

- A fifth level covers return on investment.

- Reporting results is as important as measuring them. Be strategic in crafting your results document, taking into consideration purpose, audience, timing, and format.

What to Do Next

- Identify the purpose and level of evaluation based on the learning objectives and learning goals.

- Prepare a training evaluation form, or use the one provided in Chapter 12.

- If required, develop plans for follow-up evaluations to determine skills mastery, on-the-job application, and business impact.

Additional Resources

Biech, E., ed. (2014). *ASTD Handbook: The Definitive Reference for Training & Development,* 2nd edition. Alexandria, VA: ASTD Press.

Brinkerhoff, R.O. (2006). *Telling Training's Story: Evaluation Made Simple, Credible, and Effective.* San Francisco: Berrett-Koehler.

Coscarelli, W., and S. Shrock. (2008). "Level 2: Learning—Five Essential Steps for Creating Your Tests and Two Cautionary Tales." In E. Biech, ed., *ASTD Handbook for Workplace Learning Professionals.* Alexandria, VA: ASTD Press.

Kirkpatrick, D.L. (2007). "The Four Levels of Evaluation." *Infoline* No. 0701, Alexandria, VA: ASTD Press.

Kirkpatrick, D., and J.D. Kirkpatrick. (2006). *Evaluating Training Programs: The Four Levels,* 3rd edition. San Francisco: Berrett-Koehler.

Kirkpatrick, D., and J.D. Kirkpatrick. (2007). *Implementing the Four Levels: A Practical Guide for Effective Evaluation of Training Programs.* San Francisco: Berrett-Koehler.

Kristiansen, N.S. (2004). "Making Smile Sheets Count." *Infoline* No. 0402, Alexandria, VA: ASTD Press.

Phillips, P.P., ed. (2010). *ASTD Handbook of Measuring and Evaluating Training.* Alexandria, VA: ASTD Press.

SECTION III
POST-WORKSHOP LEARNING

Chapter 10
The Follow-Up Coach

What's in This Chapter

- The benefits of follow-up to your workshop
- Dozens of ideas you can implement before, during, near the end, and after the workshop to extend learning from start to finish

---

In the blistering pace of business today, organizations have invested time and money in just about everything—technology, training, new processes, strategy planning, operational excellence, process improvement, communications, and team building, to name just a few. The common thread among the topics is results. How do we get relevant, timely, and accurate business results from all that we do for and in organizations?

The answer, I argue in this book, is project management. It is the one process or method that can be used to apply all of the components above and more to deliver business results. So it follows that training your employees in project management is a key to unlocking results.

Transitioning learners from "I tried it" to "I'll apply it" requires you to design follow-up activities and provide tools to support the participants' learning. For learning to transfer, the participants must be committed to implementing the skills, and their bosses must be willing to support the new skills.

The suggestions in this chapter can help provide much-needed support you can do before, during, and after the workshop to ensure that the project management skills are implemented and that your participants continue to grow and learn.

Before the Workshop Begins

Follow-up starts even before the workshop begins. Try some of these ideas to garner support for learning before the workshop:

- **Meet with managers.** Meet with the participants' managers to discuss what the managers expect from the workshop. Dana Robinson (2013) offers these examples of questions you can ask when exploring a manager's request for a training program:

  ○ What are the goals for your employees?

  ○ What are the measures you will use to determine success?

  ○ What must participants do more, better, or differently if your department/function is to be more effective in managing projects?

  ○ What have you observed your employees do that you believe needs to change?

- **Partner with stakeholders.** Work with managers and other stakeholders to help them determine how to help the participants upon returning from the workshop. Ask them what changes they expect to see when the participants return to the workplace. Share this information with participants during the workshop (without specifically divulging the source). Leave supervisors with a list of skills that you intend to discuss in the workshop that they can reinforce with their employees when they see them implementing the skills.

- **Explain action plans.** Several activities in the workshops help participants create a development plan for their future. Inform participants' managers about these plans, recommending that they discuss them with the participants upon returning. Consider providing workshop handouts and other content to the managers in advance to help them prepare for these vital conversations.

- **Put support into words.** Collect messages of support from the participants' managers describing how they will support transfer of skills after the workshop. Weave these messages into your workshop.

- **Personalize it.** Before the formal learning begins, ask participants to bring challenges they have that they hope will be resolved by what they learn in the workshop. Be prepared to address their challenges if the solutions aren't too complicated or too far off topic. People can benefit from hearing how others solved similar problems, and they are truly invested in addressing their own.

During the Workshop

Here are other ideas to try *during* the workshop that you can then build on after the workshop:

- **Leverage your strengths.** Remember that as the facilitator you are seen by the group as the expert. Even if you are not, they must believe you are. The best way to do this is to be prepared and work with your strengths. If you are a great facilitator but a less-than-expert project manager, lead with your facilitation skills. If you are an expert project manager, use that knowledge to inform the facilitation. If you are a great listener or fabulous communicator, model those skills for the participants so they can see what effective communication looks like.

- **Collect and share success stories from other project managers.** Stories of principles in action are powerful. You can find testimonials just about anywhere, but the ones that will resonate are those from your participants' organizations or industries. Be on the lookout for great examples of skills and knowledge application from your participants, your colleagues, a local professional association chapter, or your own experience.

- **Share a message of support from a sponsor or stakeholder within the organization.** Share a statement from project sponsors, direct managers, or executive leaders that demonstrates the organization's commitment to project management. Help participants understand that their learning really matters to the organization.

- **Deliver feedback.** If you are familiar with the book *The New One-Minute Manager* (Blanchard and Johnson 2015), then you will remember the importance of delivering timely feedback. If you observe a group exercise being done incorrectly, make the correction as soon as possible and then demonstrate the correct way to do the work. Likewise, if participants are doing a good or exceptional job, let them know.

- **Encourage participants to take notes.** There will be times throughout the workshops when participants come across great insights and ideas. They need to be ready to capture and document them for later use. The action plans provided in these workshops include space for note taking.

- **Don't skip debriefing.** Debriefing the activities reveals whether participants have understood the concepts and can help take the learning to a deeper level. It also helps them internalize the learning and see the value in it.

- **Make it practical.** Try to understand when and how your participants will be using what they are learning in the workshop. Help them to connect what they are learning to what they do back in their jobs. Remember that project management is not about how many processes you perform; it is about performing the right processes for your project.

At the Close of the Workshop

Many things come together at the end of your workshop. Be sure to allow enough time to discuss next steps. Consider implementing some of these other ideas to support and ensure follow-up:

- **Close well:** I like to use what I call "mini closings" in my workshops. Throughout the workshop at important milestones, I close a learning module by summarizing what was discussed and give participants a chance to plan next actions or goals. This is especially important at the end of the workshop. Discuss what great managers do so that each person begins to develop a picture in their mind of themselves performing as a great project manager. Help them visualize that image along with the specific steps to get there.

- **Connect participants with fellow learners.** Encourage participants to connect with each other to form learning communities or study groups. There are a number of tools available to create learning communities that are easy to use and low cost. You can help by contributing an occasional article, shortcut, great idea, or whitepaper. One of the largest IT companies in the world uses my training, and each "class" forms a study group afterward. They use lunch-and-learn sessions to share ideas on application or successes with the entire team. Guest speakers from within the company (those who have already gotten their certification) are asked to share their experiences.

- **Push practice.** The old adage that practice makes perfect is based in real-world experience and holds true especially for learning. Challenge participants to practice or employ one new template, process, or technique each day or each week. Encourage them to add a reminder to their calendars so that they don't forget once they are busy back at work.

- **Remove roadblocks and barriers.** Every new change, technique, method, and process will throw up potential barriers or roadblocks that can prevent learners from succeeding. If you are in a position to influence any of these barriers, do it. Partner with human resources and participants' managers to mitigate problems. Encourage your learners to become champions of roadblock removal for themselves, their teams, and others in the organization.

- **Encourage mentoring.** Mentoring is an integral part of talent development, especially for project management. Mentors willing to share their experience, time, and successes with others can be transformative influences on new project managers. Mentoring maintains consistency, transitions leadership, and provides a safe and usable path to knowledge and information. Encourage your participants to identify a mentor within the organization. Work with HR to identify top performers who might be willing to mentor and support new project managers and then help connect those mentors with your learners.

After the Workshop

It should be clear by now that follow-up and support for training starts before you enter the training room and to be truly effective extends long after the workshop ends.

One of the main roles of a project manager is to integrate the various organizations, groups, teams, and individuals that contribute to the success of any given project. There are many factors to consider with this diverse group of contributors. This means that project managers need to have a diverse set of skills to draw on when managing a project. The one-day workshop focused on developing six of these skills: communicating, leading, motivating, decision making, problem solving, and influencing. There is much more to learn about these and many other business skills. Professional skills that project managers may need to develop include but are not limited to the following:

- Coaching
- Contract management
- Critical thinking
- Cultural and other diversity training
- Emotional intelligence
- Meeting management
- Negotiating
- Time management
- Organization development
- Risk management
- Managing different generations in the workplace
- Team building.

Encourage participants to take advantage of any training offered on these and other topics to hone the multiple skills they need to be effective project managers. Guide them to resources that will add to their success. If a project manager works with people from other countries or cultures, for example, recommend the book *Kiss, Bow, or Shake Hands* (Morrison and Conaway 2013). If they need help with time management or productivity, recommend *Getting Things Done* (Allen 2001).

Figure 1-1 (in Chapter 1) listed helpful books, blogs, websites, and other resources to build your project management acumen. Consider sharing that list with your participants to help them build theirs. Share the Project Manager Toolkit from Chapter 14 in digital form to give participants a selection of templates they can use in their projects and teams. These valuable time-saving template tools will help project teams use project management processes more effectively.

Here are some additional ideas to follow up training *after* the workshop is done:

- **Make contact a priority.** Send a simple follow-up email to each of the participants with a new resource (tip, job aid, template, link to a great article) to reinforce one of the topics covered in the workshop. Or send a short quiz to sharpen up a project management topic. Make it fun by offering a prize for the first one to respond with all of the correct answers.

- **Leverage social media.** Tweet a question such as "Which skill did you use this week that really helped in managing a project?" Ask participants to share tips from their projects or post problems that they need ideas on how to solve.

- **Conduct a virtual book club.** Ask participants to read *The New One-Minute Manager* or other business skills resource and then share their favorite tips, ask questions, or comment on ideas using Facebook or an office intranet.

- **Schedule "check-ins" with your participants.** Touch base with participants one month after the workshop—virtually if they don't work in the same organization or location or in person if they do. Over lunch or a snack, celebrate the group's successes. Ask them to share their "wins," such as project cost savings, customer satisfaction memos, increased sales, successful delivery of a product, or a "good catch" made possible by project management processes. Social media, email, and intranet sites make it much easier to stay in touch with your participants. You will be surprised by the positive influence of an unsolicited email or note to a supervisor for an individual. It doesn't take long, and it pays huge dividends.

- **Don't forget MBWA.** Management by walking around is an effective technique for project managers—and it works for trainers too! Technology makes our jobs easier in many ways but nothing beats a quick in-person drop-in to see how people are doing, to answer questions, and to let them know that you continue to be invested in their success.

- **Create a short video or podcast.** If you have the facilities and resources available, create a short video or podcast about a specific topic and send it out to the participants as a topic refresher or to expand on a topic from the workshop. Once created, the videos or podcasts can be reused for other workshop follow-up. Over time, you could create a library of helpful resources to draw on for your learners.

- **Follow up with participants' supervisors and managers.** Four to six weeks after the workshop, contact the participants' supervisors to see how the participants are doing. Find out if they are seeing changes in behavior, language, and attitudes in one-on-one and team interactions and meetings. Mark your calendar so you remember to do this.

- **Enlist sponsors and managers to promote project management.** You've done some of the heavy lifting during the workshop; now you need help to keep up the momentum. Recruit sponsors to affirm the value of project management whenever they can internally. Ask managers to acknowledge project management accomplishments, successes, and wins through newsletters, blogs, internal intranet, and so on.

What to Do Next

Most learning occurs after the training session, when participants have a chance to use what they learned in the workshop. Remember these simple follow-up support methods as you plan to help participants keep their learning alive.

- **Be selective in what you decide to use.** You can't do everything, so decide which of these suggestions will provide the biggest impact for your learners (for example, you will need a different approach for a research firm than for a construction company).

- **Partner with sponsors and supervisors.** Make sure that the sponsors or supervisors understand their role in reinforcing learning. They can ensure their staff has opportunities to practice their new skills and gain recognition for their efforts when they succeed.

- **Determine what is and what isn't in your control.** You can give people support and tools but you can't force them to learn or make changes if they don't want to.

- **Stay in touch.** Social media, email, and intranet sites have made it so much easier to stay in touch with your participants. Become an expert in using technology to stay connected.

- **Don't forget WIIFM.** That is, what's in it for me? Yes you! As the facilitator you are learning too. If you're not, then it is time to try something different. What did you learn in the last workshop that you can apply to the next? What do you need to brush up on so you can be better prepared? What new activities, tools, or resources can you introduce to freshen up the workshop for the learners—and for yourself?

Additional Resources

This list gives a good mix of resources on training essentials for you as the facilitator and on project management for both you and your learners.

Training

Biech, E. (2005). *Training for Dummies*. Hoboken, NJ: Wiley.

Bozarth, J. (2008). *From Analysis to Evaluation: Tools, Tips, and Techniques for Trainers*. San Francisco: Pfeiffer.

Chapman, B. 2008. "Learning Technology Primer." In E. Biech, ed., *ASTD Handbook for Workplace Learning Professionals*. Alexandria, VA: ASTD Press.

Kirkpatrick, D.L., and J.D. Kirkpatrick. 2005. *Transferring Learning to Behavior*. San Francisco: Berrett-Koehler.

Robinson, D. (2013). *Training for Impact*. San Francisco: Pfeiffer.

Project Management and Interpersonal Skills

Allen, D. (2001). *Getting Things Done: The Art of Stress-Free Activity*. New York: Penguin.

Arora, M., and H. Baronikian. (2013). *Leadership in Project Management: Leading People and Projects to Success*. N.p.: Leadership Publishing House.

Blanchard, K., and S. Johnson. (2015). *The New One-Minute Manager*. New York: William Morrow.

Garrett, D. (2011). *Project Pain Reliever: A Just-In-Time Handbook for Anyone Managing Projects*. Fort Lauderdale, FL: J. Ross.

Highsmith, J. (2009). *Agile Project Management: Creating Innovative Products*, 2nd ed. Indianapolis, IN: Addison-Wesley.

Kerzner, H. (2013). *Project Management: A Systems Approach to Planning, Scheduling, and Controlling,* 11th ed. Hoboken, NJ: Wiley.

Morrison, T., and W.A. Conaway. (2015). *Kiss, Bow, or Shake Hands: The Bestselling Guide to Doing Business in More Than 60 Countries.* Avon, MA: Adams Media.

PMI. (2013). *A Guide to the Project Management Body of Knowledge: PMBOK® Guide.* Newtown Square, PA: PMI.

Thomas, W.H. (2014). *Templates for Managing Training Projects.* Alexandria, VA: ATD Press.

SECTION IV

WORKSHOP SUPPORTING DOCUMENTS AND ONLINE SUPPORT

Chapter 11

Learning Activities

What's in This Chapter

- 22 learning activities for use in the workshop sessions
- Complete step-by-step instructions for conducting the learning activities

---

To facilitate adult learning, learning activities take place regularly throughout the workshops. Their purpose is to challenge and engage learners by breaking up any monotony, providing stimulation for different types of learners, and helping them actively acquire new knowledge. Such activities enliven and invigorate the experience, and they help learning "stick."

Each learning activity provides detailed information about learning objectives, materials required, timeframe, step-by-step instructions, variations, and debriefing questions if required. Use the following instructions to prepare your workshop agenda, identify and gather materials needed, and successfully guide learners through the activity. The following learning activities provide various experiences to offer your participants in support of the topics covered in the workshop. See Chapter 15 for information on how to download these and other workshop support materials provided with this book.

Learning Activities Included in *Project Management Training*

Learning Activity 1: My Project Management Story

Learning Activity 2: Create a Project Charter

Learning Activity 3: Create a Stakeholder Register

Learning Activity 4: Create a Scope Statement

Learning Activity 5: Communication Interference

Learning Activity 6: Create a Simple WBS

Learning Activity 7: Create a Schedule Management Plan

Learning Activity 8: Create a Human Resource Plan

Learning Activity 9: Create a Contract Award

Learning Activity 10: Process Flowcharting Exercise

Learning Activity 11: Risk Categorization Exercise

Learning Activity 12: Matrix Game: Communication 101

Learning Activity 13: Create a Quality Management Plan

Learning Activity 14: Interpersonal Skills Quick Assessment

Learning Activity 15: Action Planning

Learning Activity 16: Bumper Sticker Communication Tips

Learning Activity 17: Leadership Skills: Manager or Leader?

Learning Activity 18: Inspirational Leader

Learning Activity 19: MBWA Exercise

Learning Activity 20: Motivators and De-motivators

Learning Activity 21: Problem-Solving Exercise

Learning Activity 22: Are You a Good Listener?

PROJECT MANAGEMENT training

Learning Activity 1: My Project Management Story

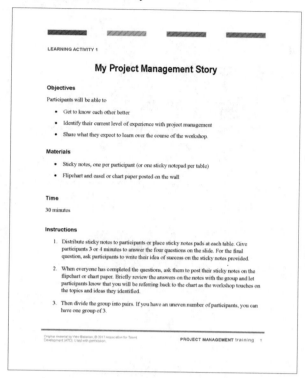

LEARNING ACTIVITY 1

My Project Management Story

Objectives

Participants will be able to

- Get to know each other better
- Identify their current level of experience with project management
- Share what they expect to learn over the course of the workshop.

Materials

- Sticky notes, one per participant (or one sticky notepad per table)
- Flipchart and easel or chart paper posted on the wall

Time

30 minutes

Instructions

1. Distribute sticky notes to participants or place sticky notes pads at each table. Give participants 3 or 4 minutes to answer the four questions on the slide. For the final question, ask participants to write their idea of success on the sticky notes provided.

2. When everyone has completed the questions, ask them to post their sticky notes on the flipchart or chart paper. Briefly review the answers on the notes with the group and let participants know that you will be referring back to the chart as the workshop touches on the topics and ideas they identified.

3. Then divide the group into pairs. If you have an uneven number of participants, you can have one group of 3.

Original material by Vivo Bielakran. © 2017 Association for Talent Development (ATD). Used with permission.

PROJECT MANAGEMENT training   1

Learning Activity 1: My Project Management Story, *continued*

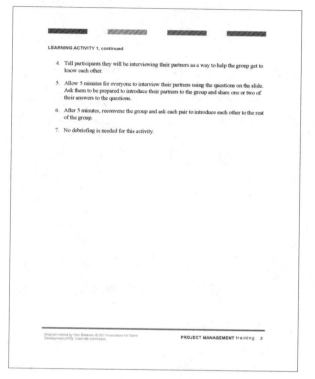

LEARNING ACTIVITY 1, continued

4. Tell participants they will be interviewing their partners as a way to help the group get to know each other.

5. Allow 5 minutes for everyone to interview their partners using the questions on the slide. Ask them to be prepared to introduce their partners to the group and share one or two of their answers to the questions.

6. After 5 minutes, reconvene the group and ask each pair to introduce each other to the rest of the group.

7. No debriefing is needed for this activity.

Original material by Vivo Bielakran. © 2017 Association for Talent Development (ATD). Used with permission.

PROJECT MANAGEMENT training   2

Learning Activity 2: Create a Project Charter

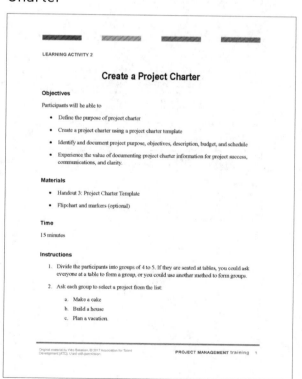

LEARNING ACTIVITY 2

Create a Project Charter

Objectives

Participants will be able to

- Define the purpose of project charter
- Create a project charter using a project charter template
- Identify and document project purpose, objectives, description, budget, and schedule
- Experience the value of documenting project charter information for project success, communications, and clarity.

Materials

- Handout 3: Project Charter Template
- Flipchart and markers (optional)

Time

15 minutes

Instructions

1. Divide the participants into groups of 4 to 5. If they are seated at tables, you could ask everyone at a table to form a group, or you could use another method to form groups.

2. Ask each group to select a project from the list:

   a. Make a cake

   b. Build a house

   c. Plan a vacation.

Original material by Vivo Bielakran. © 2017 Association for Talent Development (ATD). Used with permission.

PROJECT MANAGEMENT training   1

Learning Activity 2: Create a Project Charter, *continued*

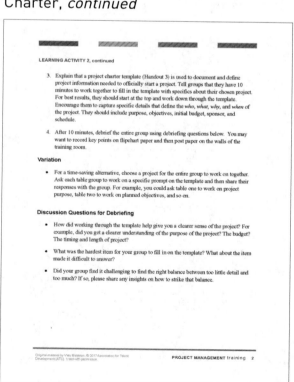

LEARNING ACTIVITY 2, continued

3. Explain that a project charter template (Handout 3) is used to document and define project information needed to officially start a project. Tell groups that they have 10 minutes to work together to fill in the template with specifics about their chosen project. For best results, they should start at the top and work down through the template. Encourage them to capture specific details that define the *who, what, why,* and *when* of the project. They should include purpose, objectives, initial budget, sponsor, and schedule.

4. After 10 minutes, debrief the entire group using debriefing questions below. You may want to record key points on flipchart paper and then post paper on the walls of the training room.

Variation

- For a time-saving alternative, choose a project for the entire group to work on together. Ask each table group to work on a specific prompt on the template and then share their responses with the group. For example, you could ask table one to work on project purpose, table two to work on planned objectives, and so on.

Discussion Questions for Debriefing

- How did working through the template help give you a clearer sense of the project? For example, did you get a clearer understanding of the purpose of the project? The budget? The timing and length of project?

- What was the hardest item for your group to fill in on the template? What about the item made it difficult to answer?

- Did your group find it challenging to find the right balance between too little detail and too much? If so, please share any insights on how to strike that balance.

Original material by Vivo Bielakran. © 2017 Association for Talent Development (ATD). Used with permission.

PROJECT MANAGEMENT training   2

Learning Activity 3: Create a Stakeholder Register

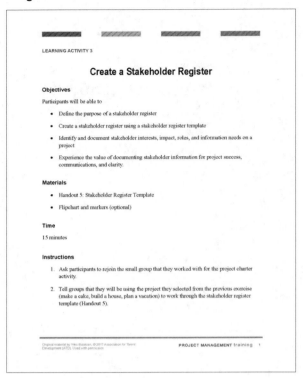

Learning Activity 3: Create a Stakeholder Register, *continued*

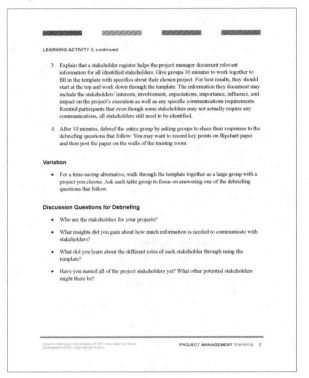

Learning Activity 4: Create a Scope Statement

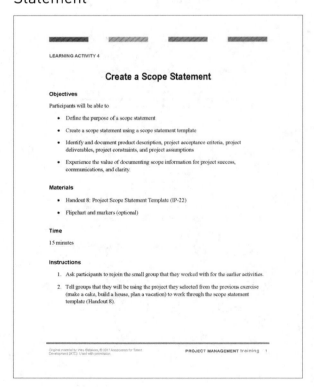

Learning Activity 4: Create a Scope Statement, *continued*

Learning Activity 5: Communication Interference

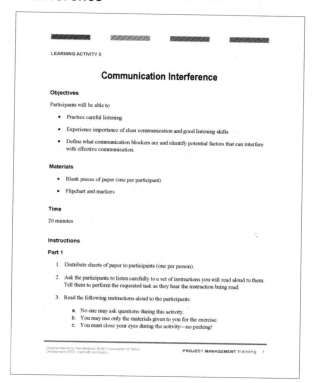

LEARNING ACTIVITY 5

Communication Interference

Objectives

Participants will be able to

- Practice careful listening

- Experience importance of clear communication and good listening skills

- Define what communication blockers are and identify potential factors that can interfere with effective communication.

Materials

- Blank pieces of paper (one per participant)

- Flipchart and markers

Time

20 minutes

Instructions

Part 1

1. Distribute sheets of paper to participants (one per person).

2. Ask the participants to listen carefully to a set of instructions you will read aloud to them. Tell them to perform the requested task as they hear the instruction being read.

3. Read the following instructions aloud to the participants:

    a. No one may ask questions during this activity.

    b. You may use only the materials given to you for the exercise.

    c. You must close your eyes during the activity—no peeking!

Learning Activity 5: Communication Interference, *continued*

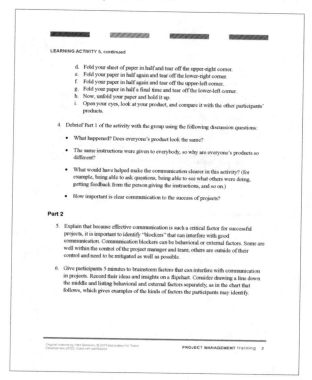

LEARNING ACTIVITY 5, continued

    d. Fold your sheet of paper in half and tear off the upper-right corner.

    e. Fold your paper in half again and tear off the lower-right corner.

    f. Fold your paper in half again and tear off the upper-left corner.

    g. Fold your paper in half a final time and tear off the lower-left corner.

    h. Now, unfold your paper and hold it up.

    i. Open your eyes, look at your product, and compare it with the other participants' products.

4. Debrief Part 1 of the activity with the group using the following discussion questions:

    - What happened? Does everyone's product look the same?

    - The same instructions were given to everybody, so why are everyone's products so different?

    - What would have helped make the communication clearer in this activity? (for example, being able to ask questions, being able to see what others were doing, getting feedback from the person giving the instructions, and so on.)

    - How important is clear communication to the success of projects?

Part 2

5. Explain that because effective communication is such a critical factor for successful projects, it is important to identify "blockers" that can interfere with good communication. Communication blockers can be behavioral or external factors. Some are well within the control of the project manager and team; others are outside of their control and need to be mitigated as well as possible.

6. Give participants 5 minutes to brainstorm factors that can interfere with communication in projects. Record their ideas and insights on a flipchart. Consider drawing a line down the middle and listing behavioral and external factors separately, as in the chart that follows, which gives examples of the kinds of factors the participants may identify.

Learning Activity 5: Communication Interference, *continued*

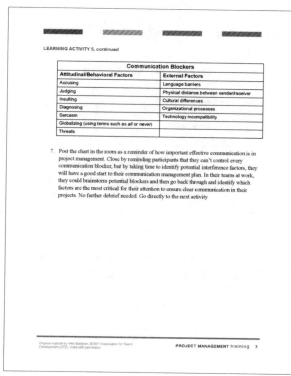

LEARNING ACTIVITY 5, continued

Communication Blockers	
Attitudinal/Behavioral Factors	**External Factors**
Accusing	Language barriers
Judging	Physical distance between sender/receiver
Insulting	Cultural differences
Diagnosing	Organizational processes
Sarcasm	Technology incompatibility
Globalizing (using terms such as *all* or *never*)	
Threats	

7. Post the chart in the room as a reminder of how important effective communication is in project management. Close by reminding participants that they can't control every communication blocker, but by taking time to identify potential interference factors, they will have a good start to their communication management plan. In their teams at work, they could brainstorm potential blockers and then go back through and identify which factors are the most critical for their attention to ensure clear communication in their projects. No further debrief needed. Go directly to the next activity.

Learning Activity 6: Create a Simple WBS

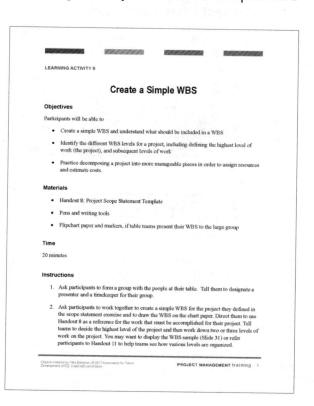

LEARNING ACTIVITY 6

Create a Simple WBS

Objectives

Participants will be able to

- Create a simple WBS and understand what should be included in a WBS

- Identify the different WBS levels for a project, including defining the highest level of work (the project), and subsequent levels of work

- Practice decomposing a project into more manageable pieces in order to assign resources and estimate costs.

Materials

- Handout 8: Project Scope Statement Template

- Pens and writing tools

- Flipchart paper and markers, if table teams present their WBS to the large group

Time

20 minutes

Instructions

1. Ask participants to form a group with the people at their table. Tell them to designate a presenter and a timekeeper for their group.

2. Ask participants to work together to create a simple WBS for the project they defined in the scope statement exercise and to draw the WBS on the chart paper. Direct them to use Handout 8 as a reference for the work that must be accomplished for their project. Tell teams to decide the highest level of the project and then work down two or three levels of work on the project. You may want to display the WBS sample (Slide 31) or refer participants to Handout 11 to help teams see how various levels are organized.

Learning Activity 6: Create a Simple WBS, *continued*

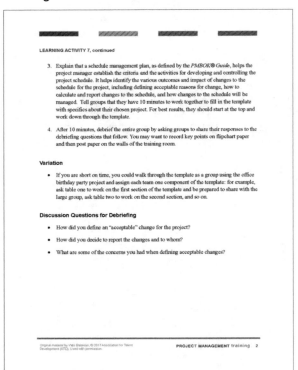

LEARNING ACTIVITY 6, continued

3. Tell them they will have 10 minutes in total to create the WBS and help their chosen spokesperson prepare to present their WBS to the group. Task their timekeepers with keeping track of time so that they complete the WBS in the time allotted.

4. After 10 minutes, call time and ask groups to present their WBS charts to the group.

5. Lead a debrief of the activity using the discussion questions below. Encourage groups to ask each other questions about their presentations.

Variations

- If you have extra time, you could allow each team to select a different project for creating the WBS. You will, however, want to "approve" their projects to make sure that the projects they have chosen are simple enough to complete the WBS creation in the time allotted.

- If you are running short on time, create a WBS together as a large group for a project you choose. I suggest using the office birthday party project. Ask teams to identify the highest level of work on the project, the next level, and then the next level after that.

Discussion Questions for Debriefing

- What was the highest level of work for the project?

- What was the next level down and so on?

- What are some of the concerns you had deciding in what work to include in the next level down?

- How does breaking the work into small packages help you to better identify what needs to be done and estimate the work costs?

Original material by Vlikx Bielakian, © 2017 Association for Talent Development (ATD). Used with permission. PROJECT MANAGEMENT training 2

Learning Activity 7: Create a Schedule Management Plan

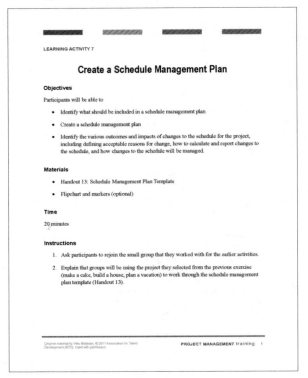

LEARNING ACTIVITY 7

Create a Schedule Management Plan

Objectives

Participants will be able to

- Identify what should be included in a schedule management plan

- Create a schedule management plan

- Identify the various outcomes and impacts of changes to the schedule for the project, including defining acceptable reasons for change, how to calculate and report changes to the schedule, and how changes to the schedule will be managed.

Materials

- Handout 13: Schedule Management Plan Template

- Flipchart and markers (optional)

Time

20 minutes

Instructions

1. Ask participants to rejoin the small group that they worked with for the earlier activities.

2. Explain that groups will be using the project they selected from the previous exercise (make a cake, build a house, plan a vacation) to work through the schedule management plan template (Handout 13).

Original material by Vikx Bielakian, © 2017 Association for Talent Development (ATD). Used with permission. PROJECT MANAGEMENT training 1

Learning Activity 7: Create a Schedule Management Plan, *continued*

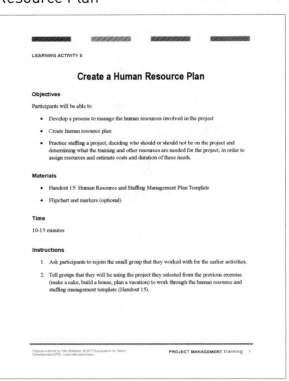

LEARNING ACTIVITY 7, continued

3. Explain that a schedule management plan, as defined by the *PMBOK® Guide*, helps the project manager establish the criteria and the activities for developing and controlling the project schedule. It helps identify the various outcomes and impact of changes to the schedule for the project, including defining acceptable reasons for change, how to calculate and report changes to the schedule, and how changes to the schedule will be managed. Tell groups that they have 10 minutes to work together to fill in the template with specifics about their chosen project. For best results, they should start at the top and work down through the template.

4. After 10 minutes, debrief the entire group by asking groups to share their responses to the debriefing questions that follow. You may want to record key points on flipchart paper and then post paper on the walls of the training room.

Variation

- If you are short on time, you could walk through the template as a group using the office birthday party project and assign each team one component of the template: for example, ask table one to work on the first section of the template and be prepared to share with the large group, ask table two to work on the second section, and so on.

Discussion Questions for Debriefing

- How did you define an "acceptable" change for the project?

- How did you decide to report the changes and to whom?

- What are some of the concerns you had when defining acceptable changes?

Original material by Vikx Bielakian, © 2017 Association for Talent Development (ATD). Used with permission. PROJECT MANAGEMENT training 2

Learning Activity 8: Create a Human Resource Plan

LEARNING ACTIVITY 8

Create a Human Resource Plan

Objectives

Participants will be able to

- Develop a process to manage the human resources involved in the project

- Create human resource plan

- Practice staffing a project, deciding who should or should not be on the project and determining what the training and other resources are needed for the project, in order to assign resources and estimate costs and duration of these needs.

Materials

- Handout 15: Human Resource and Staffing Management Plan Template

- Flipchart and markers (optional)

Time

10-15 minutes

Instructions

1. Ask participants to rejoin the small group that they worked with for the earlier activities.

2. Tell groups that they will be using the project they selected from the previous exercise (make a cake, build a house, plan a vacation) to work through the human resource and staffing management template (Handout 15).

Original material by Vikx Bielakian, © 2017 Association for Talent Development (ATD). Used with permission. PROJECT MANAGEMENT training 1

PROJECT MANAGEMENT training

Learning Activity 8: Create a Human Resource Plan, *continued*

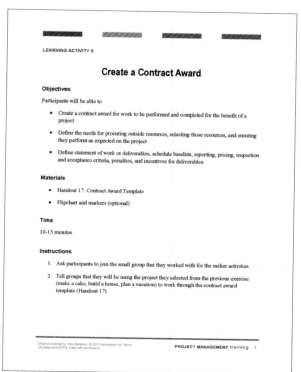

LEARNING ACTIVITY 8, continued

3. Explain that a human resource management plan helps the project manager define roles and responsibilities, how resources will be acquired, time when each resource will be needed, any specialized training requirements, and staffing plans. Tell groups that they have 10 minutes to work together to fill in the template with specifics about their chosen project. For best results, they should start at the top and work down through the template.

4. After 10 minutes, debrief the entire group by asking groups to share their responses to the debriefing questions that follow. You may want to record key points on flipchart paper and then post paper on the walls of the training room.

Variation

• If you are running short on time, you could walk through the template as a group using the project of an office birthday party and assign each team one component of the template: for example, ask table one to work on the first section of the template and be prepared to share with the large group; ask table two to work on the second section and so on.

Discussion Questions for Debriefing

• What types of resources are needed for the project?

• What type of training would they need to be successful?

• What are some of the concerns you had when deciding on resources?

• If you did not have the resources you needed in-house, how would you acquire them?

Original material by Vies Balakian, © 2017 Association for Talent Development (ATD). Used with permission.   **PROJECT MANAGEMENT** training   2

Learning Activity 9: Create a Contract Award

LEARNING ACTIVITY 9

Create a Contract Award

Objectives

Participants will be able to

• Create a contract award for work to be performed and completed for the benefit of a project

• Define the needs for procuring outside resources, selecting those resources, and ensuring they perform as expected on the project

• Define statement of work or deliverables, schedule baseline, reporting, pricing, inspection and acceptance criteria, penalties, and incentives for deliverables.

Materials

• Handout 17: Contract Award Template

• Flipchart and markers (optional)

Time

10-15 minutes

Instructions

1. Ask participants to join the small group that they worked with for the earlier activities.

2. Tell groups that they will be using the project they selected from the previous exercise (make a cake, build a house, plan a vacation) to work through the contract award template (Handout 17).

Original material by Vies Balakian, © 2017 Association for Talent Development (ATD). Used with permission.   **PROJECT MANAGEMENT** training   1

Learning Activity 9: Create a Contract Award, *continued*

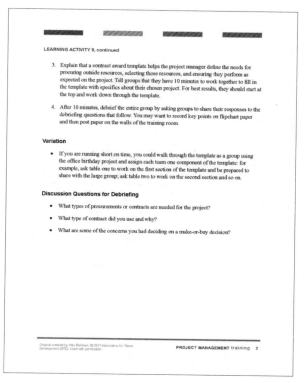

LEARNING ACTIVITY 9, continued

3. Explain that a contract award template helps the project manager define the needs for procuring outside resources, selecting those resources, and ensuring they perform as expected on the project. Tell groups that they have 10 minutes to work together to fill in the template with specifics about their chosen project. For best results, they should start at the top and work down through the template.

4. After 10 minutes, debrief the entire group by asking groups to share their responses to the debriefing questions that follow. You may want to record key points on flipchart paper and then post paper on the walls of the training room.

Variation

• If you are running short on time, you could walk through the template as a group using the office birthday project and assign each team one component of the template: for example, ask table one to work on the first section of the template and be prepared to share with the large group; ask table two to work on the second section and so on.

Discussion Questions for Debriefing

• What types of procurements or contracts are needed for the project?

• What type of contract did you use and why?

• What are some of the concerns you had deciding on a make-or-buy decision?

Original material by Vies Balakian, © 2017 Association for Talent Development (ATD). Used with permission.   **PROJECT MANAGEMENT** training   2

Learning Activity 10: Process Flowcharting Exercise

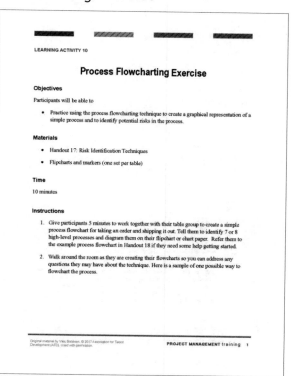

LEARNING ACTIVITY 10

Process Flowcharting Exercise

Objectives

Participants will be able to

• Practice using the process flowcharting technique to create a graphical representation of a simple process and to identify potential risks in the process.

Materials

• Handout 17: Risk Identification Techniques

• Flipcharts and markers (one set per table)

Time

10 minutes

Instructions

1. Give participants 5 minutes to work together with their table group to create a simple process flowchart for taking an order and shipping it out. Tell them to identify 7 or 8 high-level processes and diagram them on their flipchart or chart paper. Refer them to the example process flowchart in Handout 18 if they need some help getting started.

2. Walk around the room as they are creating their flowcharts so you can address any questions they may have about the technique. Here is a sample of one possible way to flowchart the process.

Original material by Vies Balakian, © 2017 Association for Talent Development (ATD). Used with permission.   **PROJECT MANAGEMENT** training   1

Learning Activity 10: Process Flowcharting Exercise, *continued*

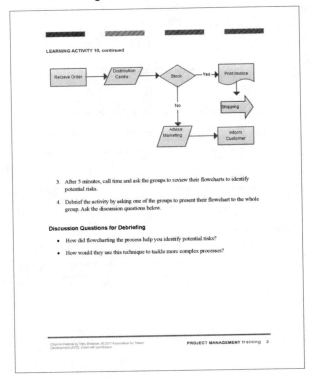

3. After 5 minutes, call time and ask the groups to review their flowcharts to identify potential risks.

4. Debrief the activity by asking one of the groups to present their flowchart to the whole group. Ask the discussion questions below.

Discussion Questions for Debriefing

- How did flowcharting the process help you identify potential risks?
- How would they use this technique to tackle more complex processes?

Learning Activity 11: Risk Categorization Exercise

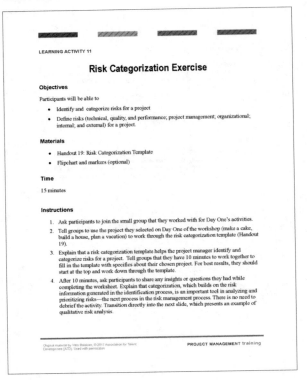

Risk Categorization Exercise

Objectives

Participants will be able to

- Identify and categorize risks for a project
- Define risks (technical, quality, and performance; project management; organizational; internal; and external) for a project.

Materials

- Handout 19: Risk Categorization Template
- Flipchart and markers (optional)

Time

15 minutes

Instructions

1. Ask participants to join the small group that they worked with for Day One's activities.

2. Tell groups to use the project they selected on Day One of the workshop (make a cake, build a house, plan a vacation) to work through the risk categorization template (Handout 19).

3. Explain that a risk categorization template helps the project manager identify and categorize risks for a project. Tell groups that they have 10 minutes to work together to fill in the template with specifics about their chosen project. For best results, they should start at the top and work down through the template.

4. After 10 minutes, ask participants to share any insights or questions they had while completing the worksheet. Explain that categorization, which builds on the risk information generated in the identification process, is an important tool in analyzing and prioritizing risks—the next process in the risk management process. There is no need to debrief the activity. Transition directly into the next slide, which presents an example of qualitative risk analysis.

Learning Activity 12: Matrix Game: Communication 101

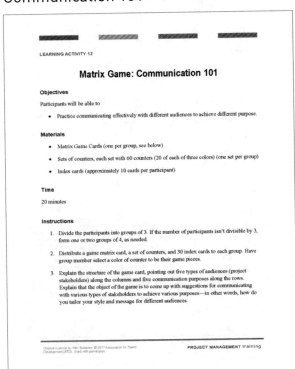

Matrix Game: Communication 101

Objectives

Participants will be able to

- Practice communicating effectively with different audiences to achieve different purpose.

Materials

- Matrix Game Cards (one per group, see below)
- Sets of counters, each set with 60 counters (20 of each of three colors) (one set per group)
- Index cards (approximately 10 cards per participant)

Time

20 minutes

Instructions

1. Divide the participants into groups of 3. If the number of participants isn't divisible by 3, form one or two groups of 4, as needed.

2. Distribute a game matrix card, a set of counters, and 30 index cards to each group. Have group member select a color of counter to be their game pieces.

3. Explain the structure of the game card, pointing out five types of audiences (project stakeholders) along the columns and five communication purposes along the rows. Explain that the object of the game is to come up with suggestions for communicating with various types of stakeholders to achieve various purposes—in other words, how do you tailor your style and message for different audiences.

Learning Activity 12: Matrix Game: Communication 101, *continued*

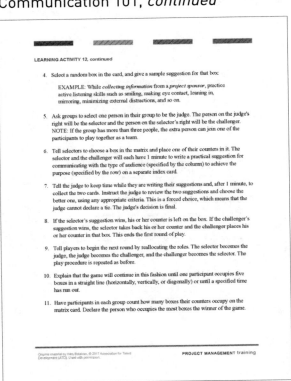

4. Select a random box in the card, and give a sample suggestion for that box.

> EXAMPLE: While *collecting information* from a *project sponsor*, practice active listening skills such as smiling, making eye contact, leaning in, mirroring, minimizing external distractions, and so on.

5. Ask groups to select one person in their group to be the judge. The person on the judge's right will be the selector and the person on the selector's right will be the challenger. NOTE: If the group has more than three people, the extra person can join one of the participants to play together as a team.

6. Tell selectors to choose a box in the matrix and place one of their counters in it. The selector and the challenger will each have 1 minute to write a practical suggestion for communicating with the type of audience (specified by the column) to achieve the purpose (specified by the row) on a separate index card.

7. Tell the judge to keep time while they are writing their suggestions and, after 1 minute, to collect the two cards. Instruct the judge to review the two suggestions and choose the better one, using any appropriate criteria. This is a forced choice, which means that the judge cannot declare a tie. The judge's decision is final.

8. If the selector's suggestion wins, his or her counter is left on the box. If the challenger's suggestion wins, the selector takes back his or her counter and the challenger places his or her counter in that box. This ends the first round of play.

9. Tell players to begin the next round by reallocating the roles. The selector becomes the judge, the judge becomes the challenger, and the challenger becomes the selector. The play procedure is repeated as before.

10. Explain that the game will continue in this fashion until one participant occupies five boxes in a straight line (horizontally, vertically, or diagonally) or until a specified time has run out.

11. Have participants in each group count how many boxes their counters occupy on the matrix card. Declare the person who occupies the most boxes the winner of the game.

Learning Activity 12: Matrix Game: Communication 101, *continued*

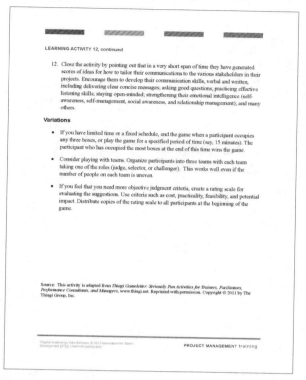

LEARNING ACTIVITY 12, continued

12. Close the activity by pointing out that in a very short span of time they have generated scores of ideas for how to tailor their communications to the various stakeholders in their projects. Encourage them to develop their communication skills, verbal and written, including delivering clear concise messages; asking good questions; practicing effective listening skills; staying open-minded; strengthening their emotional intelligence (self-awareness, self-management, social awareness, and relationship management); and many others.

Variations

- If you have limited time or a fixed schedule, end the game when a participant occupies any three boxes, or play the game for a specified period of time (say, 15 minutes). The participant who has occupied the most boxes at the end of this time wins the game.

- Consider playing with teams. Organize participants into three teams with each team taking one of the roles (judge, selector, or challenger). This works well even if the number of people on each team is uneven.

- If you feel that you need more objective judgment criteria, create a rating scale for evaluating the suggestions. Use criteria such as cost, practicality, feasibility, and potential impact. Distribute copies of the rating scale to all participants at the beginning of the game.

Source: This activity is adapted from *Thiagi Gameletter: Seriously Fun Activities for Trainers, Facilitators, Performance Consultants, and Managers*, www.thiagi.net. Reprinted with permission. Copyright © 2011 by The Thiagi Group, Inc.

Original material by Wes Balakian. © 2017 Association for Talent Development (ATD). Used with permission.   **PROJECT MANAGEMENT** training

Learning Activity 12: Matrix Game: Communication 101, *continued*

LEARNING ACTIVITY 12, Activity Resource

Matrix Game Card

	Project Sponsor	Project Team Member	Senior Management	Employee	Supplier
Inform					
Collect Information					
Persuade					
Build Rapport					
Instruct					

Original material by Wes Balakian. © 2017 Association for Talent Development (ATD). Used with permission.   **PROJECT MANAGEMENT** training

Learning Activity 13: Create a Quality Management Plan

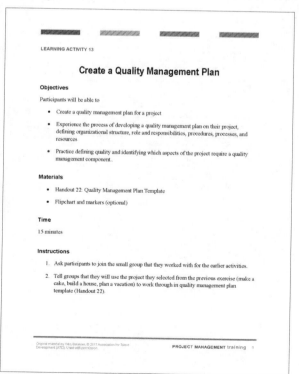

LEARNING ACTIVITY 13

Create a Quality Management Plan

Objectives

Participants will be able to

- Create a quality management plan for a project

- Experience the process of developing a quality management plan on their project, defining organizational structure, role and responsibilities, procedures, processes, and resources

- Practice defining quality and identifying which aspects of the project require a quality management component.

Materials

- Handout 22: Quality Management Plan Template

- Flipchart and markers (optional)

Time

15 minutes

Instructions

1. Ask participants to join the small group that they worked with for the earlier activities.

2. Tell groups that they will use the project they selected from the previous exercise (make a cake, build a house, plan a vacation) to work through in quality management plan template (Handout 22).

Original material by Wes Balakian. © 2017 Association for Talent Development (ATD). Used with permission.   **PROJECT MANAGEMENT** training   1

Learning Activity 13: Create a Quality Management Plan, *continued*

LEARNING ACTIVITY 13, continued

3. Explain that a quality management plan helps the project manager define how the project management team will implement the performing organization's quality policy. Tell groups that they have 10 minutes to work together to fill in the template with specifics about their chosen project. The information they document may include what will be required in the following areas to manage quality: organizational structure, role and responsibilities, procedures, processes, and resources. For best results, they should start at the top and work down through the template.

4. After 10 minutes, debrief the entire group by asking groups to share their responses to the debriefing questions that follow. You may want to record key points on flipchart paper and then post paper on the walls of the training room.

Variation

- If time is an issue, you could walk through the template as a group using the office birthday party project (or other simple project you choose) and assign each team one component of the template: for example, ask table one to work on the first section of the template and be prepared to share with the large group; ask table two to work on the second section and so on.

Discussion Questions for Debriefing

- What types of quality issues were hard to identify for the project?

- Where you able to identify roles and responsibilities for those involved in quality management plan?

- What are some of the concerns you had deciding who was going to perform the work?

- Did you find it hard to identify quality management without knowing what the stakeholders would define as acceptable quality?

Original material by Wes Balakian. © 2017 Association for Talent Development (ATD). Used with permission.   **PROJECT MANAGEMENT** training   2

Learning Activity 14: Interpersonal Skills Quick Assessment

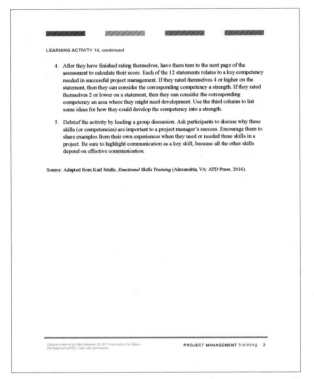

LEARNING ACTIVITY 14

Interpersonal Skills Quick Assessment

Objectives

Participants will be able to

- Identify interpersonal skill areas of strength and areas for potential development.

Materials

- Assessment 1: Interpersonal Skills Quick Assessment

Time

15 minutes

Instructions

1. Ask participants to turn to Assessment 1.

2. Explain the assessment instructions. Tell participants that they will rate themselves on the 12 statements in the assessment using a scale of 1 to 5, with 1 being never true and 5 being always true.

3. Let them know that the value of this assessment as a guide for personal development will be maximized if they solicit the feedback of others, especially on those statements where they may be somewhat uncertain about how to rate themselves. Encourage them to take a moment to reflect on each statement and decide whether or not their rating would benefit from someone else's feedback. If it would, they can circle the item number in the far left column as a reminder to seek feedback from others regarding this statement. Each statement is a potential opportunity to open up a conversation to gain valuable feedback.

Learning Activity 14: Interpersonal Skills Quick Assessment, *continued*

LEARNING ACTIVITY 14, continued

4. After they have finished rating themselves, have them turn to the next page of the assessment to calculate their score. Each of the 12 statements relates to a key competency needed in successful project management. If they rated themselves 4 or higher on the statement, then they can consider the corresponding competency a strength. If they rated themselves 2 or lower on a statement, then they can consider the corresponding competency an area where they might need development. Use the third column to list some ideas for how they could develop the competency into a strength.

5. Debrief the activity by leading a group discussion. Ask participants to discuss why these skills (or competencies) are important to a project manager's success. Encourage them to share examples from their own experiences when they used or needed these skills in a project. Be sure to highlight communication as a key skill, because all the other skills depend on effective communication.

Source: Adapted from Karl Mulle, *Emotional Skills Training* (Alexandria, VA: ATD Press, 2016).

Learning Activity 15: Action Planning

LEARNING ACTIVITY 15

Action Planning

Objectives

Participants will be able to

- Create alignment between the workshop content and the individual participant's development plan
- Connect with other participants to help support each other's learning goals.

Materials

- Handout 2: My Project Management Action Plan (use with two-day workshop)
- Index cards (two per participant)

Time

30 minutes

Instructions

1. Ask participants to take 10 minutes to review their action plans (choose appropriate handout) to identify what they will do to continue their project management learning back at their workplace. They have been doing this throughout the workshop, but now they have a chance to step back and review all five process groups and make notes. Encourage them to add details to make their learning goals SMART (specific, measurable, actionable, realistic, and timely).

2. Then ask participants to look over the list again and choose their top three goals.

3. Have them write their top three goals, their names, and their preferred methods of contact (email, telephone, or other) on two index cards (they are creating two identical cards, each with their goals, names, and contact information).

Learning Activity 15: Action Planning, *continued*

LEARNING ACTIVITY 15, continued

4. Explain that making changes can be challenging, and so it is important to find people who can help them sustain growth and change. Help participants make connections with others who are also working on project management goals by asking them to find a partner in the group. If you have an odd number of participants, you can pair up with one participant or allow one group of three. Tell participants to share their top three goals with their partners and then exchange one of their index cards with them.

5. Then have them pair up with a new partner and repeat the exchange process (step 4).

6. Now they each will have cards with goals and information for two fellow participants. Tell them that to support each other's project management journey, they will "check in" with their partners to share how they are doing with their learning goals and to see if there is anything they can do to help each other. Ask them to mark their calendars to follow up in two weeks' time. Let them know that you will send them a message to remind them to check in with each other. (Mark your own calendar at the same time so that you remember to send the reminder message.)

7. No further debrief is needed.

Learning Activity 16: Bumper Sticker Communication Tips

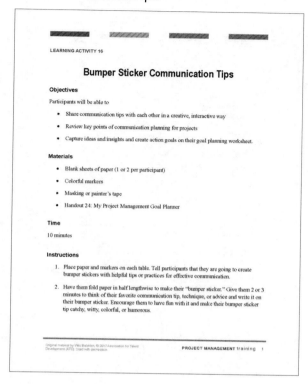

Learning Activity 16: Bumper Sticker Communication Tips, *continued*

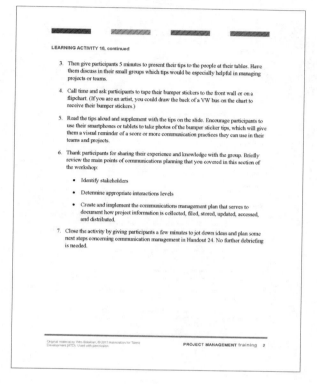

Learning Activity 17: Leadership Skills: Manager or Leader?

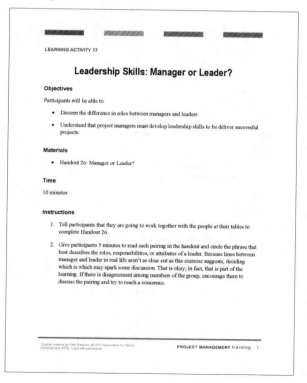

Learning Activity 17: Leadership Skills: Manager or Leader?, *continued*

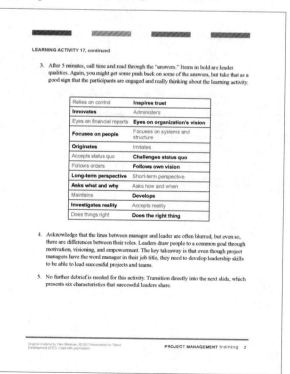

Learning Activity 18: Inspirational Leader

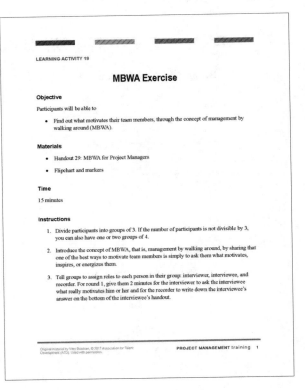

Learning Activity 19: MBWA Exercise

Learning Activity 19: MBWA Exercise, *continued*

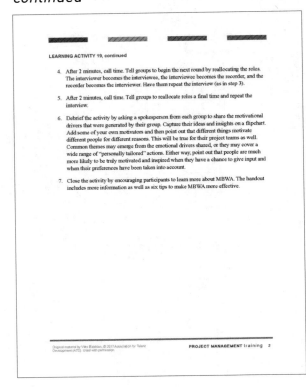

Learning Activity 20: Motivators and De-motivators

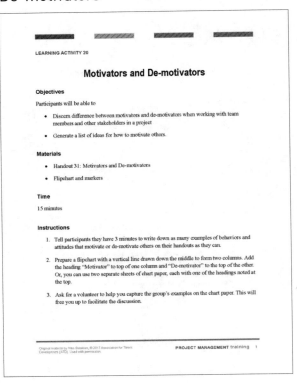

Learning Activity 20: Motivators and De-motivators, *continued*

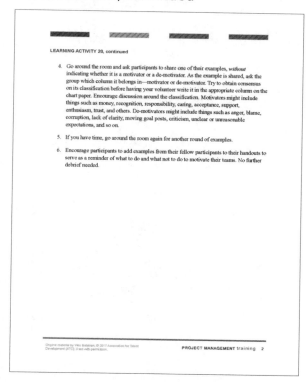

LEARNING ACTIVITY 20, continued

4. Go around the room and ask participants to share one of their examples, *without* indicating whether it is a motivator or a de-motivator. As the example is shared, ask the group which column it belongs in—motivator or de-motivator. Try to obtain consensus on its classification before having your volunteer write it in the appropriate column on the chart paper. Encourage discussion around the classification. Motivators might include things such as money, recognition, responsibility, caring, acceptance, support, enthusiasm, trust, and others. De-motivators might include things such as anger, blame, corruption, lack of clarity, moving goal posts, criticism, unclear or unreasonable expectations, and so on.

5. If you have time, go around the room again for another round of examples.

6. Encourage participants to add examples from their fellow participants to their handouts to serve as a reminder of what to do and what not to do to motivate their teams. No further debrief needed.

Original material by Vito Bialakian, © 2017 Association for Talent Development (ATD). Used with permission.

PROJECT MANAGEMENT training   2

Learning Activity 21: Problem-Solving Exercise

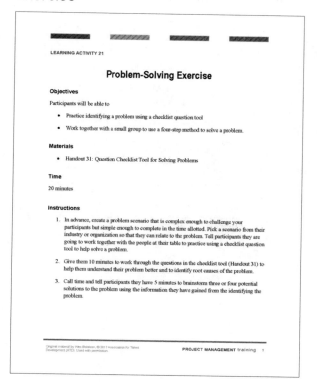

LEARNING ACTIVITY 21

Problem-Solving Exercise

Objectives

Participants will be able to

- Practice identifying a problem using a checklist question tool
- Work together with a small group to use a four-step method to solve a problem.

Materials

- Handout 31: Question Checklist Tool for Solving Problems

Time

20 minutes

Instructions

1. In advance, create a problem scenario that is complex enough to challenge your participants but simple enough to complete in the time allotted. Pick a scenario from their industry or organization so that they can relate to the problem. Tell participants they are going to work together with the people at their table to practice using a checklist question tool to help solve a problem.

2. Give them 10 minutes to work through the questions in the checklist tool (Handout 31) to help them understand their problem better and to identify root causes of the problem.

3. Call time and tell participants they have 5 minutes to brainstorm three or four potential solutions to the problem using the information they have gained from the identifying the problem.

Original material by Vito Bialakian, © 2017 Association for Talent Development (ATD). Used with permission.

PROJECT MANAGEMENT training   1

Learning Activity 21: Problem-Solving Exercise, *continued*

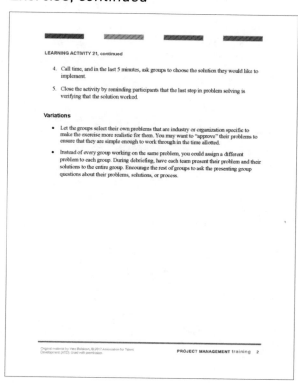

LEARNING ACTIVITY 21, continued

4. Call time, and in the last 5 minutes, ask groups to choose the solution they would like to implement.

5. Close the activity by reminding participants that the last step in problem solving is verifying that the solution worked.

Variations

- Let the groups select their own problems that are industry or organization specific to make the exercise more realistic for them. You may want to "approve" their problems to ensure that they are simple enough to work through in the time allotted.

- Instead of every group working on the same problem, you could assign a different problem to each group. During debriefing, have each team present their problem and their solutions to the entire group. Encourage the rest of groups to ask the presenting group questions about their problems, solutions, or process.

Original material by Vito Bialakian, © 2017 Association for Talent Development (ATD). Used with permission.

PROJECT MANAGEMENT training   2

Learning Activity 22: Are You a Good Listener?

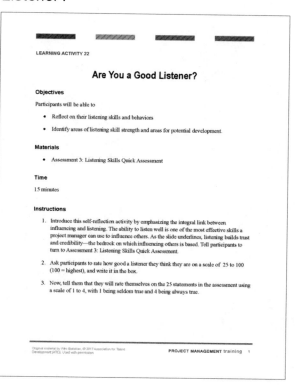

LEARNING ACTIVITY 22

Are You a Good Listener?

Objectives

Participants will be able to

- Reflect on their listening skills and behaviors
- Identify areas of listening skill strength and areas for potential development.

Materials

- Assessment 3: Listening Skills Quick Assessment

Time

15 minutes

Instructions

1. Introduce this self-reflection activity by emphasizing the integral link between influencing and listening. The ability to listen well is one of the most effective skills a project manager can use to influence others. As the slide underlines, listening builds trust and credibility—the bedrock on which influencing others is based. Tell participants to turn to Assessment 3: Listening Skills Quick Assessment.

2. Ask participants to rate how good a listener they think they are on a scale of 25 to 100 (100 = highest), and write it in the box.

3. Now, tell them that they will rate themselves on the 25 statements in the assessment using a scale of 1 to 4, with 1 being seldom true and 4 being always true.

Original material by Vito Bialakian, © 2017 Association for Talent Development (ATD). Used with permission.

PROJECT MANAGEMENT training   1

Learning Activity 22: Are You a Good Listener?, *continued*

4. After they have finished rating themselves, have them add up all their scores to come up with a total score. Scoring is as follows:

   75–100 = You're an excellent listener and communicator. Keep it up.

   50–74 = You're trying to be a good listener. Consider brushing up some of your listening skills.

   25–49 = Listening isn't one of your strong points. Spend serious time developing your listening skills.

5. Ask participants if they were surprised by their scores? How did their actual scores compare with their estimated scores?

6. Then explain that each of the 25 statements in the assessment relate to a key aspect of good listening. If they rated themselves 3 or 4 on the statement, they can consider that skill a strength. If they rated themselves 1 or 2 on a statement, they can consider it a skill they may need to develop. Have them pick three listening skills that they would like to work on and note actions they can take to become better listeners in that area.

7. This activity was meant as self-reflection and so no further debrief is needed.

8. Close by asking participants to add notes and next actions about influencing to their project management goal planners (Handout 25).

Original material by Mike Bishidan, © 2017 Association for Talent Development (ATD). Used with permission.

PROJECT MANAGEMENT training   2

Chapter 12
Assessments

What's in This Chapter

- Four assessments to use in the workshop sessions or as professional development
- Instructions on how and when to use the assessments

Assessments and evaluations are essential components of any workshop—before it begins, as it goes on, and when it concludes. To prepare an effective workshop for participants, you have to assess their needs and those of their organization. Although a formal needs assessment is outside the scope of this book, Chapter 5 provides information on how you can identify participant needs.

Using assessments during the workshop helps participants identify areas of strength and weakness, enabling them to capitalize on their strengths and improve their weaknesses to become more effective in the workplace. Assessments 1 and 3 will help participants reflect on their interpersonal skills and listening skills, respectively. Assessments can also be used during the workshop to check in on participants' learning so that you can make any needed adjustments as you go.

Assessment 2 provides a workshop evaluation that you can distribute at the end of your sessions to help you continually improve your workshop facilitation. Assessment 4: Facilitator Competencies provides an instrument to help you manage your professional development and increase the effectiveness of your training sessions. You can use this tool in several ways: as self-assessment, end-of-course feedback, observer feedback, or as a gauge for tracking professional growth with repeated ratings.

The assessments in this chapter provide instructions on how to complete the assessment and when to use it in the course of the workshop and an explanation of the assessment's purpose. See Chapter 15 for complete instructions on how to download the workshop support materials.

Assessments Included in *Project Management Training*

Assessment 1: Interpersonal Skills Quick Assessment

Assessment 2: Workshop Evaluation

Assessment 3: Listening Skills Quick Assessment

Assessment 4: Facilitator Competencies

Assessment 1: Interpersonal Skills Quick Assessment

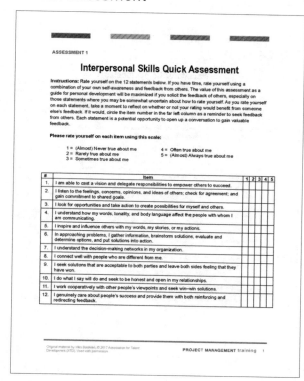

Assessment 1: Interpersonal Skills Quick Assessment, *continued*

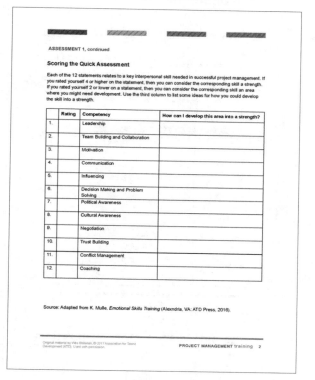

Assessment 2: Workshop Evaluation

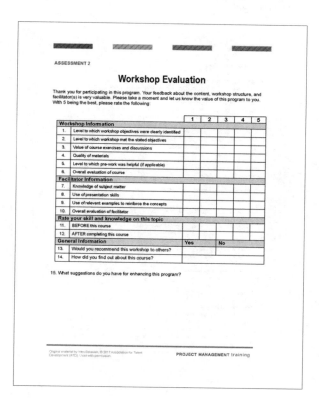

Assessment 3: Listening Skills Quick Assessment

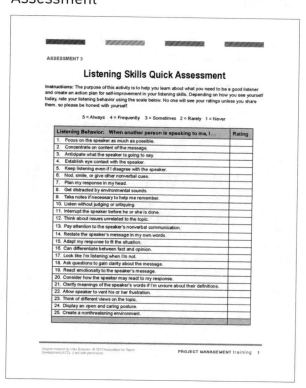

Assessment 3: Listening Skills Quick Assessment, *continued*

Scoring the Listening Assessment

Analysis: If you responded "always" (5), "frequently" (4), or "sometimes" (3) for items 3, 7, 8, 11, 12, 17, or 19, these may be areas in which you need to improve your listening skills, especially your focus on the speaker and how you filter information. You may also wish to address any of the remaining statements if you responded with "sometimes" (3), "rarely" (2), or "never" (1), particularly items 5, 6, 13, 14, 15, 20, and 23, which directly relate to providing feedback to the speaker effectively during a conversation.

Pick three listening skills that you would like to work on to develop into a strength and note actions you can take to become a better listener.

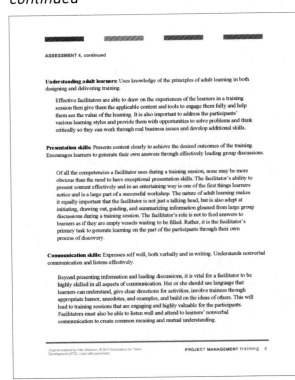

Listening Skill	How can I develop this skill into a strength?

Source: Adapted from Lisa Downs, *Listening Skills Training* (Alexandria, VA: ASTD Press, 2008).

Assessment 4: Facilitator Competencies

Facilitator Competencies

This assessment instrument will help you manage your own professional development and increase the effectiveness of your training sessions. You can use this instrument in the following ways:

Self-assessment. Use the assessment to rate yourself on the five-point scale, which will generate an overall profile and help determine the competency areas that are in the greatest need of improvement.

End-of-course feedback. Honest feedback from the training participants can lessen the possibility that facilitators deceive themselves about the 12 competencies. Trainees may not be able to rate the facilitator on all 12, so it may be necessary to ask the participants to rate only those they consider themselves qualified to address.

Observer feedback. Facilitators may observe each other's training sessions and provide highly useful information on the 12 competencies that are crucial to be effective in conducting training.

Repeat ratings. This assessment can be the basis of tracking professional growth on the competencies needed to be an effective facilitator. The repeat measure may be obtained as often as needed to gauge progress on action plans for improvement.

The Competencies

Facilitators are faced with challenges anytime they lead a training session. Many skills are necessary to help participants meet their learning needs and to ensure that the organization achieves its desired results for the training. This assessment contains a set of 12 important competencies that effective training requires. Not all seasoned facilitators have expertise in all of these competencies, but they may represent learning and growth areas for almost any facilitator.

Here is a detailed explanation of the importance of each of the dozen crucial elements of facilitator competence.

Assessment 4: Facilitator Competencies, *continued*

Understanding adult learners: Uses knowledge of the principles of adult learning in both designing and delivering training.

Effective facilitators are able to draw on the experiences of the learners in a training session then give them the applicable tools and tools to engage them fully and help them see the value of the learning. It is also important to address the participants' various learning styles and provide them with opportunities to solve problems and think critically so they can work through real business issues and develop additional skills.

Presentation skills: Presents content clearly to achieve the desired outcomes of the training. Encourages learners to generate their own answers through effectively leading group discussions.

Of all the competencies a facilitator uses during a training session, none may be more obvious than the need to have exceptional presentation skills. The facilitator's ability to present content effectively and in an entertaining way is one of the first things learners notice and is a large part of a successful workshop. The nature of adult learning makes it equally important that the facilitator is not just a talking head, but is also adept at initiating, drawing out, guiding, and summarizing information gleaned from large group discussions during a training session. The facilitator's role is not to feed answers to learners as if they are empty vessels waiting to be filled. Rather, it is the facilitator's primary task to generate learning on the part of the participants through their own process of discovery.

Communication skills: Expresses self well, both verbally and in writing. Understands nonverbal communication and listens effectively.

Beyond presenting information and leading discussions, it is vital for a facilitator to be highly skilled in all aspects of communication. Her or she should use language that learners can understand, give clear directions for activities, involve trainees through appropriate humor, anecdotes, and examples, and build on the ideas of others. This will lead to training sessions that are engaging and highly valuable for the participants. Facilitators must also be able to listen well and attend to learners' nonverbal communication to create common meaning and mutual understanding.

Assessment 4: Facilitator Competencies, *continued*

Emotional intelligence: Respects learners' viewpoints, knowledge, and experience. Recognizes and responds appropriately to others' feelings, attitudes, and concerns.

Because learners may have many different backgrounds, experience levels, and opinions in the same training sessions, facilitators must be able to handle a variety of situations and conversations well, and be sensitive to others' emotions. They must pay close attention to the dynamics in the room, be flexible enough to make immediate changes to activities during training to meet the needs of learners, and create an open and trusting learning environment. Attendees should feel comfortable expressing their opinions, asking questions, and participating in activities without fear of repercussion or disapproval. Monitoring learners' emotions during a training session also helps the facilitator gauge when it may be time to change gears if conflict arises, if discussion needs to be refocused on desired outcomes, or if there is a need to delve deeper into a topic to encourage further learning.

Training methods: Varies instructional approaches to address different learning styles and hold learners' interest.

All learners have preferred learning styles, and one of the keys to effective training facilitation is to use a variety of methods to address them. Some people are more visual ("see it") learners, and others are more auditory ("hear it") or kinesthetic ("do it") learners. An effective facilitator must be familiar with a variety of training methods to tap into each participant's style(s) and maintain interest during the training session. These methods may include such activities as small group activities, individual exercises, case studies, role plays, simulations, and games.

Subject matter expertise: Possesses deep knowledge of training content and applicable experience to draw upon.

Facilitators must have solid background knowledge of the training topic at hand and be able to share related experience to help learners connect theory to real-world scenarios. Anecdotes and other examples to illustrate how the training content relates to participants' circumstances and work can enhance the learning experience and encourage learners to apply the information and also to use the tools they have been given. It is also crucial that facilitators know their topics inside and out, so they can answer the trainees' questions and guide them toward problem-solving and skill development.

Assessment 4: Facilitator Competencies, *continued*

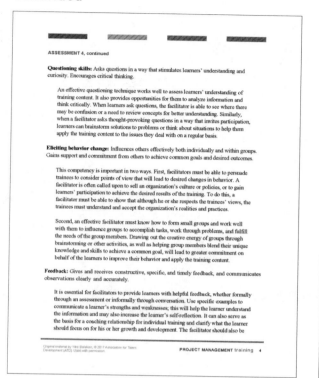

ASSESSMENT 4, continued

Questioning skills: Asks questions in a way that stimulates learners' understanding and curiosity. Encourages critical thinking.

An effective questioning technique works well to assess learners' understanding of training content. It also provides opportunities for them to analyze information and think critically. When learners ask questions, the facilitator is able to see where there may be confusion or a need to review concepts for better understanding. Similarly, when a facilitator asks thought-provoking questions in a way that invites participation, learners can brainstorm solutions to problems or think about situations to help them apply the training content to the issues they deal with on a regular basis.

Eliciting behavior change: Influences others effectively both individually and within groups. Gains support and commitment from others to achieve common goals and desired outcomes.

This competency is important in two ways. First, facilitators must be able to persuade trainees to consider points of view that will lead to desired changes in behavior. A facilitator is often called upon to sell an organization's culture or policies, or to gain learners' participation to achieve the desired results of the training. To do this, a facilitator must be able to show that although he or she respects the trainees' views, the trainees must understand and accept the organization's realities and practices.

Second, an effective facilitator must know how to form small groups and work well with them to influence groups to accomplish tasks, work through problems, and fulfill the needs of the group members. Drawing out the creative energy of groups through brainstorming or other activities, as well as helping group members blend their unique knowledge and skills to achieve a common goal, will lead to greater commitment on behalf of the learners to improve their behavior and apply the training content.

Feedback: Gives and receives constructive, specific, and timely feedback, and communicates observations clearly and accurately.

It is essential for facilitators to provide learners with helpful feedback, whether formally through an assessment or informally through conversation. Use specific examples to communicate a learner's strengths and weaknesses; this will help the learner understand the information and may also increase the learner's self-reflection. It can also serve as the basis for a coaching relationship for individual training and clarify what the learner should focus on for his or her growth and development. The facilitator should also be

Original material by Wes Balakian, © 2017 Association for Talent Development (ATD). Used with permission.

PROJECT MANAGEMENT training   **4**

Assessment 4: Facilitator Competencies, *continued*

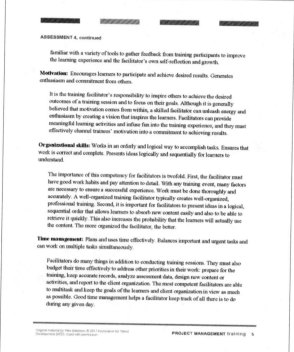

ASSESSMENT 4, continued

familiar with a variety of tools to gather feedback from training participants to improve the learning experience and the facilitator's own self-reflection and growth.

Motivation: Encourages learners to participate and achieve desired results. Generates enthusiasm and commitment from others.

It is the training facilitator's responsibility to inspire others to achieve the desired outcomes of a training session and to focus on their goals. Although it is generally believed that motivation comes from within, a skilled facilitator can unleash energy and enthusiasm by creating a vision that inspires the learners. Facilitators can provide meaningful learning activities and infuse fun into the training experience, and they must effectively channel trainees' motivation into a commitment to achieving results.

Organizational skills: Works in an orderly and logical way to accomplish tasks. Ensures that work is correct and complete. Presents ideas logically and sequentially for learners to understand.

The importance of this competency for facilitators is twofold. First, the facilitator must have good work habits and pay attention to detail. With any training event, many factors are necessary to ensure a successful experience. Work must be done thoroughly and accurately. A well-organized training facilitator typically creates well-organized, professional training. Second, it is important for facilitators to present ideas in a logical, sequential order that allows learners to absorb new content easily and also to be able to retrieve it quickly. This also increases the probability that the learners will actually use the content. The more organized the facilitator, the better.

Time management: Plans and uses time effectively. Balances important and urgent tasks and can work on multiple tasks simultaneously.

Facilitators do many things in addition to conducting training sessions. They must also budget their time effectively to address other priorities in their work: prepare for the training, keep accurate records, analyze assessment data, design new content or activities, and report to the client organization. The most competent facilitators are able to multitask and keep the goals of the learners and client organization in view as much as possible. Good time management helps a facilitator keep track of all there is to do during any given day.

Original material by Wes Balakian, © 2017 Association for Talent Development (ATD). Used with permission.

PROJECT MANAGEMENT training   **5**

Assessment 4: Facilitator Competencies, *continued*

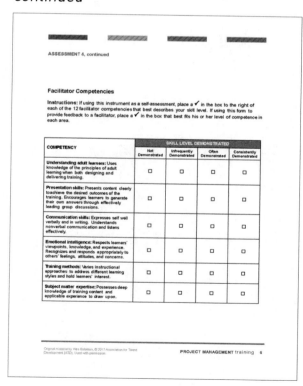

ASSESSMENT 4, continued

Facilitator Competencies

Instructions: If using this instrument as a self-assessment, place a ✓ in the box to the right of each of the 12 facilitator competencies that best describes your skill level. If using this form to provide feedback to a facilitator, place a ✓ in the box that best fits his or her level of competence in each area.

COMPETENCY	SKILL LEVEL DEMONSTRATED			
	Not Demonstrated	Infrequently Demonstrated	Often Demonstrated	Consistently Demonstrated
Understanding adult learners: Uses knowledge of the principles of adult learning when both designing and delivering training.	☐	☐	☐	☐
Presentation skills: Presents content clearly to achieve the desired outcomes of the training. Encourages learners to generate their own answers through effectively leading group discussions.	☐	☐	☐	☐
Communication skills: Expresses self well verbally and in writing. Understands nonverbal communication and listens effectively.	☐	☐	☐	☐
Emotional intelligence: Respects learners' viewpoints, knowledge, and experience. Recognizes and responds appropriately to others' feelings, attitudes, and concerns.	☐	☐	☐	☐
Training methods: Varies instructional approaches to address different learning styles and hold learners' interest.	☐	☐	☐	☐
Subject matter expertise: Possesses deep knowledge of training content and applicable experience to draw upon.	☐	☐	☐	☐

Original material by Wes Balakian, © 2017 Association for Talent Development (ATD). Used with permission.

PROJECT MANAGEMENT training   **6**

Assessment 4: Facilitator Competencies, *continued*

ASSESSMENT 4, continued

COMPETENCY	SKILL LEVEL DEMONSTRATED			
	Not Demonstrated	Infrequently Demonstrated	Often Demonstrated	Consistently Demonstrated
Questioning skills: Asks questions in a way that stimulates learners' understanding and curiosity. Encourages critical thinking.	☐	☐	☐	☐
Eliciting behavior change: Influences others effectively, both individually and within groups. Gains support and commitment from others to achieve common goals and desired outcomes.	☐	☐	☐	☐
Feedback: Gives and receives constructive, specific, and timely feedback and communicates observations clearly and accurately.	☐	☐	☐	☐
Motivation: Encourages learners to participate and achieve desired results. Generates enthusiasm and commitment from others.	☐	☐	☐	☐
Organizational skills: Works in an orderly and logical way to accomplish tasks. Ensures work is correct and complete. Presents ideas logically and sequentially for learners to understand.	☐	☐	☐	☐
Time management: Plans time effectively. Balances important and urgent tasks and can work on multiple tasks simultaneously.	☐	☐	☐	☐

Original material by Wes Balakian, © 2017 Association for Talent Development (ATD). Used with permission.

PROJECT MANAGEMENT training   **7**

Chapter 13
Handouts

What's in This Chapter

- 34 handouts for use in the workshop sessions
- Refer to Chapter 15 for instructions on how to download the handouts

---

Handouts comprise the various materials you will provide to the learners throughout the course of the workshop. In some cases, the handouts will simply provide instructions for worksheets to complete, places to take notes, and so forth. In other cases, they will provide important and practical materials for use in and out of the training room, such as reference materials, tip sheets, samples of completed forms, flowcharts, and other useful content.

The workshop agendas in Chapters 1-3 and the learning activities in Chapter 11 provide instructions for how and when to use the handouts within the context of the workshop. See Chapter 15 for complete instructions on how to download the workshop support materials.

Handouts Included in *Project Management Training*

Handout 1: Project Management Process Groups

Handout 2: My Project Management Action Plan

Handout 3: Project Charter Template

Handout 4: Potential Stakeholders

Handout 5: Stakeholder Register Template

Handout 6: Stakeholder Needs and Expectations Questionnaire

Handout 7: Requirements Management Plan Template

Handout 8: Scope Statement Template

Handout 9: Scope Management Plan Template

Handout 10: Communications Management Plan Template

Handout 11: Work Breakdown Structures

Handout 12: WBS Dictionary

Handout 13: Schedule Management Plan Template

Handout 14: Estimate Activity Durations

Handout 15: Human Resource and Staffing Management Plan Template

Handout 16: Contract Options

Handout 17: Contract Award Template

Handout 18: Risk Identification and Diagramming Techniques

Handout 19: Project Risk Categorization Worksheet

Handout 20: Risk Responses

Handout 21: Four Key Data Points for Controlling Project Costs

Handout 22: Quality Management Plan Template

Handout 23: 10 Things Great Project Managers Do Every Day!

Handout 24: Project Management Knowledge Requirements

Handout 25: My Project Management Goal Plan

Handout 26: Manager or Leader?

Handout 27: Inspirational Leadership

Handout 28: Leadership Power

Handout 29: MBWA for Project Managers

Handout 30: Motivation Techniques

Handout 31: Motivators and De-motivators

Handout 32: Question Checklist Tool for Solving Problems

Handout 33: Stakeholder Power–Interest Grid

Handout 34: My Project Management Development Plan

Handout 1: Project Management Process Groups

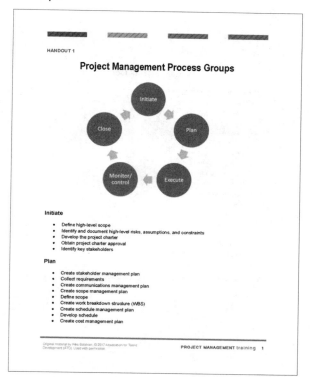

Handout 1: Project Management Process Groups, *continued*

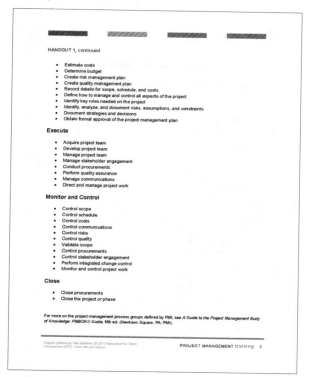

Handout 2: My Project Management Action Plan

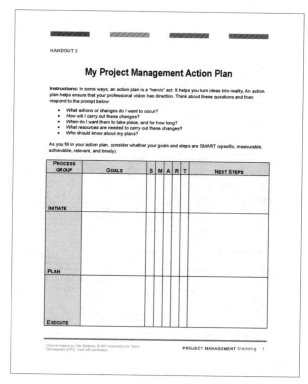

Handout 2: My Project Management Action Plan, *continued*

Handout 3: Project Charter Template

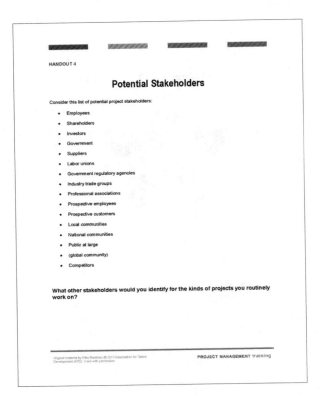

HANDOUT 3

Project Charter Template

Project Name:	Prepared by:		Date:
Project Purpose	Identify the customers who are to receive and benefit from the product developed by the project and the need the product is intended to meet (either as a problem to solve or as an opportunity to exploit).		
Planned Objectives	Identify what product or service is to be delivered at the end of the project and at any interim points. Describe the product sufficiently to enable the project team to create it and for agreement to be reached at product delivery time that the product has been correctly produced.		
High-Level Project Description	Briefly explain the requirements for the project and a description of the project to afford an understanding of known needs and tasks to accomplish the project.		
High-Level Product Description	Briefly identify major deliverables to be created by this project.		
Planned Schedule	Identify what milestones will be needed to reach project objectives.		
Initial Budget	Use a rough order of magnitude estimate to show budget requirements (a "ballpark" estimation of project's level of effort and cost to complete).		
Program or Portfolio Links	Identify how the project links to the work of the organization and any programs being managed in the organization.		
Assignment of Project Manager, Responsibility, and Authority	Often the project manager will have already been decided before hand or during the charter. Identify who the project manager is and their responsibility during the project and the authority level they have (decision making, budget, approving, and so on).		
Name and Title of Sponsor	Identify the project sponsor (persons or groups) and explain what sponsor authority will be within the project.		
Other	Identify and explain any other matters that are important for the initiation and conduct of the project. Focus on charter issues of importance between the project sponsor and the project manager. This section is not for describing the project plan.		
Approval	Sponsor		Date

Original material by Wes Balakian, © 2017 Association for Talent Development (ATD). Used with permission.

PROJECT MANAGEMENT training

Handout 4: Potential Stakeholders

HANDOUT 4

Potential Stakeholders

Consider this list of potential project stakeholders:

- Employees
- Shareholders
- Investors
- Government
- Suppliers
- Labor unions
- Government regulatory agencies
- Industry trade groups
- Professional associations
- Prospective employees
- Prospective customers
- Local communities
- National communities
- Public at large
- (global community)
- Competitors

What other stakeholders would you identify for the kinds of projects you routinely work on?

Original material by Wes Balakian, © 2017 Association for Talent Development (ATD). Used with permission.

PROJECT MANAGEMENT training

Handout 5: Stakeholder Register Template

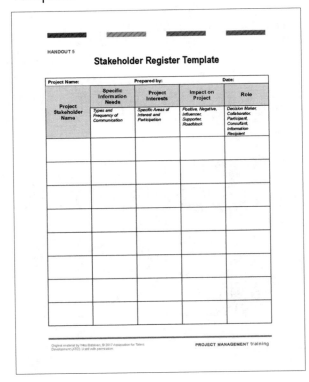

HANDOUT 5

Stakeholder Register Template

Project Name:		Prepared by:		Date:
Project Stakeholder Name	Specific Information Needs — Types and Frequency of Communication	Project Interests — Specific Areas of Interest and Participation	Impact on Project — Positive, Negative, Influencer, Supporter, Roadblock	Role — Decision Maker, Collaborator, Participant, Consultant, Information Recipient

Original material by Wes Balakian, © 2017 Association for Talent Development (ATD). Used with permission.

PROJECT MANAGEMENT training

Handout 6: Stakeholder Needs and Expectations Questionnaire

HANDOUT 6

Stakeholder Needs and Expectations Questionnaire

Instructions: You have been identified as a stakeholder for this project (a stakeholder is anyone who will affect or be affected by the project). You can help this project be successful by answering the following questions:

Project		Date
Stakeholder	Ext.	Department

A. Objectives—What results would you require, expect, or desire from the project? Categories of objectives include function, cost, time, surprises, flexibility, effectiveness.

Item	Expectation
1	
2	
3	
4	

B. Measures—What measures could be used to validate that these objectives are met?

1	
2	
3	
4	

C. Impact—What changes do you expect your area to make to adjust to this change?

1	
2	
3	
4	

D. Involvement—What do you see as your role or your area's role?

E. Your Deliverables and Roles—What items or changes do you think you and your area should provide for the project to be effective? Who would be responsible for these deliverables?

Deliverable	Responsible
1	
2	
3	

Original material by Wes Balakian, © 2017 Association for Talent Development (ATD). Used with permission.

PROJECT MANAGEMENT training

Handout 7: Requirements Management Plan Template

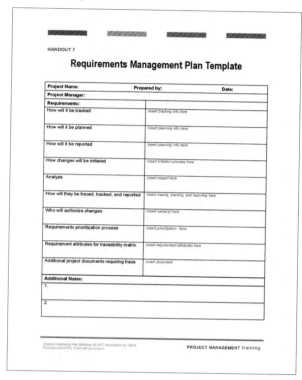

Handout 8: Scope Statement Template

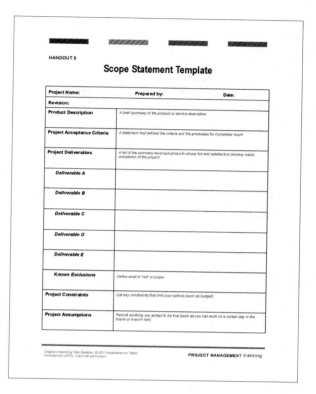

Handout 9: Scope Management Plan Template

Handout 10: Communications Management Plan Template

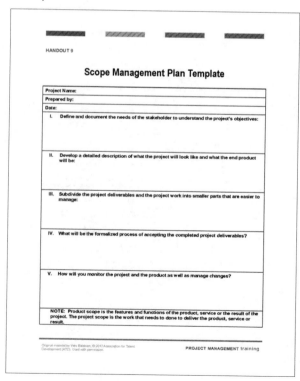

Handout 11: Work Breakdown Structures

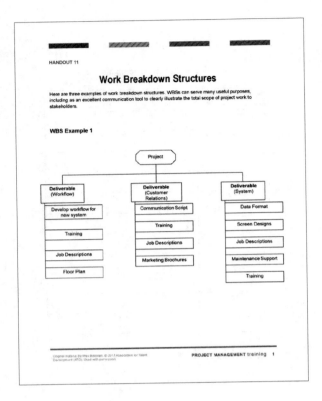

Handout 11: Work Breakdown Structures, *continued*

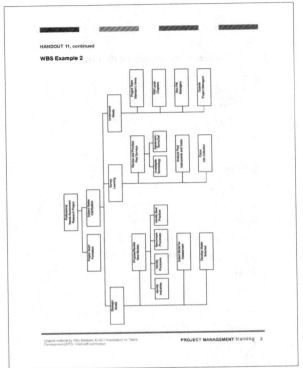

Handout 11: Work Breakdown Structures, *continued*

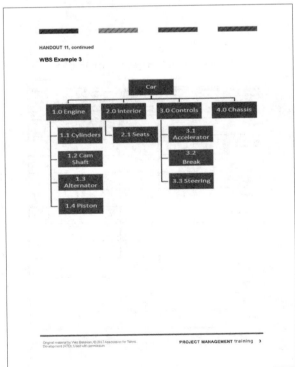

Handout12: WBS Dictionary

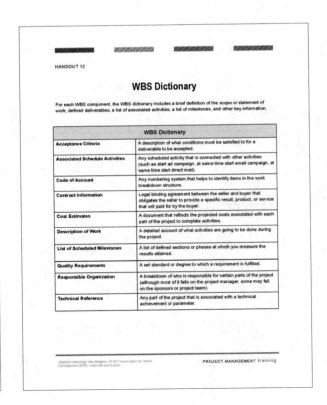

Handout 13: Schedule Management Plan Template

Schedule Management Plan Template

Project Name:	Prepared by:	Date:

Person(s) authorized to request schedule changes (see Schedule Change Request):

Name:	Title:	Location:
Name:	Title:	Location:
Name:	Title:	Location:

Person(s) to whom Schedule Change Request forms must be submitted for approval:

Name:	Title:	Location:
Name:	Title:	Location:
Name:	Title:	Location:

Acceptable reasons for changes to project schedule (for example, delays due to material or personnel availability; weather; need to resolve related issues before proceeding, acceleration permitted due to early completion of a phase or process, and others)

Describe how you will calculate and report on the projected impact of any schedule changes (time, cost, quality, and so on):

Describe any other aspects of how changes to the project schedule will be managed:

Handout 14: Estimate Activity Durations

Estimate Activity Durations

When estimating in the project world, we need to have a way to definitively articulate time and costs. Here are some typical techniques used for estimating activity durations.

Single-Point Estimate. In simpler projects, estimates are typically documented as single-point values (one number). For example, a single-point estimate may be documented as 5 days (with no plus/minus flexibility). Single-point estimates are generally a way to estimate with less confidence.

Top-Down Estimate. Using expert judgment (also known as top-down estimate) is a simple and quick way to produce a single-point estimate. Top-down estimates take less time and are usually less accurate. Use them when you need it fast but accuracy is not critical.

Bottom-Up Estimate. In bottom-up estimating, those who are will do the work participate in the estimating process. Typically, they include project team members, the developer, and so on. Together with the project manager they develop estimates at the task level (and work breakdown structure if you have developed one). Bottom-up estimating takes more time but is more accurate.

Probabilistic Estimate. Another technique, often used in more complex projects, is to use sophisticated mathematics to determine probabilistic distributions for each activity, resulting in a time range estimate instead of a single time estimate. A probabilistic estimate, for example, may be documented as a graphical curve indicating the probability of an activity finishing at any given time on the curve. Probabilistic estimates generally provide for more confident expectations. They often use a method such as three-point estimating to predict a range of outcomes.

Three-Point Estimate. Three-point estimates, which are sometimes called PERT (program evaluation review technique) estimates, use this formula:

$$t_c = \frac{t_o + 4t_d + t_c}{s}$$

$$E = \frac{4 + 6 + 10}{6} \quad E = 6.333$$

This formula is equivalent to the common PERT formula: E=O+4ML+P/6

Where

O = Optimistic estimate
ML (or M) = Most likely estimate
P = Pessimistic estimate

Estimates in the three-point technique should be made by the person or group of people who have expert familiarity with the activity. If you do not have this many people who can give this range, estimates can come from one or two people who have enough experience to give you the pessimistic, optimistic, and most probable data.

In most of today's project management software, it is common to estimate activity durations in terms of work periods (activity durations). The project team determines how best to define work periods for their particular project (typically, days, shifts, hours, or weeks).

Handout 15: Human Resource and Staffing Management Plan Template

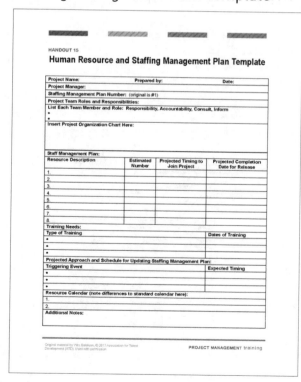

Human Resource and Staffing Management Plan Template

Project Name:	Prepared by:	Date:

Project Manager:

Staffing Management Plan Number: (original is #1)

Project Team Roles and Responsibilities:

List Each Team Member and Role: Responsibility, Accountability, Consult, Inform
-
-
-

Insert Project Organization Chart Here:

Staff Management Plan:

Resource Description	Estimated Number	Projected Timing to Join Project	Projected Completion Date for Release
1.			
2.			
3.			
4.			
5.			
6.			
7.			
8.			

Training Needs:

Type of Training	Dates of Training
•	
•	
•	

Projected Approach and Schedule for Updating Staffing Management Plan:

Triggering Event	Expected Timing
•	
•	
•	

Resource Calendar (note differences to standard calendar here):

1.
2.

Additional Notes:

Handout 16: Contract Options

Contract Options

	Contract Options		
	Fixed Price	**Cost Reimbursable**	**Time and Materials**
Contract Forms	FP = Fixed price FPIF = Fixed price incentive fee FPEPA = Fixed price economic price adjustment	CR = Cost reimbursable CPFF = Cost plus fixed fee CPPC = Cost plus percent of cost CPIF = Cost plus incentive fee	T&M = Time and materials T&E = Time and expense
Advantages	• Less work for buyer to manage • Less cost risk to buyer • Seller has incentive to control costs • Buyer knows total cost	• Simpler SOW • Sometimes lower cost because seller doesn't need to factor in as much risk	• Quick to create SOW • Good choice for staff augmentation
When Best to Use	You know precisely what you need to be done.	You need help in determining what needs to be done.	You need to augment staff in the short term or you need someone right away.
Disadvantages	• Seller may attempt to add-on with change orders • Needs a detailed SOW when changes must be controlled closely	• Buyer must closely control each seller invoice to avoid overpaying • Seller has a moderate incentive to control costs	• Seller has no incentive at all to control costs or to work efficiently • Requires daily management by the buyer
Scope of Work (SOW)	Highly detailed—must define all the work specifically	Moderately detailed—seller to help define the work	Briefly detailed—often specified on a daily basis

Note: The PMBOK® Guide identifies three types of contractual agreements common in project management. PMI, A Guide to the Project Management Body of Knowledge: PMBOK® Guide, fifth edition, Newtown Square, PA: PMI.

Handout 17: Contract Award Template

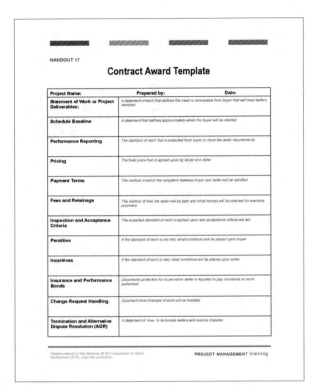

HANDOUT 17

Contract Award Template

Project Name:	Prepared by:	Date:
Statement of Work or Project Deliverables:	A statement of work that defines the need or deliverable from buyer that will meet sellers standard	
Schedule Baseline	A statement that defines approximately when the buyer will be needed	
Performance Reporting	The standard of work that is expected from buyer to meet the seller requirement	
Pricing	The fixed price that is agreed upon by buyer and seller	
Payment Terms	The method in which the obligation between buyer and seller will be satisfied	
Fees and Retainage	The method of how the seller will be paid and what monies will be retained for warranty purposes	
Inspection and Acceptance Criteria	The expected standard of work is agreed upon and acceptance criteria are set	
Penalties	If the standard of work is not met, what conditions will be placed upon buyer	
Incentives	If the standard of work is met, what conditions will be placed upon seller	
Insurance and Performance Bonds	Documents protection for buyer when seller is required to pay insurance on work performed	
Change Request Handling	Document how changes of work will be handled	
Termination and Alternative Dispute Resolution (ADR)	A statement of how to terminate sellers and resolve disputes	

Original material by Wes Balakian, © 2017 Association for Talent Development (ATD). Used with permission.

PROJECT MANAGEMENT training

Handout 18: Risk Identification and DiagrammingTechniques

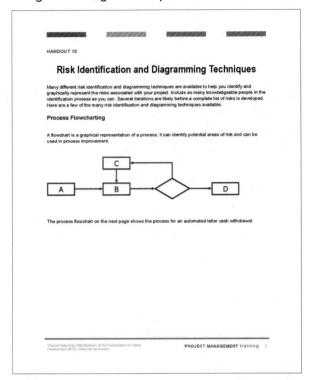

HANDOUT 18

Risk Identification and Diagramming Techniques

Many different risk identification and diagramming techniques are available to help you identify and graphically represent the risks associated with your project. Include as many knowledgeable people in the identification process as you can. Several iterations are likely before a complete list of risks is developed. Here are a few of the many risk identification and diagramming techniques available.

Process Flowcharting

A flowchart is a graphical representation of a process. It can identify potential areas of risk and can be used in process improvement.

The process flowchart on the next page shows the process for an automated teller cash withdrawal.

Original material by Wes Balakian, © 2017 Association for Talent Development (ATD). Used with permission.

PROJECT MANAGEMENT training   1

Handout 18: Risk Identification and DiagrammingTechniques, *continued*

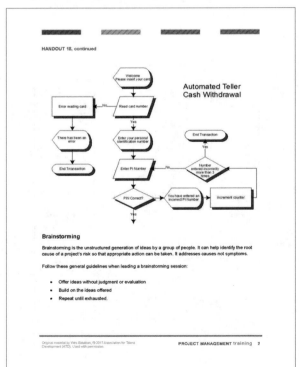

HANDOUT 18, continued

Automated Teller Cash Withdrawal

Brainstorming

Brainstorming is the unstructured generation of ideas by a group of people. It can help identify the root cause of a project's risk so that appropriate action can be taken. It addresses causes not symptoms.

Follow these general guidelines when leading a brainstorming session:

- Offer ideas without judgment or evaluation
- Build on the ideas offered
- Repeat until exhausted.

Original material by Wes Balakian, © 2017 Association for Talent Development (ATD). Used with permission.

PROJECT MANAGEMENT training   2

Handout 18: Risk Identification and DiagrammingTechniques, *continued*

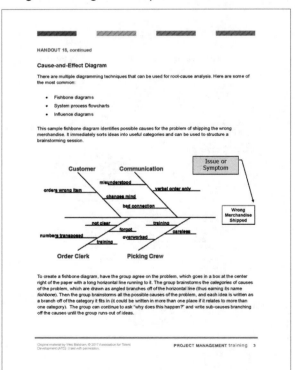

HANDOUT 18, continued

Cause-and-Effect Diagram

There are multiple diagramming techniques that can be used for root-cause analysis. Here are some of the most common:

- Fishbone diagrams
- System process flowcharts
- Influence diagrams

This sample fishbone diagram identifies possible causes for the problem of shipping the wrong merchandise. It immediately sorts ideas into useful categories and can be used to structure a brainstorming session.

To create a fishbone diagram, have the group agree on the problem, which goes in a box at the center right of the paper with a long horizontal line running to it. The group brainstorms the categories of causes of the problem, which are drawn as angled branches off of the horizontal line (thus earning its name fishbone). Then the group brainstorms all the possible causes of the problem, and each idea is written as a branch off the category it fits in (it could be written in more than one place if it relates to more than one category). The group can continue to ask "why does this happen?" and write sub-causes branching off the causes until the group runs out of ideas.

Original material by Wes Balakian, © 2017 Association for Talent Development (ATD). Used with permission.

PROJECT MANAGEMENT training   3

PROJECT MANAGEMENT training

Handout 18: Risk Identification and DiagrammingTechniques, *continued*

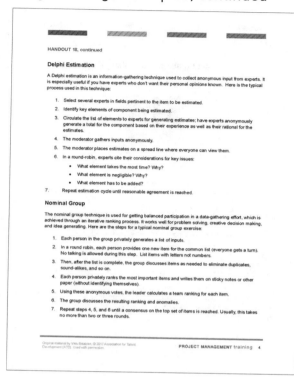

HANDOUT 18, continued

Delphi Estimation

A Delphi estimation is an information-gathering technique used to collect anonymous input from experts. It is especially useful if you have experts who don't want their personal opinions known. Here is the typical process used in this technique:

1. Select several experts in fields pertinent to the item to be estimated.
2. Identify key elements of component being estimated.
3. Circulate the list of elements to experts for generating estimates; have experts anonymously generate a total for the component based on their experience as well as their rational for the estimates.
4. The moderator gathers inputs anonymously.
5. The moderator places estimates on a spread line where everyone can view them.
6. In a round-robin, experts cite their considerations for key issues:
   - What element takes the most time? Why?
   - What element is negligible? Why?
   - What element has to be added?
7. Repeat estimation cycle until reasonable agreement is reached.

Nominal Group

The nominal group technique is used for getting balanced participation in a data-gathering effort, which is achieved through an iterative ranking process. It works well for problem solving, creative decision making, and idea generating. Here are the steps for a typical nominal group exercise:

1. Each person in the group privately generates a list of inputs.
2. In a round robin, each person provides one new item for the common list (everyone gets a turn). No talking is allowed during this step. List items with letters not numbers.
3. Then, after the list is complete, the group discusses items as needed to eliminate duplicates, sound-alikes, and so on.
4. Each person privately ranks the most important items and writes them on sticky notes or other paper (without identifying themselves).
5. Using these anonymous votes, the leader calculates a team ranking for each item.
6. The group discusses the resulting ranking and anomalies.
7. Repeat steps 4, 5, and 6 until a consensus on the top set of items is reached. Usually, this takes no more than two or three rounds.

Handout 18: Risk Identification and DiagrammingTechniques, *continued*

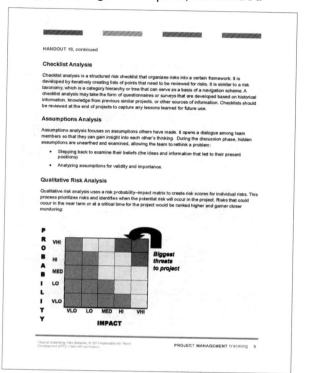

HANDOUT 18, continued

Checklist Analysis

Checklist analysis is a structured risk checklist that organizes risks into a certain framework. It is developed by iteratively creating lists of points that need to be reviewed for risks. It is similar to a risk taxonomy, which is a category hierarchy or tree that can serve as a basis of a navigation scheme. A checklist analysis may take the form of questionnaires or surveys that are developed based on historical information, knowledge from previous similar projects, or other sources of information. Checklists should be reviewed at the end of projects to capture any lessons learned for future use.

Assumptions Analysis

Assumptions analysis focuses on assumptions others have made. It opens a dialogue among team members so that they can gain insight into each other's thinking. During the discussion phase, hidden assumptions are unearthed and examined, allowing the team to rethink a problem:

- Stepping back to examine their beliefs (the ideas and information that led to their present positions)
- Analyzing assumptions for validity and importance.

Qualitative Risk Analysis

Qualitative risk analysis uses a risk probability–impact matrix to create risk scores for individual risks. This process prioritizes risks and identifies when the potential risk will occur in the project. Risks that could occur in the near term or at a critical time for the project would be ranked higher and garner closer monitoring:

Handout 18: Risk Identification and DiagrammingTechniques, *continued*

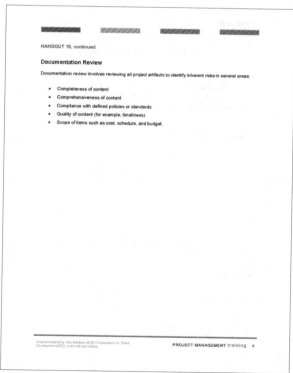

HANDOUT 18, continued

Documentation Review

Documentation review involves reviewing all project artifacts to identify inherent risks in several areas:

- Completeness of content
- Comprehensiveness of content
- Compliance with defined policies or standards
- Quality of content (for example, timeliness)
- Scope of items such as cost, schedule, and budget.

Handout 19: Project Risk Categorization Worksheet

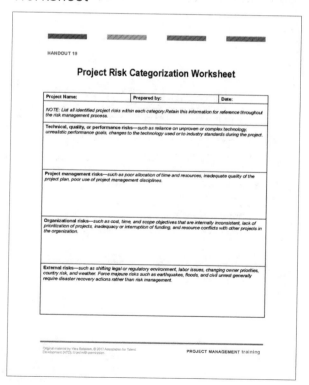

HANDOUT 19

Project Risk Categorization Worksheet

Project Name:	Prepared by:	Date:

NOTE: List all identified project risks within each category. Retain this information for reference throughout the risk management process.

Technical, quality, or performance risks—*such as reliance on unproven or complex technology, unrealistic performance goals, changes to the technology used or to industry standards during the project.*

Project management risks—*such as poor allocation of time and resources, inadequate quality of the project plan, poor use of project management disciplines.*

Organizational risks—*such as cost, time, and scope objectives that are internally inconsistent, lack of prioritization of projects, inadequacy or interruption of funding, and resource conflicts with other projects in the organization.*

External risks—*such as shifting legal or regulatory environment, labor issues, changing owner priorities, country risk, and weather. Force majeure risks such as earthquakes, floods, and civil unrest generally require disaster recovery actions rather than risk management.*

Handout 20: Risk Responses

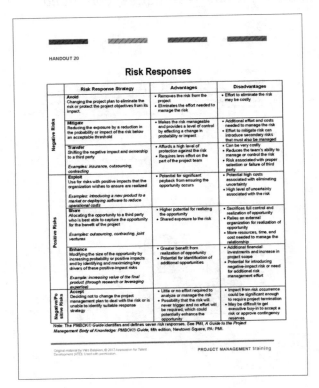

Handout 21: Four Key Data Points for Controlling Project Costs

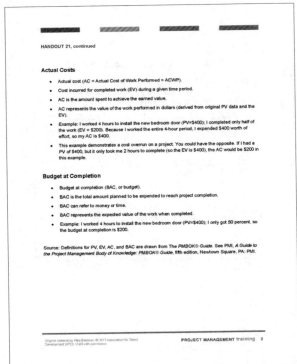

Handout 21: Four Key Data Points for Controlling Project Costs, *continued*

Actual Costs

- Actual cost (AC = Actual Cost of Work Performed = ACWP).
- Cost incurred for completed work (EV) during a given time period.
- AC is the amount spent to achieve the earned value.
- AC represents the value of the work performed in dollars (derived from original PV data and the EV).
- Example: I worked 4 hours to install the new bedroom door (PV=$400); I completed only half of the work (EV = $200). Because I worked the entire 4-hour period, I expended $400 worth of effort, so my AC is $400.
- This example demonstrates a cost overrun on a project. You could have the opposite. If I had a PV of $400, but it only took me 2 hours to complete (so the EV is $400), the AC would be $200 in this example.

Budget at Completion

- Budget at completion (BAC, or budget).
- BAC is the total amount planned to be expended to reach project completion.
- BAC can refer to money or time.
- BAC represents the expected value of the work when completed.
- Example: I worked 4 hours to install the new bedroom door (PV=$400); I only got 50 percent, so the budget at completion is $200.

Source: Definitions for PV, EV, AC, and BAC are drawn from The PMBOK® Guide. See PMI, *A Guide to the Project Management Body of Knowledge: PMBOK® Guide,* fifth edition, Newtown Square, PA: PMI.

Handout 22: Quality Management Plan Template

Project Name:	Prepared by:	Date:
Description of Project Quality System:		
Describe in as much detail as needed specifically what will be required in each of the following areas to manage quality on this project.		
ORGANIZATIONAL STRUCTURE		
ROLES AND RESPONSIBILITIES		
PROCEDURES		
PROCESSES		
RESOURCES		
Describe how each of the following aspects of quality management will be addressed on this project:		
QUALITY CONTROL		
QUALITY ASSURANCE		
QUALITY IMPROVEMENT		

Handout 23: 10 Things Great Project Managers Do Every Day!

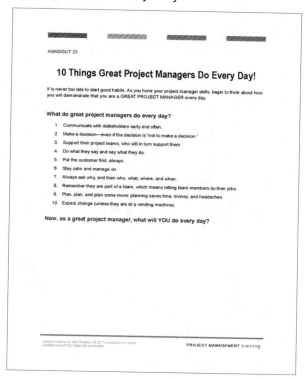

Handout 24: Project Management Knowledge Requirements

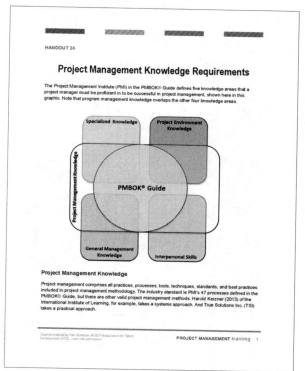

Handout 24: Project Management Knowledge Requirements, *continued*

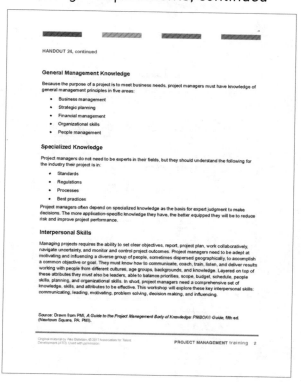

Handout 25: My Project Management Goal Plan

Handout 25: My Project Management Goal Plan, *continued*

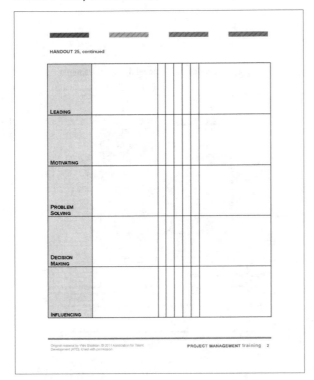

LEADING				
MOTIVATING				
PROBLEM SOLVING				
DECISION MAKING				
INFLUENCING				

Handout 26: Manager or Leader?

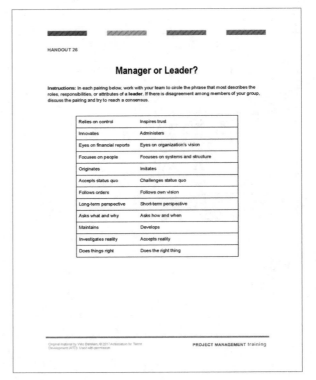

Manager or Leader?

Instructions: In each pairing below, work with your team to circle the phrase that most describes the roles, responsibilities, or attributes of a **leader**. If there is disagreement among members of your group, discuss the pairing and try to reach a consensus.

Relies on control	Inspires trust
Innovates	Administers
Eyes on financial reports	Eyes on organization's vision
Focuses on people	Focuses on systems and structure
Originates	Imitates
Accepts status quo	Challenges status quo
Follows orders	Follows own vision
Long-term perspective	Short-term perspective
Asks what and why	Asks how and when
Maintains	Develops
Investigates reality	Accepts reality
Does things right	Does the right thing

Handout 27: Inspirational Leadership

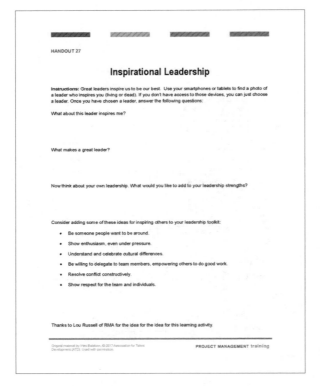

Inspirational Leadership

Instructions: Great leaders inspire us to be our best. Use your smartphones or tablets to find a photo of a leader who inspires you (living or dead). If you don't have access to those devices, you can just choose a leader. Once you have chosen a leader, answer the following questions:

What about this leader inspires me?

What makes a great leader?

Now think about your own leadership. What would you like to add to your leadership strengths?

Consider adding some of these ideas for inspiring others to your leadership toolkit:

- Be someone people want to be around.
- Show enthusiasm, even under pressure.
- Understand and celebrate cultural differences.
- Be willing to delegate to team members, empowering others to do good work.
- Resolve conflict constructively.
- Show respect for the team and individuals.

Thanks to Lou Russell of RMA for the idea for the idea for this learning activity.

Handout 28: Leadership Power

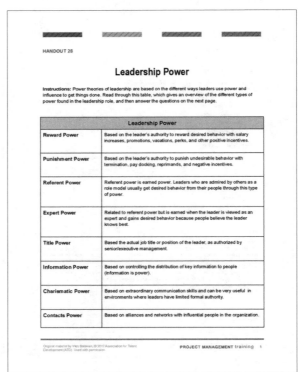

Leadership Power

Instructions: Power theories of leadership are based on the different ways leaders use power and influence to get things done. Read through this table, which gives an overview of the different types of power found in the leadership role, and then answer the questions on the next page.

Leadership Power	
Reward Power	Based on the leader's authority to reward desired behavior with salary increases, promotions, vacations, perks, and other positive incentives.
Punishment Power	Based on the leader's authority to punish undesirable behavior with termination, pay docking, reprimands, and negative incentives.
Referent Power	Referent power is earned power. Leaders who are admired by others as a role model usually get desired behavior from their people through this type of power.
Expert Power	Related to referent power but is earned when the leader is viewed as an expert and gains desired behavior because people believe the leader knows best.
Title Power	Based the actual job title or position of the leader, as authorized by senior/executive management.
Information Power	Based on controlling the distribution of key information to people (information is power).
Charismatic Power	Based on extraordinary communication skills and can be very useful in environments where leaders have limited formal authority.
Contacts Power	Based on alliances and networks with influential people in the organization.

Handout 28: Leadership Power, *continued*

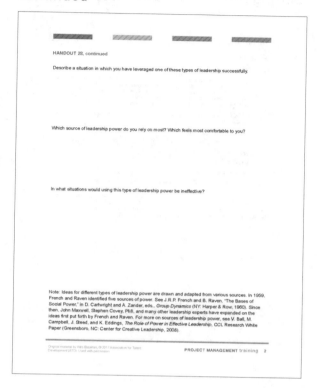

HANDOUT 28, continued

Describe a situation in which you have leveraged one of these types of leadership successfully.

Which source of leadership power do you rely on most? Which feels most comfortable to you?

In what situations would using this type of leadership power be ineffective?

Note: Ideas for different types of leadership power are drawn and adapted from various sources. In 1959, French and Raven identified five sources of power. See J.R.P. French and B. Raven, "The Bases of Social Power," in D. Cartwright and A. Zander, eds., *Group Dynamics* (NY: Harper & Row, 1960). Since then, John Maxwell, Stephen Covey, PMI, and many other leadership experts have expanded on the ideas first put forth by French and Raven. For more on sources of leadership power, see V. Ball, M. Campbell, J. Steed, and K. Eddings, *The Role of Power in Effective Leadership*, CCL Research White Paper (Greensboro, NC: Center for Creative Leadership, 2008).

PROJECT MANAGEMENT training   2

Handout 29: MBWA for Project Managers

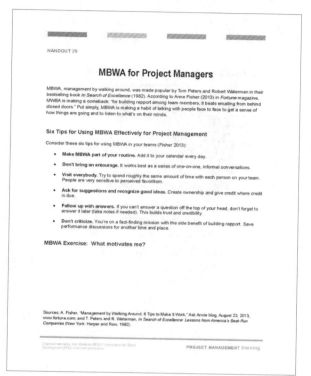

HANDOUT 29

MBWA for Project Managers

MBWA, management by walking around, was made popular by Tom Peters and Robert Waterman in their bestselling book *In Search of Excellence* (1982). According to Anne Fisher (2013) in *Fortune* magazine, MWBA is making a comeback: "for building rapport among team members, it beats emailing from behind closed doors." Put simply, MBWA is making a habit of talking with people face to face to get a sense of how things are going and to listen to what's on their minds.

Six Tips for Using MBWA Effectively for Project Management

Consider these six tips for using MBWA in your teams (Fisher 2013):

- **Make MBWA part of your routine.** Add it to your calendar every day.
- **Don't bring an entourage.** It works best as a series of one-on-one, informal conversations.
- **Visit everybody.** Try to spend roughly the same amount of time with each person on your team. People are very sensitive to perceived favoritism.
- **Ask for suggestions and recognize good ideas.** Create ownership and give credit where credit is due.
- **Follow up with answers.** If you can't answer a question off the top of your head, don't forget to answer it later (take notes if needed). This builds trust and credibility.
- **Don't criticize.** You're on a fact-finding mission with the side benefit of building rapport. Save performance discussions for another time and place.

MBWA Exercise: What motivates me?

Sources: A. Fisher, "Management by Walking Around: 6 Tips to Make It Work," Ask Annie blog, August 23, 2013, www.fortune.com; and T. Peters and R. Waterman, *In Search of Excellence: Lessons from America's Best-Run Companies* (New York: Harper and Row, 1982).

PROJECT MANAGEMENT training

Handout 30: Motivation Techniques

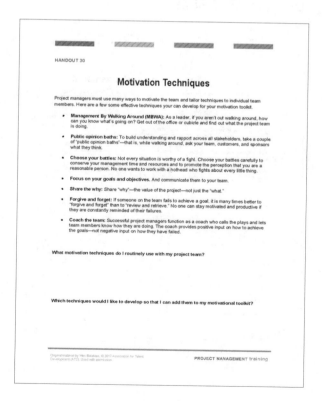

HANDOUT 30

Motivation Techniques

Project managers must use many ways to motivate the team and tailor techniques to individual team members. Here are a few some effective techniques your can develop for your motivation toolkit.

- **Management By Walking Around (MBWA):** As a leader, if you aren't out walking around, how can you know what's going on? Get out of the office or cubicle and find out what the project team is doing.
- **Public opinion baths:** To build understanding and rapport across all stakeholders, take a couple of "public opinion baths"—that is, while walking around, ask your team, customers, and sponsors what they think.
- **Choose your battles:** Not every situation is worthy of a fight. Choose your battles carefully to conserve your management time and resources and to promote the perception that you are a reasonable person. No one wants to work with a hothead who fights about every little thing.
- **Focus on your goals and objectives.** And communicate them to your team.
- **Share the why:** Share "why"—the value of the project—not just the "what."
- **Forgive and forget:** If someone on the team fails to achieve a goal, it is many times better to "forgive and forget" than to "review and retrieve." No one can stay motivated and productive if they are constantly reminded of their failures.
- **Coach the team:** Successful project managers function as a coach who calls the plays and lets team members know how they are doing. The coach provides positive input on how to achieve the goals—not negative input on how they have failed.

What motivation techniques do I routinely use with my project team?

Which techniques would I like to develop so that I can add them to my motivational toolkit?

PROJECT MANAGEMENT training

Handout 31: Motivators and De-motivators

HANDOUT 31

Motivators and De-motivators

Instructions: Take a few minutes to think of examples of behaviors and attitudes that motivate or de-motivate you and others and write them in the appropriate columns below. Be prepared to share some of your examples with the group. As other participants share their ideas, add them below to supplement your list of what to do and what not to do in motivating and leading project teams.

Motivators	De-motivators

PROJECT MANAGEMENT training

Handout 32: Question Checklist Tool for Solving Problems

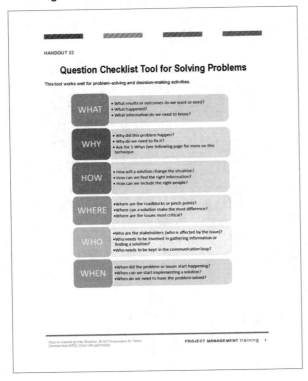

Handout 32: Question Checklist Tool for Solving Problems, *continued*

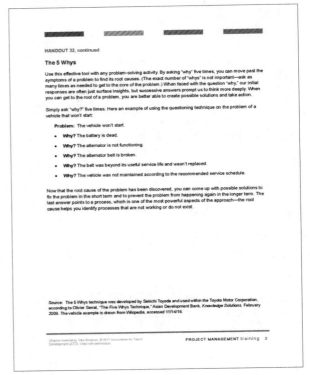

Handout 33: Stakeholder Power–Interest Grid

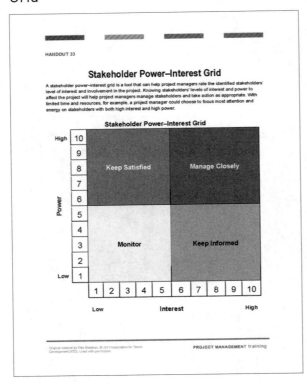

Handout 34: My Project Management Development Plan

Chapter 14
Project Manager Toolkit

What's in This Chapter

- 15 tools and templates to help project managers manage successful projects

Managing projects requires the ability to set clear objectives, report, plan, work collaboratively, navigate uncertainty, and monitor and control project outcomes. Project managers must know how to communicate, influence, lead, problem solve, listen, and deliver results working with many different people. In addition, they must be able to balance priorities, scope, budgets, schedules, human resources, risks, and a host of other factors. The training in the workshops in this book is designed to help participants begin to develop these skills.

And while it is true that project management is about more than filling in templates or using a particular software program, such tools can help save time and make project management easier and more effective. This chapter presents a Project Manager Toolkit that pulls together all the templates from the workshops plus additional templates and tools. Your participants will be able to put these tools to work immediately when they return to their projects and teams.

You may distribute a print copy of the Project Manager Toolkit to your participants at the close of your workshop or send it to them digitally a week or two after the workshop is completed as follow-up support for their learning. Consider creating a cover sheet for the toolkit with contact information for you and other resources they can reach out to if they have questions about using the tools.

The tools are created and made available to you and your workshop participants by True Solutions Inc. (TSI), which also publishes a set of more than 100 templates on a wide range of project management processes and tasks to help project managers navigate their myriad responsibilities. In addition, ATD has published a book of templates for training projects by W.H. Thomas called *Templates for Managing Training Projects*.

Tools Included in the Project Manager Toolkit

Tool 1: Communications Requirements Analysis Worksheet

Tool 2: Communications Management Plan Template

Tool 3: Requirements Management Plan Template

Tool 4: Project Charter Template

Tool 5: Project WBS Example

Tool 6: Scope Management Plan Template

Tool 7: Scope Statement Template

Tool 8: Human Resource and Staffing Management Plan Template

Tool 9: Stakeholder Register Template

Tool 10: Project Stakeholder Needs and Expectations Questionnaire

Tool 11: Contract Award Template

Tool 12: Quality Management Plan Template

Tool 13: Project Risk Categorization Worksheet

Tool 14: Schedule Management Plan Template

Tool 15: Project Issues Tool: What Went Wrong?

Tool 1: Communications Requirements Analysis Worksheet

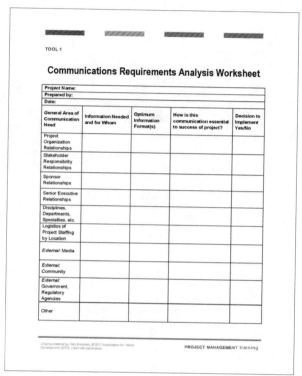

Tool 2: Communications Management Plan Template

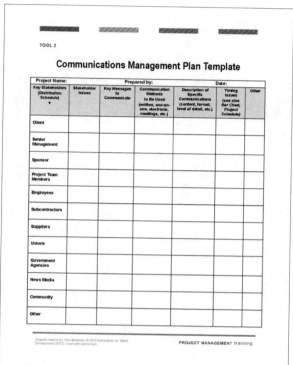

Tool 3: Requirements Management Plan Template

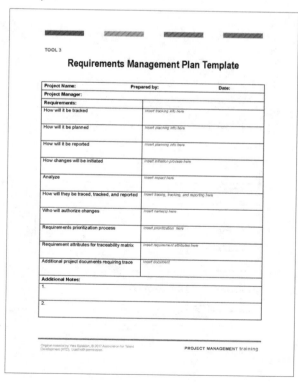

Tool 4: Project Charter Template

Tool 5: Project WBS Example

Project WBS Example

Here is an example of a work breakdown structure (WBS). The project in this example is divided along functional lines. Other formats for breaking down a project might include by subsystem or timed phases. The purpose of the WBS is to structure the work into smaller elements that

- Define all effort to be expended and assign responsibility to an identified organization
- Are manageable, so that specific authority and responsibility can be assigned
- Are independent or have limited dependence on other ongoing elements
- Can be integrated to show the total package
- Are measurable in terms of progress
- Present the total program as a summation of subdivided elements
- Enable thorough planning to be performed
- Enable costs and budgets to be established
- Enable time, cost, and performance to be tracked
- Link objectives to company resources in a logical manner
- Enable schedules and status reporting procedures to be tracked
- Establish responsibility assignments for each element.

PROJECT MANAGEMENT training   1

Tool 5: Project WBS Example, *continued*

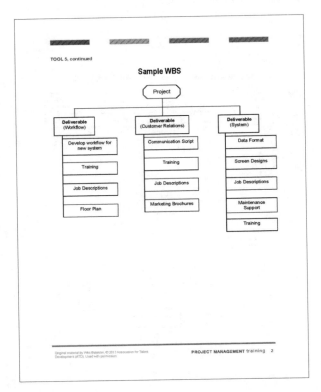

Sample WBS

PROJECT MANAGEMENT training   2

Tool 6: Scope Management Plan Template

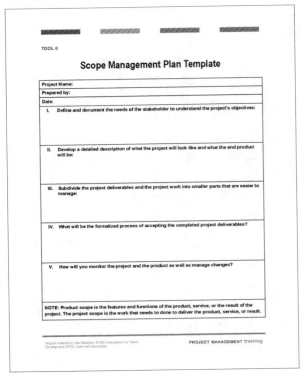

Scope Management Plan Template

Project Name:
Prepared by:
Date:

I. Define and document the needs of the stakeholder to understand the project's objectives:

II. Develop a detailed description of what the project will look like and what the end product will be:

III. Subdivide the project deliverables and the project work into smaller parts that are easier to manage:

IV. What will be the formalized process of accepting the completed project deliverables?

V. How will you monitor the project and the product as well as manage changes?

NOTE: Product scope is the features and functions of the product, service, or the result of the project. The project scope is the work that needs to done to deliver the product, service, or result.

PROJECT MANAGEMENT training

Tool 7: Scope Statement Template

Scope Statement Template

Project Name:	Prepared by:	Date:
Revision:		
Product Description	A brief summary of the product or service description	
Project Acceptance Criteria	A statement that defines the criteria and the processes for completed result	
Project Deliverables	A list of the summary-level sub-products whose full and satisfactory delivery marks completion of the project	
Deliverable A		
Deliverable B		
Deliverable C		
Deliverable D		
Deliverable E		
Known Exclusions	Define what is "not" in scope	
Project Constraints	List any constraints that limit your options (such as budget)	
Project Assumptions	Record anything you accept to be true (such as you can work on a certain day in the future or it won't rain)	

PROJECT MANAGEMENT training

PROJECT MANAGEMENT training

Tool 8: Human Resource and Staffing Management Plan Template

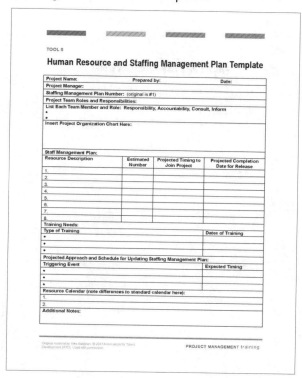

Tool 9: Stakeholder Register Template

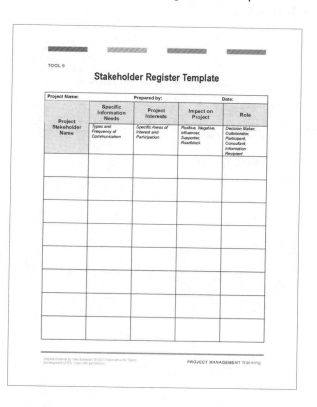

Tool 10: Project Stakeholder Needs and Expectations Questionnaire

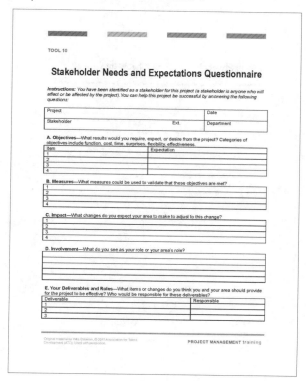

Tool 11: Procurement Contract Award Template

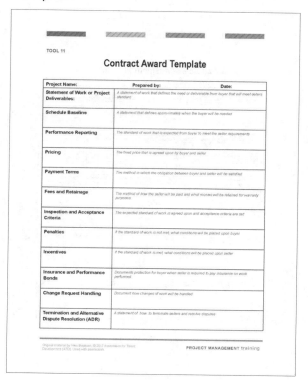

Tool 12: Quality Management Plan Template

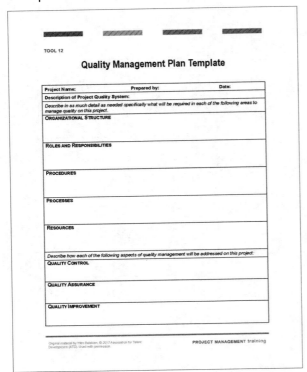

TOOL 12

Quality Management Plan Template

Project Name:	Prepared by:	Date:

Description of Project Quality System:

Describe in as much detail as needed specifically what will be required in each of the following areas to manage quality on this project.

ORGANIZATIONAL STRUCTURE

ROLES AND RESPONSIBILITIES

PROCEDURES

PROCESSES

RESOURCES

Describe how each of the following aspects of quality management will be addressed on this project:

QUALITY CONTROL

QUALITY ASSURANCE

QUALITY IMPROVEMENT

Original material by Wes Balakian, © 2017 Association for Talent Development (ATD). Used with permission.

PROJECT MANAGEMENT training

Tool 13: Project Risk Categorization Worksheet

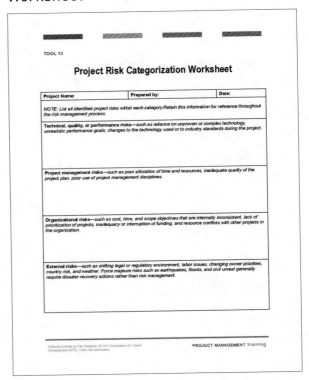

TOOL 13

Project Risk Categorization Worksheet

Project Name:	Prepared by:	Date:

NOTE: List all identified project risks within each category. Retain this information for reference throughout the risk management process.

Technical, quality, or performance risks—such as reliance on unproven or complex technology, unrealistic performance goals, changes to the technology used or to industry standards during the project.

Project management risks—such as poor allocation of time and resources, inadequate quality of the project plan, poor use of project management disciplines.

Organizational risks—such as cost, time, and scope objectives that are internally inconsistent, lack of prioritization of projects, inadequacy or interruption of funding, and resource conflicts with other projects in the organization.

External risks—such as shifting legal or regulatory environment, labor issues, changing owner priorities, country risk, and weather. Force majeure risks such as earthquakes, floods, and civil unrest generally require disaster recovery actions rather than risk management.

Original material by Wes Balakian, © 2017 Association for Talent Development (ATD). Used with permission.

PROJECT MANAGEMENT training

Tool 14: Schedule Management Plan Template

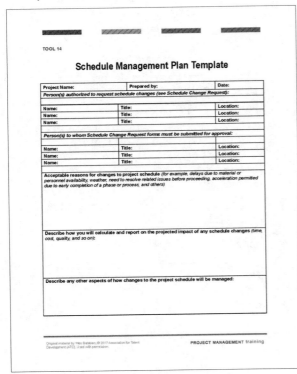

TOOL 14

Schedule Management Plan Template

Project Name:	Prepared by:	Date:

Person(s) authorized to request schedule changes (see Schedule Change Request):

Name:	Title:	Location:
Name:	Title:	Location:
Name:	Title:	Location:

Person(s) to whom Schedule Change Request forms must be submitted for approval:

Name:	Title:	Location:
Name:	Title:	Location:
Name:	Title:	Location:

Acceptable reasons for changes to project schedule *(for example, delays due to material or personnel availability, weather, need to resolve related issues before proceeding, acceleration permitted due to early completion of a phase or process, and others)*:

Describe how you will calculate and report on the projected impact of any schedule changes *(time, cost, quality, and so on)*:

Describe any other aspects of how changes to the project schedule will be managed:

Original material by Wes Balakian, © 2017 Association for Talent Development (ATD). Used with permission.

PROJECT MANAGEMENT training

Tool 15: Project Issues Tool: What Went Wrong?

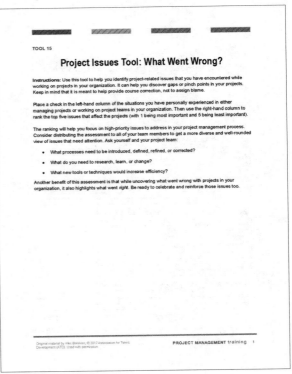

TOOL 15

Project Issues Tool: What Went Wrong?

Instructions: Use this tool to help you identify project-related issues that you have encountered while working on projects in your organization. It can help you discover gaps or pinch points in your projects. Keep in mind that it is meant to help provide course correction, not to assign blame.

Place a check in the left-hand column of the situations you have personally experienced in either managing projects or working on project teams in your organization. Then use the right-hand column to rank the top five issues that affect the projects (with 1 being most important and 5 being least important).

The ranking will help you focus on high-priority issues to address in your project management process. Consider distributing the assessment to all of your team members to get a more diverse and well-rounded view of issues that need attention. Ask yourself and your project team:

- What processes need to be introduced, defined, refined, or corrected?
- What do you need to research, learn, or change?
- What new tools or techniques would increase efficiency?

Another benefit of this assessment is that while uncovering what went wrong with projects in your organization, it also highlights what went *right*. Be ready to celebrate and reinforce those issues too.

Original material by Wes Balakian, © 2017 Association for Talent Development (ATD). Used with permission.

PROJECT MANAGEMENT training 1

Tool 15: Project Issues Tool: What Went Wrong?, *continued*

TOOL 15, continued

Project Issues Tool

Check Issues You Have Encountered In Your Projects:	Project-Related Issues	Rank the Top 5 (1=most important; 5=least important)
	Time allocated to the project was reduced, but scope wasn't.	
	The wrong people were selected in forming the team (wrong fit, wrong skillsets, and so on).	
	Project hand-offs were poorly executed because they were not defined or agreed to up front.	
	Project progress was not measured or documented.	
	Project requirements or project success criteria were not fully defined.	
	Project communication (formal and informal) was unreliable or ill-defined.	
	Risks were poorly managed or not identified.	
	Project team meetings were poorly planned or otherwise inefficient.	
	Project team roles and responsibilities were not clearly defined.	
	Milestones were missed because they were not acknowledged or documented.	
	Project activities/tasks durations were not accurately estimated.	
	No room for errors or unforeseen delays because project was too tightly scheduled.	
	There were no consequences associated with missed deadlines or other failures.	
	The project was not formally closed.	
	There was no attempt to analyze the lessons learned or best practices experienced during the project so that other projects could benefit.	
	The original budget for the project was grossly underestimated.	
	There was no formal change management process.	
	Project changes were poorly documented or controlled.	
	The project manager could not motivate the team members because functional managers did not support the effort (for example, people were pulled off project work to work on other items).	
	The level of complexity was not clearly communicated to the customers, leading them to have unrealistic expectations of the project team.	

PROJECT MANAGEMENT training   2

Chapter 15

Online Supporting Documents and Downloads

What's in This Chapter

- Instructions to access supporting materials
- Options for using tools and downloads
- Licensing and copyright information for workshop programs
- Tips for working with the downloaded files

The ATD Workshop Series is designed to give you flexible options for many levels of training facilitation and topic expertise. As you prepare your program, you will want to incorporate many of the handouts, assessments, presentation slides, and other training tools provided as supplementary materials with this volume. We wish you the best of luck in delivering your training workshops. It is exciting work that ultimately can change lives.

Access to Free Supporting Materials

To get started, visit the ATD Workshop Series page: www.td.org/workshopbooks. This page includes links to download all the free supporting materials that accompany this book, as well as up-to-date information about additions to the series and new program offerings.

These downloads, which are included in the price of the book, feature ready-to-use learning activities, handouts, assessments, and presentation slide files in PDF format. Use these files to deliver your workshop program and as a resource to help you prepare your own materials. You may download and use any of these files as part of your training delivery for the workshops, provided no changes are made to the original materials. To access this material, you will be asked to log into the ATD website. If you are not an ATD member, you will have to create an ATD account.

If you choose to re-create these documents, they can only be used within your organization; they cannot be presented or sold as your original work. Please note that all materials included in the book are copyrighted and you are using them with permission of ATD. If you choose to re-create the materials, per copyright usage requirements, you must provide attribution to the original source of the content and display a copyright notice as follows:

© 2017 ATD. Adapted and used with permission.

Customizable Materials

You can also choose to customize this supporting content for an additional licensing fee. This option gives you access to a downloadable zip file with the entire collection of supporting materials in Microsoft Word and PowerPoint file formats. Once purchased, you will have indefinite and unlimited access to these materials through the My Downloads section of your ATD account. Then, you will be able to customize and personalize all the documents and presentations using Microsoft Word and PowerPoint. You can add your own content, change the order or format, include your company logo, or make any other customization.

Please note that all the original documents contain attribution to ATD and this book as the original source for the material. As you customize the documents, remember to keep these attributions intact (see the copyright notice above). By doing so, you are practicing professional courtesy by respecting the intellectual property rights of another trainer (the author) and modeling respect for copyright and intellectual property laws for your program participants.

ATD offers two custom material license options: *Internal Use* and *Client Use*. To determine which license option you need to purchase, ask yourself the following question:

Will I or my employer be charging a person or outside organization a fee for providing services or for delivering training that includes any ATD Workshop content that I wish to customize?

If the answer is yes, then you need to purchase a *Client Use* license.

If the answer is no, and you plan to customize ATD Workshop content to deliver training at no cost to employees within your own department or company only, you need to purchase the *Internal Use* license.

Working With the Files

PDF Documents

To read or print the PDF files you download, you must have PDF reader software such as Adobe Acrobat Reader installed on your system. The program can be downloaded free of cost from the Adobe website: www.adobe.com. To print documents, simply use the PDF reader to open the downloaded files and print as many copies as you need.

PowerPoint Slides

To use or adapt the contents of the PowerPoint presentation files (available with the Internal Use and Client Use licenses), you must have Microsoft PowerPoint software installed on your system. If you simply want to view the PowerPoint documents, you only need an appropriate viewer on your system. Microsoft provides various viewers at www.microsoft.com for free download.

Once you have downloaded the files to your computer system, use Microsoft PowerPoint (or free viewer) to print as many copies of the presentation slides as you need. You can also make handouts of the presentations by choosing the "print three slides per page" option on the print menu.

You can modify or otherwise customize the slides by opening and editing them in Microsoft PowerPoint. However, you must retain the credit line denoting the original source of the material, as noted earlier in this chapter. It is illegal to present this content as your own work. The files will open as read-only files, so before you adapt them you will need to save them onto your hard drive. Further use of the images in the slides for any purpose other than presentation for these workshops is strictly prohibited by law.

The PowerPoint slides included in this volume support the three workshop agendas:

- Two-Day Workshop
- One-Day Workshop
- Half-Day Workshop.

For PowerPoint slides to successfully support and augment your learning program, it is essential that you practice giving presentations with the slides *before* using them in live training situations. You should be confident that you can logically expand on the points featured in the presentations and discuss the methods for working through them. If you want to fully engage your participants, become familiar with this technology before you use it. See the sidebar that follows for a cheat sheet to help you navigate through the presentation. A good practice is to insert comments into PowerPoint's notes feature, which you can print out and use when you present the slides. The workshop agendas in this book show thumbnails of each slide to help you keep your place as you deliver the workshop.

NAVIGATING THROUGH A POWERPOINT PRESENTATION	
Key	**PowerPoint "Show" Action**
Space bar or Enter or Mouse click	Advance through custom animations embedded in the presentation or advance to next slide if no animations to show
Backspace	Back up to the last projected element of the presentation
Escape	Abort the presentation
B or b	Blank the screen to black
B or b (repeat)	Resume the presentation
W or w	Blank the screen to white
W or w (repeat)	Resume the presentation

About the Author

Wes Balakian is CEO of True Solutions Inc., a Dallas-based global project management consulting and training organization. He is a published author, accomplished speaker, strategic facilitator, and program manager delivering strategic planning and program management consulting services to a variety of organizations including military, nonprofit, governmental, and commercial entities throughout the world. During his career, he has been a management consultant, a college professor, a corporate executive, and a business owner. Before founding True Solutions Inc., he held management positions with several Fortune 100 companies and served as a senior strategic planning and performance management consultant and adviser to many global corporations.

As a strategic facilitator Wes has worked with boards of directors and executive management to develop strategic initiatives that have delivered positive results to *Fortune*'s Global 1000 companies. Wes's innovative style has helped him become a proven leader in program management, portfolio management, project planning, and delivery of business solutions across industries. He is well versed in corporate culture and strategic alignment as it relates to organizational maturity, business process, logistics, and manufacturing and is known for his practical expertise as a successful mentor and facilitator. His experience includes development of critical business process improvement strategies and short- and long-term strategic planning for executive management teams. He has extensive knowledge in implementation and management of complex, business-to-business process solutions for client relationship management and workforce optimization. Wes has consulted or worked for many global organizations, including J.P. Morgan, Texas Instruments, Verizon, MCI, EDS, Flowserve, Cisco Systems, and Hewlett-Packard.

As a true project management evangelist with a long history of volunteerism, Wes has been instrumental in changing the way program and project management is delivered, perceived, and globally received. His award-winning programs have been taught and used by dozens of organizations, including Oracle, Saudi Telecom, Aramco, Shell, Ericsson, MBFS (Mercedes-Benz Financial Services), Sabre, Delta Airlines, U.S. Department of Defense, U.S. Air Force, U.S. Department of Homeland Security, General Services Administration, Federal Reserve Bank, and the city of Dallas. Balakian, who is a PMP® credential holder, has authored several books on project management and PMP® exam preparation. He has been a contributing leader of the Project Management Institute (PMI) since 1999 and has held positions on PMI's board.

Wes holds an advanced master's certificate in project management from George Washington University's School of Business. He recently graduated from PMI's Leadership Institute Master Class in Budapest.

PMP is the registered trademark of the Project Management Institute, Inc.

About ATD

The Association for Talent Development (ATD), formerly ASTD, is the world's largest association dedicated to those who develop talent in organizations. These professionals help others achieve their full potential by improving their knowledge, skills, and abilities.

ATD's members come from more than 120 countries and work in public and private organizations in every industry sector.

ATD supports the work of professionals locally in more than 125 chapters, international strategic partners, and global member networks.

1640 King Street
Alexandria, VA 22314
www.td.org
800.628.2783
703.683.8100

HOW TO PURCHASE ATD PRESS PUBLICATIONS

ATD Press publications are available worldwide in print and electronic format.

To place an order, please visit our online store: www.td.org/books.

Our publications are also available at select online and brick-and-mortar retailers.

Outside the United States, English-language ATD Press titles may be purchased through the following distributors:

United Kingdom, Continental Europe, the Middle East, North Africa, Central Asia, Australia, New Zealand, and Latin America
Eurospan Group
Phone: 44.1767.604.972
Fax: 44.1767.601.640
Email: eurospan@turpin-distribution.com
Website: www.eurospanbookstore.com

Asia
Cengage Learning Asia Pte. Ltd.
Phone: (65)6410-1200
Email: asia.info@cengage.com
Website: www.cengageasia.com

Nigeria
Paradise Bookshops
Phone: 08033075133
Email: paradisebookshops@gmail.com
Website: www.paradisebookshops.com

South Africa
Knowledge Resources
Phone: +27 (11) 706.6009
Fax: +27 (11) 706.1127
Email: sharon@knowres.co.za
Web: www.kr.co.za

For all other territories, customers may place their orders at the ATD online store: **www.td.org/books**.

0215145.62220